PRAISE FOR

Fast Times in Palestine

"It's love in the time of occupation as Pamela Olson . . . takes us on the emotional roller coaster of her very personal experience of life in Ramallah—and in doing so lays bare the human drama of a people . . . determined to live free."

—Tony Karon, senior editor, *Time*

"Olson does not merely report on the world of others; she steps into their shoes and sees the world through their eyes. *Fast Times in Palestine* is a heroic and touching journey to self-awareness that will awaken the reader to a more humane perspective on the Arab world."

—Richard Forer, author of *Breakthrough: Transforming Fear into Compassion*

"Olson's masterful storytelling, imagery, and wit take the reader on a transformative journey through Palestine."

—Anna Baltzer, author of *Witness in Palestine*

"A moving, inspiring account of life in Palestine that's enormously informative yet reads like a novel."

—Rebecca Vilkomerson, executive director, Jewish Voice for Peace

"Pamela Olson leads the reader on an exciting, funny, at times heart-wrenching journey, carefully deciphering complex political and historical issues. Olson is a talented writer, intelligent and exceptional in her ability to convey both tragedy and hope, remaining morally grounded and refreshingly honest."
    —Ramzy Baroud, author of *My Father Was a Freedom Fighter*

"As an Israeli whose life was shaped by the Israeli-Palestinian conflict, I found *Fast Times in Palestine* moving and refreshing. Pamela Olson comes to the Middle East with a blank slate and is therefore able to hold up an undistorted mirror to the reality she encounters."
    —Miko Peled, author of *The General's Son*

"Pamela Olson operates in a great tradition of American explorers, from Martha Gellhorn to Susan Meiselas to Rachel Corrie—open-minded women who have thrown off a lot of tired received wisdom about a fearful part of the world in order to see it for themselves, then brought that understanding back to their own culture. This book is a triumph of sympathy and observation."
    —Philip Weiss, editor of *Mondoweiss*

"*Fast Times in Palestine* will open your eyes to the human story inside the political drama. Mixing humor, memoir, political intrigue, romance, and sociological commentary, Olson's heartfelt work will change how you understand the Middle East."
    —Patricia Ryan Madson, author of *Improv Wisdom*

"In a field overcrowded with arcane academic texts and strident polemics, Pamela Olson has broken through with a refreshing read that packs gritty journalism into a fast-paced, intimate personal narrative."
—Max Blumenthal, author of *Republican Gomorrah*

"Part adventure story, part searing reportage, part love story, and wholly absorbing . . . If you want to know what everyday life is like for the Palestinian people, go to Palestine; if you can't, read this book."
—Dr. Kenneth Ring, co author of *Letters from Palestine*

Fast Times in Palestine

A Love Affair with a Homeless Homeland

Pamela J. Olson

SEAL PRESS

FAST TIMES IN PALESTINE
A Love Affair with a Homeless Homeland

Copyright © 2013 Pamela J. Olson

Published by
Seal Press
A Member of the Perseus Books Group
1700 Fourth Street
Berkeley, California

www.sealpress.com
www.pamolson.org

Library of Congress Cataloging-in-Publication Data is available.

ISBN: 978-1-58005-482-9

10 9 8 7 6 5 4 3 2 1

Cover design by Gopa & Ted2, Inc.
Interior design by Domini Dragoone
Cartography by Mike Morgenfeld, Chris Henrick, and Kaitlin Jaffe
Printed in the United States of America
Distributed by Publishers Group West

Contents

*For Fayez, Yusif, Dan, Muzna, and the people of Jayyous
for their unreasonably warm welcomes*

For my parents, my nephews, Lusan, and Karam

And for my teachers

Yes, quaint and curious war is!
You shoot a fellow down
You'd treat if met where any bar is,
Or help to half-a-crown.

—Thomas Hardy, *The Man He Killed*

"I saw only what was happening in my immediate
neighborhood, but I saw and heard quite enough to be able to
contradict many of the lies that have been circulated . . .
It is . . . necessary to try and establish the truth, so far as it is
possible. This squalid brawl in a distant city is more important
than might appear at first."

—George Orwell, *Homage to Catalonia*

CHAPTER 1

From the Midwest to the Middle East

Do you have the patience to wait
till your mud settles and the water is clear?
Can you remain unmoving
till the right action arises of itself?

—Lao-tzu, *Tao Te Ching*

"Why are you coming to Israel?"

The wide, suspicious eyes of the young Israeli border guard were unnerving after all the laid-back hospitality in Jordan.

"I'm just a tourist," I said, probably too nonchalantly.

"What kind of tourist?"

"Well, I'm a Christian," I said, starting to sweat and wishing I'd worn a cross like I'd been advised, "and I want to see the holy sites."

"What holy sites?"

His tone suggested he'd never heard of any "holy sites" in Israel.

"You know," I said carefully, as if one of us might be slightly insane, "like Jerusalem, the Sea of Galilee, Nazareth—"

"Why Nazareth? What's in Nazareth?" he cut me off sharply.

It was just a random Biblical name as far as I was concerned. I didn't know then it was an Arab town in Israel or what that meant. I certainly didn't know that the outcome of this, the first of what would be many Israeli interrogations, would profoundly affect the course of my life. But I had clearly picked the wrong answer.

"Because, I mean, that's where Jesus was born and grew up and—"

"What? He was *what*?"

"He was . . . Oh, right! Sorry, obviously he wasn't *born* there—"

"Where was he born?!"

"He was born in . . . uh . . ."

Christ. I'd sung about where Jesus was born every Sunday morning growing up in eastern Oklahoma. But I had just finished reading a Middle East guidebook, so all my associations were shifted, everything was a jumble in my head, a border guard with an assault rifle slung over his shoulder was breathing down my neck, and I couldn't think.

Just start at the beginning, I told my fevered mind. *There was a woman on a donkey, and they went to an inn, and everybody sings O Little Town of—*

"Bethlehem!" I smiled and shrugged expansively as if it were the most basic knowledge in the universe, trying desperately to look relaxed rather than relieved.

The guard finally calmed down. I just hoped he wouldn't figure out the connection between me and the two men behind me. If he did, we could all be in trouble.

DEGREE OF FREEDOM

This wasn't where I expected to end up at age twenty-three—jobless, planless, and lying through my teeth to Israeli border security.

I had graduated a year earlier, in 2002, with a physics degree from Stanford only to realize I had no interest in spending any more of my young years in a basement lab doing problem sets. Several friends were heading to Wall Street, but I had even less interest in finance than in physics. The things I enjoyed most during college—travel, writing, languages, politics, sports—didn't sound like serious career options for a math-and-science type like me.

Beyond that was only a massive mental block, an abyss of vague fear and paralysis. And I had no idea why.

Feeling dazed and ashamed, I took a job at a pub near the Stanford campus because it had the best dollars-to-stress ratio of any job I could think of, and the popular image of bartenders was almost sexy enough to make up for the savage beating my ego was taking.

After I settled in with the job, I joined a jujitsu club, one of those things I had always wanted to do but never had the time. I noticed a purple belt named Michel who had powerful shoulders, light olive skin, and slate blue eyes.

He asked me out after practice one evening. He didn't have to ask twice.

Over dinner he mentioned he was from Lebanon, a country I knew so little about I couldn't think of any intelligent questions to ask. I decided to start small. When he dropped me off at the end of the night, I asked him how to say "Thank you" in Arabic.

"*Shukran,*" he said.

I repeated the strange word, tasting it in my mouth.

He bowed his head slightly in an utterly charming way and said, "No problem. Anytime."

We had only three months together before he took a job in another city, but they were three very good months. He talked incessantly about his native Beirut and its picturesque beaches, forested mountains, crazy nightclubs, world-class food, and gorgeous women, which surprised me. I'd always hazily pictured the Middle East as a vast desert full of cave-dwelling, Kalashnikov-wielding, misogynistic bearded maniacs, and I figured anyone without an armored convoy and a PhD in Middle Eastern studies should probably stay out of it. But Michel made Lebanon sound fabulous, and when he spoke with his Lebanese friends in Arabic and I couldn't understand, it drove me crazy. So I borrowed a friend's primer and started studying Arabic.

As the weeks passed, I began to notice a curious thing: I was actually pretty happy most of the time. I spent forty hours a week in a fantastic pub, and the rest of my time was wide open to enjoy friends and books, sandwiches and sunsets. I knew I'd been vaguely unhappy most of my life, but I never realized the extent of it until the fog gradually lifted and left me in an unfamiliar landscape so bright it almost hurt my eyes.

My ears burned, though, whenever I asked my patrons at the pub, in all seriousness, if they wanted fries with that. All this happiness and free time flew in the face of my deeply ingrained rural middle-class upbringing. Whenever I started hyperventilating about it, I took a deep breath and reminded myself that God and society could take care of themselves for a year or two whether or not I was staring at Excel spreadsheets all day. After that, if nothing better came along, I could always dust myself off, buy an Ann Taylor suit on credit, and put together a quasi-fictitious résumé like everyone else.

ONE AFTERNOON IN March of 2003, I found a copy of *The Wave*, a San Francisco magazine, left behind at the pub. The Iraq War had just begun, and it was full of articles about the Arab world. I flipped it open to a satirical piece about spending Spring Break in the Middle East. It listed the major countries of the region (including Lebanon), their most impressive tourist attractions, and why the people of each country wanted to kill us.

I knew it was supposed to be a joke, but it bothered me. Curious, I biked to the Stanford Bookstore and picked up a Lonely Planet guidebook called *From Istanbul to Cairo on a Shoestring*, expecting to see nothing but dire travel warnings. To my astonishment, it recommended the route as one of the most romantic, historically rich, and friendly in the world, and no more dangerous than Brazil or Thailand.

A month later, a friend in France named Olivier wrote to me and said he had three weeks of vacation coming up in September, and why didn't we meet up somewhere?

I had some money saved by now and was planning on traveling in the fall to a destination as yet unknown. I sent him an offhand list of half a dozen Mediterranean countries and told him to pick one, already imagining a lush late summer of Greek and Italian islands.

He wrote back: "What do you think about Egypt?"

My heart sank into my toes when I read it. I didn't even remember putting Egypt on the list. But I had given him his choice, and the Middle East was cheaper than Europe, which meant I could travel longer. Plus it bothered me that I didn't know enough to have an informed opinion on the Iraq War. My political science classes had been full of disconnected anecdotes and competing theories that left me unsure what to believe. The post-9/11 newspapers and magazines hadn't been much help, either. Here was a chance to bypass all that and have a look for myself. It was nice, anyway, to think my Arabic studying suddenly had a purpose.

THE SINAI

As my plane landed in Cairo in September 2003, it was clear that reading a guidebook hadn't remotely prepared me for the Middle East. My knowledge of the culture was almost nil, my Arabic skills were pitiful, and I felt ridiculous in my cargo shorts, ponytail, and bare sunburned face. All the other women wore stylish, diaphanous headscarves and subtle, lovely makeup, and if the aim of that getup was to make them less attractive, it had failed miserably. When one of the more exquisite women—all luminous skin, full rose lips, and steady eyes—caught me looking at her and smiled kindly at me, I ducked my head like a frightened child.

Just then, two boisterous college-age Egyptian guys walked up to me and asked, "Where you from?"

"Uh, America," I said, too taken aback to wonder whether it was wise to reveal my nationality on my first day in the Arab world when my country was at war with an Arab state.

"Ah, America!" They seemed delighted by the revelation. "First time in Egypt?"

"Yes."

"Welcome to Egypt!" They smiled and bounced away toward passport control.

As OLIVIER AND I traveled from the pyramids in the north to Luxor in the south, no one mentioned the Iraq War, and all thought of politics was lost in the dusty, sweaty shuffle of catching buses, finding restaurants, haggling over prices, and visiting tombs and museums.

When our cultural duty was finally done, we headed to Egypt's Sinai Peninsula, a remote triangle of mountainous desert wedged between the Gulf of Suez and the Gulf of Aqaba, for some rest and relaxation. Our first stop was Dahab, a backpacker's resort on the gulf coast whose main pedestrian drag ran right along the water. Past the flat, shallow reef tables was a drop-off populated by living corals and psychedelic tropical fish, then the sapphire sea filling a mile-deep crack in the earth. The jagged gold-brown Sinai Mountains rose behind Dahab to the west, and twenty miles east across the Gulf of Aqaba sat the hazy, sandy mountains of Saudi Arabia.[1]

We settled in at a $3-a-night camp and stretched out on brightly colored cushions in a Bedouin-style sitting area next to the sea. I put a Dire Straits tape on the camp's sound system, ordered a strawberry milkshake, watched the little aquamarine waves breaking against the reefs, and finally felt like I was on vacation.

Olivier had to leave after three days to catch his plane back to Paris. I was planning on following my guidebook's itinerary through Jordan, Syria, Lebanon, and Turkey over the next three months. But I was in no mood to pick up and be a tourist again anytime soon. I bade Olivier adieu and ordered another hookah.

A few days later, I gathered enough steam to hike two hours north to a tiny Bedouin village, a loose collection of grass huts and a few dozen camels tethered to a flat spit of desert between the mountains and the sea. There was no electricity; the only illumination came from the sun, the moon, the stars, and candles. I hadn't made any plans or reservations, but I was soon invited to have dinner and sleep on a foam mattress in one of the grass huts, for a nominal fee.

The next morning I hiked farther north to a turquoise lagoon

---

1. For a map of the Middle East, including Israel and the Sinai, see the map on p. 296.

where I came across an Estonian free diver named Dan. His hair was salty and sun-bleached and he wore a silver hoop earring, a wooden bead necklace, and a wry, dimpled smile. He dove deep into the blue depths with his weight belt, wetsuit, and carefully trained breath-holding ability while I snorkeled around the coral gardens and tried not to touch anything poisonous.

When the shadows of the Sinai Mountains were getting long, Dan and I moseyed back to the Bedouin village and found a spacious octagonal thatched shelter with a gas stove that served as a hotel and restaurant. We sat on cushions in the candlelight and talked for hours while our host prepared a dinner of fish and rice and vegetables and Bedouin flatbread. I felt more at ease than I had in months, and I soon felt like I'd known Dan for years.

Our host, who called himself Abraham, wore a traditional white Egyptian tunic and a thin white scarf fashioned into a loose turban around his head. He served us food by candlelight and told tales about Egypt and Israel dropping bombs on the Sinai, about treasures hidden in caves by fleeing Bedouins, and about smuggling on boats and camels across borders his people don't recognize. His manner of speech was bemused and ponderous, and he always had a clever, ironic expression on his face. He told us the names of the seasonal winds and said he liked octopus season best because "it's no bones, just good, white meat."

The next morning I walked back to Abraham's place to drink some tea before I departed. Then I completely failed to depart. Dan and I floated lazily among the bright yellow butterfly fish, iridescent parrotfish, and flashy lionfish, waited three hours for breakfast while the sun climbed, snorkeled again, waited three hours for dinner while the sun descended, and passed out contentedly on our cushions. The next day we did the same.

At night we went swimming at the village's sandy beach under a new moon and got a surprise. Our moving hands and feet stirred up trails of bright pinpoints of light in the water. We laughed in wonder and Dan said, "It's like a fairy tale." Abraham later told us they were billions and billions of tiny bioluminescent plankton, but we felt like we were swimming in swirling fields of sparkling water stars.

The beauty of the world filled our senses completely. Every day the sun hurtled across a flawless sky, then the galaxy floated by like a majestically slow comet. The sea shone deep blue against the Mars-like Saudi landscape. The coral gardens were incomprehensible miracles, hovering explosions of form and color below the water's surface. There was no sense of time, just an endlessly marvelous present. For the first time I understood the meaning of the phrase, "My cup runneth over."

Dan was due to leave the Sinai after four days. As we were parting in Dahab, he took me aside and said, "There's something I haven't told you. I'm not really Estonian. I grew up in Siberia, and a few years ago I moved to Israel. I'm an Israeli citizen now." He fiddled with a strap on his backpack. "Sorry for not telling you earlier. It's just easier not to say you're Israeli around here. But if you plan on visiting Israel, my house is your house any time."

Eye of the Storm

I caught a ferry to Jordan and spent a week hiking around the southern Jordanian deserts. Along the way, through some process of cultural osmosis, I began to learn how to greet people in the local ways, how to spot a petty scam artist, what the local prices ought to be, and how to cut down on mild harassment from unmarried young men—namely by covering my knees and shoulders and wearing a fake wedding ring.

When I made my way up north to the capital, Amman, I liked it immediately. The best view of the city was from the hilltop ruins of the Roman Citadel at sunset. The expansive sky glowed pink and purple, the boxy white houses on the city's seventeen hills shone sand-colored, and the minarets glowed with green neon amid wheeling flocks of pigeons while the calls to prayer echoed in stereo.

I took the advice of an Irish backpacker I'd met in southern Jordan and stayed at the Al Sarayya Hotel despite its astronomical price of 14 Jordanian dinars ($20) per night. It was in the old downtown area where hospitality is still a way of life. I almost felt bad talking with shopkeepers and waiters there, because many refused to charge me for food and services after we'd chatted long enough to feel like friends.

The manager of the hotel was a droll and charming man named Fayez who'd been trained as an electrical engineer. He was an intelligent, clean-cut chain-smoker, tall and thin and distinguished looking, the kind of guy you'd expect to see patiently explaining something obscure but important on CNN. I sat in his office with a few other guests, and he offered us porcelain cups of sweet Arabic coffee, on the house. Someone asked about the stuffed white wolf sitting on top of one of his filing cabinets. Fayez explained that a reporter had nicked it from one of Saddam's palaces. He'd left it in Fayez's office and made him promise not to sell it.

"But I don't know," Fayez mused sardonically. "Probably I could get a few thousand for him on eBay. What do you think?"

My scalp began to prickle in an odd and unnerving way. This was war loot. And it wasn't from a historical event that could safely be categorized as something done in other times and other places by other people. This was here and now, and it was my country that had done the invading.

Jordan, sandwiched between Iraq and Israel, is a jumping-off point for journalists on their way to Baghdad and Jerusalem. The Al Sarayya was a favorite among independent journalists, filmmakers, and foreign aid workers. Every evening they congregated in Fayez's office to share their stories over bottomless cups of sweet, strong tea and Arabic coffee.

A Swedish woman told us that a waiter in Baghdad once started talking to an Iraqi-born Swede she was traveling with. The rest of the Swedes were impatient and wanted service, but the Iraqi-born Swede told them to wait. The waiter was telling him that his sister and her family had been on a minibus a few days earlier, and the bus had stopped for an American soldier at a checkpoint. The soldier waved them through. But as they were passing, a woman reached for a baby bottle. The soldier emptied his ammunition clip into the bus, killing six people. Apparently he'd thought she was reaching for a grenade.

As their stories went on and on, my palms began sweating and my heart beat faster. I was almost shaking. Strangely, it wasn't the horror of the stories themselves that upset me the most. It was the prickling realization of how thoroughly I had been misled by my own press and government. They'd made the war sound so clean and under control, abstract and far away. Here, it sounded like nothing short of a blood-soaked catastrophe.

Then again, maybe these "independent journalists" were lying or exaggerating, trying to impress each other and tourists like me with their big talk.

There was only one way to find out. My head began buzzing as I realized what was possible here. It was nice enough drinking tea with Bedouins and gazing at the stone monuments of bygone eras. But here was a chance to witness history *as it was being made.*

I asked about expeditions to Baghdad the next day and was offered a ride in a shared taxi for $200. I wasn't sure what I would do once I got there. I figured I could meet people like I had in Cairo, Dahab, and Amman, and things would work out somehow.

In the evening, I told two journalists about my plan and asked if it sounded wise.

"Are you a reporter?" one asked.

"No."

"Foreign aid worker?"

"No."

They narrowed their eyes. "Then why do you want to go?"

I shrugged. "Just to see."

They looked at me like they couldn't tell whether I was a maniac or an idiot. Then they made it vividly clear that the violence in Baghdad was far too random and gruesome for tourists.

I chafed at their patronizing tones, but I wasn't suicidal. I grudgingly took their advice.

The next evening Fayez invited me to dinner with two men, Yusif and Sebastian, who were on vacation from their work in the West Bank of the Palestinian territories. Sebastian was a young, slim Canadian paramedic with close-cropped brown hair. Yusif was a skinny, white, blond British Muslim who had the aristocratic aura of a wandering ascetic. His face was drawn tight with laugh lines, his teeth were crooked, and his age was impossible to guess. There was something childlike, almost impish about him, yet he irresistibly commanded respect and attention. His words seemed to come from a deep well of spiritual confidence that was either brilliant or insane, yet he was humble and friendly. I had never met anyone remotely like him.

They were on their way to Petra, the ancient Nabatean city carved into the living rock of a canyon in southern Jordan. Its most striking landmark is a matchless monument called Al Khazneh, which famously served as the final resting place of the Holy Grail in the film *Indiana Jones and the Last Crusade*. The massive, shimmering, rose-hued tomb, exquisitely ornamented and symmetrical, is accessible only through a mile-long crack in a mountain.

Sebastian found me the next day and invited me to join him and Yusif. I hesitated. I'd already gone to Petra a week earlier, and going again would cut into my dwindling time and funds. But I had, after all, just been invited to one of the most magical places on earth in the company of one of the most intriguing people I had ever met. I didn't hesitate long.

Along the way, Yusif mentioned he had trained in survival in the Sudan from age fourteen to twenty-two, and he claimed to have met Osama bin Laden during that time. Yusif had also lived in a cave in southern Spain for several years. Now he was on the town council of a hilltop Palestinian village called Jayyous.[2] He spoke fluent Arabic. Sebastian and I once watched him silence an entire busload of Jordanians with his sing-song recitation of the Quran.

---

2. Rhymes with "stray moose," accent on the second syllable.

Both men talked compulsively about their experiences in Palestine. Yusif was sometimes offhand, almost clinical as he told his stories. Other times he was wide-eyed, like a kid describing a crime so outrageous he feared no one would believe him.

Their stories were difficult to take at face value. But I had learned in Fayez's office that the American government gives Israel more than $3 billion a year, making it the largest recipient of U.S. foreign aid in the world. I hadn't planned on visiting Israel because if my passport got stamped at the Israeli border, I wouldn't be allowed to visit Syria or Lebanon. But if their stories were true, it seemed like something I should know. If I called their bluff and things weren't really so bad, I could take that as a lesson learned, hang out with Dan in Israel, and then move on and forget about it.

As we were heading back to Amman, I asked Yusif and Sebastian if I could go with them when they went back to the West Bank.

"You're welcome to join us," Sebastian said, "but you might get turned back at the Israeli border if the guards suspect you plan on visiting the West Bank. It's better not to mention anything about that."

"And it's probably best if we pretend we don't know each other," Yusif said in his clipped patrician accent. "The interrogations will be much simpler that way."

So, green and wide-eyed, I wandered into the Holy Land, an empty vessel.

CHAPTER 2

Olives, Tea, and Assault Rifles

I was hungry and you gave me food;
I was thirsty and you gave me something to drink;
I was a stranger and you welcomed me.

—Matthew 25:35

After I finally remembered where Jesus was born, the guards asked only a few more questions and did a perfunctory baggage search before releasing me into northern Israel. The woman at passport control was even kind enough not to stamp my passport.

I emerged onto a twilit courtyard. My heart rate was still unsteady from the stress of the bizarre interrogation, and I knew that if my new friends were turned back I'd be stranded here. But for now I was just glad to be off the tourist trail, lying to foreign authority figures about things I didn't understand and heading to places about which my guidebook had nothing to say. I was unaccountably pleased by the fact that I had no idea what would happen next.

Half an hour later, to my immense relief, Yusif and Sebastian emerged together and discreetly indicated I should follow them to an ink-blue sedan with a Palestinian driver and his young son. We squeezed in and motored off.

"We're going to Cana first," Sebastian said once we were under-way. "It's an Arab town in Israel near Nazareth, famous for being the place where Jesus turned water into wine."

"My friend Rami lives there," Yusif said. "I met him when he was studying at Cambridge. We used to smoke *nargila* together in one of the courtyards."[1]

"Rami's father is an Arab member of the Knesset," Sebastian added impressively.

I nodded knowingly. I didn't want to admit I had no idea what that meant.

We soon pulled up to a breezy stone house of three stories. Rami, a fresh-faced man with dark hair, olive skin, and an easy confidence, greeted his old friend Yusif and invited us in. The bright living room was decorated with an air of casual sophistication. Rami's mother welcomed us with tea and snacks.

Sebastian and Yusif had been invited to stay the night, which I hadn't realized. Before I could ask if there was a hostel in town, they invited me to stay as well and gave me a place of honor in the old-est daughter's room. They treated all of us to a lush dinner on the family's rooftop veranda. Everyone spoke flawless English, and the food—grilled lamb, homemade *tabouleh*, *baba ghannouj*, and fluffy pita bread—was divine.

I'd become used to a certain level of hospitality in the Middle East. *Ahlan wa sahlan*, heard incessantly in the Arab world, is usually translated as "Welcome," but a more literal translation is "Be at ease, like one of the family." I'd begun to take for granted that I would have a soft landing whenever I wandered off the beaten track. But this was bordering on outrageous. I kept rubbing my eyes and wondering what the catch was.

Walking through the living room to wash up after dinner, I noticed an embroidered map of Israel plus the Palestinian territories—the West Bank and Gaza Strip, occupied by Israel since 1967—hanging

---

1. *Nargila* is the word Palestinians use for "hookah" or water pipe, usually smoked with flavored tobacco.

on one wall. The word "Palestine" and the names of several cities were stitched onto the map in Arabic along with an upraised fist.

In Jordan I had learned a little about the fallout from the 1948 war that led to Israel's creation, in which three-quarters of a million Palestinians fled or were driven from their homes and never allowed to return. Palestinians call it *Al Nakba* (The Catastrophe). For Israelis, it was their War of Independence.

By now I had learned that Rami's family were among the minority of Palestinians who remained in Israel after 1948 and became Israeli citizens,[2] and that the Knesset was Israel's parliament. I was surprised to see this map and symbol in the home of a man who worked in Israel's government.

INTO THE WEST BANK

The next morning, Rami treated us to breakfast at a hilltop restaurant owned by a friend of his. Afterward he toured us around Cana's two rival churches, both of which claimed to be built on the site of the First Miracle. At noon we settled into another café and ordered a *nargila*. Rami told us that after he'd graduated from Cambridge, he'd opened a club in Germany.

"But I sold it and left. I didn't sell it because it was a failure. I sold it because it was a success. It made me afraid it would tempt me to leave here. Sometimes I think I would like to live somewhere else. But I don't feel like I can leave here now."

I wanted to ask him why, but I suspected it would be a long time before I was ready to understand his answer, and the day was too nice to try to tease a lecture out of him.

In the evening, Rami drove us south for an hour or so, then turned east. The border between Israel and the West Bank is known as the Green Line, and we crossed it. Yusif said we were driving on a "settler road," which meant it was built on Palestinian land but only cars with

---

2. Palestinian-Israelis are a 20 percent minority within Israel, frequently referred to as "Arab-Israelis."

yellow Israeli license plates were allowed to drive on it. Palestinian cars with green license plates were forbidden.

Suddenly I began to feel nervous. Everything had been smooth up to this point, but now I was entering a bona fide conflict zone. For all I knew it was full of broken, angry, unreasonable people who might look upon me as an enemy. An odd queasiness in my stomach reached a fever pitch as we drove deeper into Palestinian land on an Israeli road in an Israeli-plated car driven by a Palestinian-Israeli.

In the twilight, Rami pulled over onto the shoulder of the highway. Yusif pointed to a pile of debris blocking a side street and told us to grab our things and climb over it quickly.

"We don't want any Israeli soldiers to see Rami and ask why he's transporting people into a Palestinian area," he explained.

Jesus, I thought dizzily. *What's left of Palestine doesn't even have the dignity of a proper gateway. Just this ridiculous pile of garbage.*

We thanked Rami and said good-bye, and then Yusif and Sebastian and I were climbing over the dusty pile of rubbish, and then . . .

We were in Palestine.

JAYYOUS

Men in leather jackets were waiting on the other side of the barrier next to a small fleet of battered yellow taxis. Each offered a friendly smile and a hearty "*Salaam alaykum!*" (peace be upon you). All of them seemed to know Yusif. One offered us a free ride into Jayyous. He and Yusif chatted cheerfully along the way. As we rolled deeper into Palestinian territory, my stomach calmed wonderfully and my whole frame relaxed.

The driver dropped us off in front of a house where half a dozen men were sitting on the porch in a circle of white plastic lawn chairs sharing an ornate *nargila*. Yusif greeted everyone and introduced me. The house belonged to Amjad, a barrel-chested mechanical engineer with a neatly clipped black moustache. One of the other men asked in English where I was from. "Oklahoma," I said.

"Ah." He looked confused. "You are Japanese?"

I smiled and shook my head. Another man in Egypt had made the same mistake. "No, not Yokohama. Oklahoma."

"So you are from America?" Amjad asked. He had a booming voice, and his question might have sounded like an accusation if not for the amused expression on his face.

I paused. "Yes."

He laughed. "You are ashamed?" I wasn't ashamed, but I said nothing. It seemed wise to keep a low profile until I had a better idea of what was going on. "Do not worry," he said reassuringly. "It is a good country. Good people. Just your government is bad. Arab people, we understand bad governments. Our governments are very bad."

Yusif shook his head. "It seems like the nicest people have the worst governments."

"Ah, Oklahoma!" the other man said, finally putting the pieces together. "Yes, Oklahoma City. It is a dangerous place?"

I couldn't imagine what he was talking about. Cowboys? Indians? "Dangerous?"

"Wasn't there a bombing?"

"A—? Oh, right. Yeah, well, there was one bombing."

"But it was a very big bombing, yes? Many people killed."

"Sure, it was very big. But it was one bombing almost ten years ago." We were in occupied Palestine and this guy was worried about Oklahoma being dangerous? I supposed that was what happened if you knew nothing about a place except its bombings.

Just then a goat came limping up the stairs and shyly peeked around at us. A man shooed it away, and it looked so startled and goofy, I laughed out loud. No one else did. Yusif whispered to me, "The goats are living under the house because Amjad's brother and father have been kicked off their land by the Israelis. They have nowhere else to put them." I nodded, chastened, and made a mental note not to laugh at any more goats.

A man with a large black beard and kind eyes walked by on the street and said in a sonorous voice, "*Salaam alaykum*" (peace be upon you). Everyone answered, *"Wa alaykum al salaam"* (and upon you be peace), as he joined us in the circle. He was wearing a long white robe and a *keffiya*, the black-and-white checkered headscarf made famous by Yasser Arafat. Yusif said something to him in Arabic. He turned to me.

"Ah, you are new here." He bowed his head politely. *"Ahlan wa sahlan.* You are very welcome here. My name is Suleiman. Yusif wants me to sing for you." He took a deep breath and gathered his thoughts. "Do you know about Solomon and the Queen of Sheba?"

"Of course. They're in the Bible, right?"

"Yes, they are in the Bible. They are also in the Quran." I felt chastened again. After two months in the Middle East, I still knew almost nothing about Islam.

Suleiman smiled. "Yes, in Islam, we believe Solomon and his father David were wise rulers favored by God. But in Arabic, we call them Suleiman and Daoud. And Yusif"—he leaned back and indicated our blond British friend—"is Arabic for Joseph. Same same." I nodded. Suleiman seemed pleased. "Listen, I will tell you the story."

He cleared his throat and began to intone in that not-quite-singing, not-quite-speaking way people recite the Quran. The others stopped their conversations to listen in. His voice was deep and clear as it swept us away to the wisdom and poetry of ages long past under desert moons and painted tiles. In my mind, Bible stories had always been associated with itchy Sunday mornings on hard wooden pews. But sitting in the Holy Land hearing a man sing with such mesmerizing expressiveness transformed the old stories into something startlingly human-scale, yet more beautiful, rich, and real.

When he finished, everyone enjoyed a moment of reflective, appreciative silence. I smiled and thanked him, and he nodded graciously. Someone got up to make another pot of tea, and conversation resumed.

It was baffling to see everyone so full of energy and good humor, with smile lines around their eyes and warm welcomes for wandering foreigners, when wars and occupations were going on all around. I could only shake my head and laugh at myself. The longer I traveled in the Middle East, the more I realized how little I knew this world.

THE WALL

The next morning hundreds of villagers got up early and headed out to their land. It was late October and the olive harvest was in full swing. I tagged along to help out, hoping to earn my keep for once. My karmic balance sheet was getting embarrassingly overdrawn.

Jayyous is built on a hilltop, and the land below it undulates and gradually flattens out until it meets the coastal plains of central Israel and the Mediterranean Sea fifteen miles to the west. We caravanned down the hill in donkey carts and tractors and on foot, excited for a long, fun day in the groves.

But our procession was stopped short at the bottom of the hill by a twenty-foot-high chain-link fence topped with razor wire. Two smoothly paved access roads flanked the fence. The land on either side of the roads was blasted bare. The whole two-hundred-foot-wide structure was bounded by trenches and six-foot pyramid-shaped piles of razor wire. This massive ribbon of metal, concrete, and emptiness snaked through the Biblical hills in jarring contrast to the ancient aesthetic. A bright red sign said in Hebrew, English, and Arabic: MORTAL DANGER—MILITARY ZONE. ANYONE WHO PASSES OR DAMAGES THE FENCE ENDANGERS HIS LIFE.

I was shocked to be confronted by such an aggressive-looking structure on a peaceful olive harvest morning. Everyone else gathered patiently around the locked gate and found places to sit in the warm, dusty morning. I swallowed my fear and followed suit. I noticed that one of the donkey carts had AGAINST TERRORISM scrawled in white paint across the back. I heard a boy say something about *simsim* while pointing to the donkey cart.

"*Simsim?*" I asked, and pointed toward the donkey cart. The boy hesitated, then nodded. "So *simsim* means 'donkey'?" I envisioned myself learning Arabic one word at a time and slowly developing a native command, like Kevin Costner in *Dances with Wolves*.

The boy looked at me blankly. One of his friends whispered something, and all the other boys burst into laughter. Seeing my bewildered expression, Yusif whispered out of the corner of his mouth, "I think

'Simsim' is the nickname of the boy in the cart." I looked at Simsim and winced apologetically. He smiled and shook his head.

I passed time with another group of kids by drawing on the back of an old envelope. They wrote a little English for me, and I wrote a little Arabic. I spelled my name "Bamila" since there's no *P* in Arabic, and *Bam* sounds unnervingly similar to *bomb*.

After nearly an hour of waiting, I caught Yusif's eye. "Who owns the olive groves we're going to?"

"People mostly own and work their own groves, which are passed down from generation to generation."

"How much of Jayyous's land is on the other side of that fence?"

"Most of it," he said. "About 75 percent. More than ten square kilometers."

"Seventy-five percent?"

"Yeah, you can see. The Fence goes right up next to the village. There are places where it's just a few meters from people's houses."

"Where's the border between the West Bank and Israel?"

"About four kilometers that way."

I squinted through the Fence in confusion. "Why would Israel build a fence here instead of on the border?"

"They say they're building it to stop suicide bombers. But hundreds of Palestinians cross the Green Line illegally every day to work in Israel. If a bomber wants to get through, he can. If he doesn't, the next one will. If there's a decrease in bombers, it's not because of the Wall."[3]

"So why are they building it, and why this route?"

He sighed as if he had been through this many times. "Jayyous has some of the most fertile land in the West Bank. They've got something like fifteen thousand olive trees, fifty thousand fruit and citrus trees, mangos, avocados, almonds, apricots, more than a hundred

---

3. This structure is referred to as Al Jedar ("the Wall") by Palestinians in Arabic. In English they use "Fence" and "Wall" interchangeably. In rural areas it is a fence/road/trench/razor wire/buffer zone structure like the one described here. In urban areas it is a twenty-five-foot-tall concrete wall embedded with sniper towers. Most Israelis call it the "Separation Barrier" or "Security Fence." See the map on p. 300 to view the route of the wall in the Jayyous area.

greenhouses, and six good water wells. Also, Jayyous sits near Israel's narrowest point. There's only about twenty kilometers between the Green Line and the sea right here."

My eyes narrowed. "So what, you're saying Israel is trying to take Jayyous's land?"

He shrugged. "It wouldn't be the first time. Anyway, look, once we get through the Fence, there's nothing stopping us from marching directly to Tel Aviv. You tell me what sense that makes."

I couldn't think of any. "How much land was destroyed to build the Wall? The scar looks enormous."

"Yeah, it was a lot. About twenty-five hundred olive trees were destroyed. And even when Israel offers compensation, no one takes it. It's never anywhere near the value of what was lost, and it makes it look like a transaction instead of what it is. It would be an insult to accept that, and it's considered treason if you do."

"Has anyone tried to climb over the Wall or tear it down?"

"Electronic sensors can call an army Jeep to investigate any possible breach in minutes. And they've been known to shoot people on sight."

A chill went down my spine. I looked at the Fence, at the villagers gathered around it, and back at Yusif. It all sounded insane. There had to be more to this than he was telling me. I had called Dan, the Russian-Israeli I'd met in the Sinai, and we were due to meet at the end of the week. I hoped he'd help me understand things a little better.

"Are they going to let us through today?" I asked.

"Maybe."

"What happens if they don't?"

"As you see. We wait."

OLIVE RAIN

Two hours later, around 10:30 AM, when the day was getting good and hot, an armored Jeep turned on its engine and kicked up dust as it powered up to the army access road next to the Fence. It had been sitting two hundred yards from us the entire time, hidden by a rise in the land. Two young Israeli soldiers with flak jackets and helmets and M16 assault rifles got out and opened the gates. We passed single file as our documents were examined. Most of us seemed to get through.

The party that had been postponed at the gate resumed as we forgot all about the Fence and set about the day's business. Rows of olive trees were evenly spaced on gently rolling hills, hemmed in beautifully by white stone retainer walls that curved in harmony with the natural topography. Their leaves were green on one side, silvery on the other, and when the wind rustled the leaves, the trees seemed to shimmer. The olives faded from bright green to dark purple. A fine chalky dust saturated the trees, muting the colors to sea foam green and deep lavender.

People began whacking at the trees with wooden sticks to knock the olives onto tarps spread out below. I watched until I thought I had an idea of what to do and set to work. After a while I noticed Yusif looking at me funny. "You're not supposed to whack it quite so . . . randomly," he said. "It takes some amount of finesse to be gentle to the trees and still get the olives." I paid closer attention and soon developed a halfway-decent olive whack.

I noticed a guy around twenty years old wearing a T-shirt over his head to keep the sun off his face. Yusif said he was the mayor's youngest son, Mohammad. He was the most energetic and charismatic of the cheerful harvesters. He didn't speak a word of English, so we could only say "*Marhaba!*" (Hi!) whenever we ran into each other. But his enormous brown eyes exuded such intense and benevolent interest in everything and everyone around him, I started calling him "Mohammad the Charmer" in my mind. The fact that his lack of English skills was an exception drove home how many people in this tiny town spoke English as a second language. Jayyous was the same size as my hometown, about three-thousand people. But in Stigler, Oklahoma, even the high school Spanish teacher didn't really speak Spanish.

I got thirsty after a while and went looking for water. Along the way I ran into Azhar, the mayor's dark-eyed youngest daughter, an ethereally beautiful and unnervingly self-possessed eleven-year-old whose name means "flower" in Arabic. She was peeling a clementine (*kalamentina* in Arabic). When she finished peeling it, she offered half to me.

"*Shukran*," I thanked her. She smiled.

Azhar's half of the clementine was halfway to her mouth when Sebastian wandered by also looking for water. Instead of eating her portion, she offered it to him. "*Shukran*," he said.

I blinked in disbelief. Sebastian and I weren't just strangers—we were foreigners who hadn't even bothered to learn much of her language before visiting her country. She had every right in the world to be suspicious of us. Instead she was giving us her food without a second thought. I couldn't help but think I'd been an ogre as a child compared to her. I wouldn't even give my little sister half of anything unless someone forced me to.

When I got tired of whacking, I began climbing the trees and combing olives from their shaded inner branches using a hand-held plastic rake. The tallest trees didn't stand much more than fifteen feet high, but within each compact canopy was a vast and unique treasury of olives and leaves and sunlight and space. Olive branches have long been symbols for power, beauty, prestige, peace, and plenty, and it was easy to see why. Olives can be used for oil, pickling, lotion, soap, even fuel. Some of these trees were older than the Renaissance, and combing their willowlike branches felt like a sacrament. Wild herbs and brambles flourished at their feet, and the leaves shimmering softly over acres and acres seemed too diffusely beautiful for this world.

At one point I noticed a lizard high in a tree looking at me curiously. I picked it up and held it in my hand, and it shifted to a slightly paler hue—a chameleon! I jumped out of the tree and showed it to Azhar. I moved a black olive toward the frightened animal's open mouth to see if it would flick its long tongue out or turn black or something. Before I could find out, Azhar stilled my arm. She clucked her tongue, shook her head, and said gently, "*Haraam*."

Yusif had told me *haraam* meant something forbidden by the laws of Islam, or any basically sinful or indecent thing. Harassing a helpless creature apparently qualified in Azhar's mind. I nodded, tossed the olive away, and let the chameleon go on a white stone wall.

Once a tree was done, people would gather up the tarps and sit together, consolidating the fallen olives, twigs, and leaves into piles and removing the twigs by hand. The prettiest green olives were put in buckets for pickling and the rest would be bagged up, sorted from the leaves, and turned into olive oil in Jayyous's Italian olive press. It was nice to sit after standing for so long, and often we would get so deep into a conversation we'd have the pile clean as a whistle and still be picking at specks and talking away. Eventually someone would come over with an empty grain sack, and we'd scoop them in and break it up and move on.

Always there was the soft, heavy patter of olives landing on tarps all around, a rich olive rain. It was a pregnant sound that promised good things, not the least of which was this day, chatting and whacking and picking under a clear blue sky.

It was a welcome relief when lunch was called. Hot and hungry, we gathered around a tarp loaded down with bread and jam, hummus and pickled olives from past harvests, homemade falafel and crumbly white cheese, tomatoes and fresh yogurt and *halaweh* (a confection made from sesame paste). Some of the younger kids, packs of nieces and nephews and cousins, ran around shrieking and laughing and throwing olives at each other. It reminded me of the golden days in Stigler when my cousins and I used to climb trees and pick mulberries, gather eggs and shell peas, chase cows and play by the creek on my grandfather's land.

As I was drinking my tea after the meal, I glanced up at Jayyous perched on its hilltop. Its white houses contrasted beautifully with the dark pine trees in the village, the shimmering olive groves surrounding it, and the clear blue sky. I remembered seeing similar scenes in Renaissance paintings when I was a kid and wondering if places like that still existed.

It struck me all of a sudden that this wasn't merely an interesting conflict zone. In many ways, Jayyous was an enviable place to call home.

AFTER SEVERAL MORE hours of picking and a last batch of olives loaded into sacks and hauled onto a waiting truck, we headed toward home. After the day's gaiety, I wasn't prepared for what awaited us. The Fence was closed and locked. No soldier was manning it. Once again we had no choice but to put down our supplies, gather around the gate, and wait. An old woman in a white headscarf glanced up at the most devastated of Jayyous's once-productive hillsides. Her eyes followed the Fence and its clear-cut and bulldozed perimeter, a huge area that used to be home and now meant a threat of death to any Palestinian who dared approach. Her eyes narrowed as she took in the piles of razor wire surrounding the structure, which were designed to corral not goats or sheep but human beings.

"*Haraam!*" she exploded suddenly and shook her fist at it. "*Haraam!*" Another old woman patted her on the shoulder to calm her. She looked down feebly and shook her head.

An hour later it was time for the evening prayer. There was still no sign of anyone to let us back home. The men laid a tarp down on a rocky ledge. One man led the prayer while the others prayed in their jeans and dusty work shoes, silhouetted against a lovely setting sun. Another man went off by himself to pray next to a pile of razor wire. As I watched him pray solemnly, imprisoned and humiliated on his own land, I felt something I'd never felt before, as if I'd been kicked in the stomach by my best friend.

It was nearly dark when the soldiers finally arrived. As the once-merry villagers lined up somberly, making sure to behave while the young Israeli soldiers questioned them, checked their documents, and waved them uncaringly through, my shoulders bowed and my head ducked. A horrified weight of sorrow settled on my heart. I felt like I couldn't bear to watch this awful scene, to quietly accept it. But there was nothing I could do.

After a few moments, it dawned on me that I was wrong. I leveled my head. I straightened my shoulders. If nothing else, I could at least try to face this situation with as much honesty and dignity as I could muster.

With that I realized something else. I had always assumed, watching scenes like this on the news, that the people who bore such things must either not quite care about life as much as I did, or they must have some kind of supernatural coping mechanism I couldn't begin to fathom. Because if anything like this happened to me, I assumed I would utterly fall apart. Now I felt ridiculous for ever imagining such a thing. Here I was, and unendurable things were happening right in front of me to people who were no different from me at all. And they were bearing the situation with dignity, not because they didn't care or because they were saints. They simply had no other options except being miserable, which wouldn't help anything, or resisting. And this was a point in time when resistance was probably futile.

Instead of feeling destroyed, to my surprise, I felt energized by a clarity of purpose I'd never felt before. Suddenly the conflict in this part of the world was no longer a blank horror. It was merely an extremely difficult series of challenges whose basic units were human beings. Enough people of good will could surely find a way to resolve them, and maybe after I learned a great deal more I could find a way to help. Either way, if the people of Jayyous could go through this every day and still go home and joke around on the porch—and apparently I could, too, because what else was I going to do, sit around and mope?—I wondered what else I might be able to bear that I never imagined I could.

SURROUNDED

Yusif took me to the house of a man named Thaher that night to show me a small apartment on his roof where he said I was welcome to stay as long as I liked. Thaher was the brother of Azhar and Mohammad the Charmer. Their father, Fayez Salim (better known as Abu Nael[4]), was the mayor of Jayyous, a stout, spry patriarch with a thick

---

4. When a Palestinian man has a son, he takes on the nickname *Abu*, which means "Father of," plus the name of his eldest son. The mother becomes *Umm*, or "Mother of," plus the name of her eldest son.

grey moustache who had worn a baseball cap, jeans, and a corduroy work shirt while he harvested. Yusif said he was heavily in debt from trying to help Jayyous's farmers cope with these new realities. Most of his eight hundred olive trees had been destroyed to build the Wall.

Azhar tagged along with us. She was young enough that she didn't wear the *hijab* (headscarf) yet, but she carried a little purse and flipped her hair back like I used to do as a preteen, trying to look more mature than her years.

The apartment had a gas stove, a sink, a foam mattress on the floor, and a shower in the corner. The view from the roof was spectacular. To the west, four kilometers beyond the Fence, was the Green Line, the boundary between the dark farmland of the West Bank and the endless lights of an Israeli suburb. Far in the distant haze, twenty miles to the southwest, the Art Deco skyscrapers of Tel Aviv were lit up against the dark span of the Mediterranean. Clusters of lights also surrounded us within the West Bank.

"Towns with white lights are Palestinian villages," Yusif explained, "and yellow ones are Israeli settlements built on Palestinian land." My mouth went dry as I realized what I was seeing. I had heard about Israeli settlements in the West Bank, and that the settlements were illegal under international law.[5] But it didn't really register until I saw it with my own eyes. Jayyous was literally surrounded by them. I could see at least four from where we were standing. The nearest one, Zufin, had been built on Jayyous land on the other side of the Wall.

"They try to take the hilltops so they can keep track of what everyone is doing," Yusif said.

"But why would Israelis want to move here?"

"Some settlers are ideological. They think the land has to be 'redeemed' by Jewish settlement so the Messiah will come. Others are 'economic settlers,' which means they live here because it's heavily

---

5. The Fourth Geneva Convention forbids an occupier from transferring its civilians into occupied territory.

subsidized by the Israeli government. They can live in a much nicer home in a settlement than in Israel for the same money."

"How many Israeli settlers live in the West Bank and Gaza?"

"About four hundred thousand."

"How many Palestinians?"

"Two and a half million in the West Bank, a million and a half in Gaza."

As I took in the surreal vista with the Wall in the foreground blasting and isolating land from its owners, and settlements blinking yellow from every compass direction, I felt a sudden, irrational urge to cover Azhar's eyes.

I AWOKE THE next morning with a thrill of trepidation in my heart. The Wall in this region had been completed just a few months earlier, and Israel had declared the area between the Wall and the Green Line to be a closed military zone called the "Seam Zone." Jayyous residents were ordered to apply for permits to access the land that fell behind the Wall.

At first they refused. The idea of applying for permits to access their own land was too ludicrous to contemplate. In order to pre-empt expected resistance, the Israeli army waived the application process and simply delivered several hundred permits. The people of Jayyous reluctantly accepted them, afraid they might otherwise be barred from their land entirely. It was a bitter decision, but at the time it seemed the lesser of two great evils. Unfortunately, the permits were insufficient in number and distributed seemingly at random. Several were made out to children, the elderly, people who lived abroad, and even dead people. Many farmers, landowners, and workers were denied.

Today was the first day the new permit system would go into effect. If too many people were denied passage, Yusif said it might result in a minor revolt: demonstrations, stone throwing, tear gas, rubber bullets, and possible escalation. He said I should be there to see it, but I should stay well back.

The scene at the gate was tense as the soldiers spoke to the anxious Palestinians. Azhar held my hand, alert and serene as usual. A cameraman who looked European was filming. The incident wouldn't have been out of place on the evening news. It was bizarre to see it for myself, and to see the characters around me as three-dimensional human beings instead of two-dimensional news objects—as if I had fallen through the looking glass.

In the end, only a few people were denied passage. Some were furious, and a few wept quietly on their way home. But the outrage wasn't enough to risk a confrontation that might turn violent. Jayyous relented. We picked olives again, but it wasn't quite the same.

Rania's House

In the evening, back in Jayyous, Yusif and I walked across town to visit Rania, a young Palestinian woman who taught English with Yusif's organization. Her mother had doubts about Rania's new job, and Yusif wanted to talk with her and ease her fears.

Yusif was wearing a white tunic and an elegant white turban, which made him look more stereotypically Muslim than most Jayyousis. As we walked down Jayyous's narrow Main Street, everyone greeted Yusif with a hearty, "*Salaam alaykum!*" to which he invariably replied, "*Wa alaykum al salaam!*" People always seemed happy and honored to see each other even if they had seen each other several times that day. Most of the men wore slacks and work shirts while teachers and college students wore pressed shirts and ties. Some of the older men sported black-and-white *keffiya* headscarves, which Yusif said were a traditional symbol of the *fellahin* (farmers), somewhat like cowboy hats in the U.S. Younger women usually wore a *hijab* (headscarf) and *jilbab* (long, flowing dress-coat), and they were master artisans with eye shadow and eyeliner. Older women wore the old-fashioned loose white headscarves and traditional black robes embroidered down the front in intricate patterns of bright red and green.

As we walked, nearly every child shouted an excited "Hallo! What's your name?" in my direction. Dozens of greetings bombarded me from side streets, windows, and rooftops. Once I glanced up and saw three adorable little girls sitting on a windowsill with their legs dangling through protective metal bars, smiling and waving as if they'd spotted a celebrity, or maybe a talking polar bear.

The air was redolent with Jayyous's characteristic scent of night-blooming jasmine commingled with burnt garbage.[6] The jasmine's fragrance was like wedding-cake-scented perfume, thick and sweet and overpowering. Most houses along the street were white with front stoops or porches, a balcony or two, and flat roofs crowned by black water tanks, TV antennae, and colorful clotheslines. Some were accented with decorative arches or columns, iron filigree, a Quran verse engraved over the front door or a flowering vine spilling over a privacy wall.

In the center of town, the mosque's ornate minaret rose proud and white over its aquamarine dome. Beside it was a humble court-yard with concrete benches under small leafy trees. Crumbling Ottoman-era ruins came into view next, then stores selling dry goods, soft drinks, candy, and school supplies. Political graffiti was scrawled across most of the walls. The houses in the center of town were notice-ably more splendid than the newer homes on the outskirts, reflecting the toughness of recent times.

When we reached Rania's house, Yusif introduced everyone and then withdrew to the parlor with Rania's mother. The interior was the same immaculate white as Thaher's and Amjad's houses. I caught a glimpse of the parlor's overstuffed couches, patterned in hues of rose and gold with wood trim.

The rest of the house was furnished more simply. The bright, spa-cious living room with its big curtained windows had only a TV on a stand in front of foam cushions on the floor. Rania invited me into her bedroom, where a Canadian girl named Amy was sitting on the bed.

---

6. Trash collection is difficult in many Palestinian villages because of checkpoints, narrow roads, lack of funds, etc., so garbage is often disposed of by burning.

She introduced herself and said she was teaching English with Rania at the Jayyous community center.

"But I'm hoping to go to the Gaza Strip soon," she said. "Someone offered to put me on a list to get permission to go there."

"She is leaving us!" Rania wailed. "And when she leaves, there will be no one to teach English with me. The girls, all of our students . . ."

Dinner was called soon. We sat on plastic chairs around their white plastic dinner table for a feast of chicken and rice with fresh yogurt and shepherd's salad (diced tomatoes and cucumbers with lemon juice and olive oil). I ate until I was stuffed, and before I could protest, Rania's mother heaped another generous serving onto my plate and smiled suggestively, urging me to finish it off.

"Oh God," I whispered to Yusif. "How do you say 'I'm about to explode' in Arabic?"

Before he could open his mouth, I said, "Actually, on second thought, never mind. It's probably better if I don't know how to say those words in Arabic."

YUSIF'S ISLAM

After leaving Rania's house, we found Sebastian and started a *nargila* circle on Amjad's porch. I'd begun looking forward to the evening ritual. The rhythm of passing the pipe, changing the coals, and replacing the tobacco was its own time-space universe. All else fell away while we chatted and watched the night. Yusif had brought rose-flavored tobacco from Jordan, and the scent was heavenly.

"That guy Suleiman said Muslims revere King Solomon," I said to Yusif. "I had no idea he was in the Quran. I guess I don't know much about Islam."

"There's a lot of overlap," he said. "Islam, Christianity, and Judaism all started with the patriarch Abraham, or 'Ibrahim' in Arabic. The Quran respects Christians and Jews as 'People of the Book,' meaning the Bible. But we believe Mohammad was God's last prophet and the Quran is the final revelation."

"Do Muslims believe in Jesus?"

"Of course. He was one of the great prophets of Allah. But he wasn't His son."

"What about *jihad*?" If I was going to embarrass myself, I might as well get it all out in one go. Yusif's views might not represent the entire Muslim world, but it was a start.

Yusif shook his head. "The word 'jihad' is used wrong all the time. It just means the struggle to be righteous, to be a good person. The extremists use it wrong, and the Western press repeats what they say. In the Quran it says, 'If anyone killed a person—unless it be for murder or for spreading mischief in the land—it would be as if he slew all mankind; and if anyone saved a life, it would be as if he saved the lives of all people.' There are certain times when violence can be justified, but it should be a last resort. But, Pamela, you see the situation here. Most Palestinians would accept a state on the West Bank and Gaza, but Israel isn't even willing to offer that."

I didn't know if this was true or not. I decided to leave it until I could do more research on my own. "Does the Quran say women have to wear the *hijab*?" No one had bothered me about not wearing one, but I wondered if they didn't secretly think of me the way Americans would think about a French woman walking around topless.

"The Quran says people should dress modestly, both men and women," he said. "The headscarf is more of a traditional custom. Actually the tight, colorful scarves most young women wear these days, I think it's a Turkish style."

"But doesn't it just hypersexualize the hidden parts?" I asked. "Anyway, look what Palestinian women do to their eyes! And have you *seen* the women in Cairo?"

"I hear erotic underwear is a huge industry in Saudi Arabia," Sebastian mused.

"Saudi Arabia," Yusif scoffed. "It's always the worst Muslims who make a big show of repressing their women. The Saudi royals brag about having control of the holy places, and then they go to Dubai and Aqaba and get whores and gamble and drink."

"That reminds me of a joke in my hometown," I said. "What's the difference between a Baptist and a Methodist?" They looked at me blankly. "Oh, right. So the Baptists are supposedly the more uptight denomination, while the Methodists are more laid-back. Anyway, the answer is: A Methodist will talk to you if he runs into you at the liquor store."

Sebastian laughed and Yusif shook his head. "It's the same everywhere."

QAIS

Amjad the barrel-chested engineer lived with his brother Amir, a clean-shaven, soft-spoken shepherd, and their father, Abu Amjad. Abu Amjad didn't say much. He was just a constant, kindly, watery-eyed presence who could never quite manage to flick the ash off the end of his cigarette before it tumbled onto his flannel shirt.

One day I was deemed to have been around long enough to be a regular instead of a guest, so I started taking my turn with tea and coffee duty. Amir taught me the proper method of making tea with loose black tea leaves, fresh mint or *maramiya* (wild sage), and plenty of sugar. The result is a sweet, strong, aromatic brew.

I brought my first masterpiece of tea out to the group only to find that my chair had been taken by a guy in a black leather jacket whose black hair spilled rakishly into his dark eyes. I poured a cup for him.

"*Spacibo,*" he said with a smile.

"*Pozhaluista,*" I answered politely. We met eyes as he raised his glass to his lips. Then we froze. Suddenly it occurred to both of us that we were speaking Russian.

"*Ti Russkaya?*" he asked, his eyes wide.

"*Nyet, Amerikanskaya.*"

"*Zachem ti govorish po-Russky?*" (Why do you speak Russian?)

"*Zachem ti govorish po-Russky?*" I asked with a laugh. Hearing a perfect Russian accent on Amjad's porch was like meeting an old friend in the most unexpected place.

"I studied in Russia for a year and a half," he said in Russian as someone moved over and gave me a chair next to his. "And you?"

"I studied in Moscow for a semester during college. *Ti Russky ili . . . Palestinsky?*" His skin was pale enough that he could have passed for a Russian, or at least a Chechen.

"I am Palestinian, of course. My name is Qais."[7]

"*Ochen priyatno.*" (Nice to meet you.) I was surprised how fluidly I was speaking Russian. My brain had apparently a chance to stir and settle since I'd last studied the language, or maybe it only seemed easier after struggling with Arabic for so long. "Did you like Russia?" I asked.

"Yes, very much. It was . . . very free. Not like this place, where they say, 'You can't do this, and you can't do that,' and everything is forbidden." I couldn't tell whether he was talking about the culture or the occupation. Maybe both. "But I realized the subject I was studying, *reklama*, was not good for me." I had to rack my brain to remember what *reklama* meant. I recalled an image of posters plastered on walls in Moscow. Ah yes—advertising. "So I came back to Palestine. Now I study physiotherapy at the American University in Jenin. I am happy to be back, but I miss Russia very much."

"I miss it, too. And I miss speaking Russian, so it's nice to practice with you. You speak very well." His vocabulary was much bigger than mine, and his grammar and accent were flawless. He was far more advanced than he should have been for having lived there only a year and a half. With his good looks and debonair confidence, I expected him to be cocky about it, but I was pleasantly surprised. When I made mistakes, he either ignored them or corrected me gently. If he suspected something was out of my vocabulary range, he would patiently ask, "*Ti znaesh shto takoe . . . ?*" (Do you know what exactly is . . . ?) If I didn't, he would explain, switching to English if necessary. Memories of Russia flooded our minds as we compared notes on the food, people, jokes, and slang.

After a while I remembered something that had been bothering me. "You know how people say '*ya khuy*' all the time? What does it mean?"

In Russian, *ya khuy* means "I am a penis." I had no idea what it

---

meant in Arabic, but I heard it all the time: "*Ya khuy*, please pass the tea." "*Ya khuy*, where are you going?" "Welcome, *ya khuy!*"

Qais laughed, probably imagining what a startling thing that was for me to hear respectable Muslims soberly announce at the beginning of nearly every utterance. "In Arabic, *ya* means . . ." He thought a moment. "It means you are speaking to someone. So if I say, *Ya Pamela*, it means I am speaking to you."

"I see. Like the English word 'hey.'"

"*Da*, maybe. But more polite, I think. And *akhuy* . . ." He glanced sideways at me, and I suppressed a giggle. "In Arabic, it means 'my brother.' Everyone calls each other 'my brother,' so that's why you hear it a lot."

Someone in the circle said "*ya akhuy*" just then, and we looked at each other and laughed. Jayyous was a conservative town, and Qais and I were unmarried young people, which meant we'd probably never have a chance to be alone together. But our shared language created its own island of intimacy. All night as we talked, we felt like kids getting away with breaking the rules.

RAMADAN

The next evening, a razor-thin crescent moon hovering in the rosy glow of the setting sun signaled the beginning of Ramadan, the holy month of fasting. For the observant, it meant no food or drink or smoking or sex from sunrise until sunset for the next twenty-eight days. I decided to try to observe it, both out of respect for the people around me and to see what it was like.

Back in my rooftop apartment that night, I also had to decide what my trip to Palestine was going to be. I'd expected to skip through the Holy Land in a week or ten days and then bounce on to the bazaars and castles of Syria, the nightclubs and mountains of Beirut, the fantastic carved cave houses of Cappadocia in central Turkey, and finally Istanbul, the Gateway to Europe on the Bosphorus Strait. My passport hadn't been stamped by Israel, so unless I got unlucky on the way out, I had seven weeks to see all that and much more.

It had occurred to me, though, that I could stay in Jayyous and help Rania teach English during Ramadan. I had been in the Holy Land only a week so far, and already I'd had such a variety of shocking experiences I'd be sorting them out for years. There was much more to learn, several people I wanted to know better, and something in the atmosphere that I deeply enjoyed—a preternatural friendliness and curiosity, artless and disarming, mixed with a healthy, humorous cynicism that I never expected. I wasn't ready to leave.

But staying for a month would mean cramming Syria, Lebanon, and Turkey—by many accounts the biggest prizes of the trip—into three short weeks in the cold of December. I'd have to skip so many things I planned on seeing. Ancient things. Carved stone things. Crusader castles, mighty rivers, hot Lebanese clubs . . . And all for one Stigler-sized farm town in the occupied West Bank?

My scalp prickled with a heavy sense that whatever decision I made tonight might resonate for the rest of my life. It made me feel tired and irritable. I thumbed through the Syria and Lebanon sections of my guidebook one last time, sighed, and went to sleep.

Behind the Fence

On the third day of Ramadan, I tagged along with Yusif and Sebastian
to Nablus, the largest city in the northern West Bank. Idyllically situated in a long valley between two rolling mountains, it's historically
known as the Uncrowned Queen of Palestine. Its *casbah*, or Old City, is
one of the most spectacular and intact in the Middle East. The town's
specialties include olive oil soap made in ancient factories and *kunafa*,
a warm, cheesy dessert covered in spiced shredded wheat, smothered
in vanilla-citrus syrup, and topped with crushed pistachios. But I was
most excited to visit the Turkish baths. My guidebook said Nablus had
some of the oldest functioning public baths in the world.

The city is about twenty miles from Jayyous, but we had to take
a dizzying series of winding back roads to get there. Each time we hit

a checkpoint or roadblock, we had to get out of our car, climb over the roadblock or walk through the checkpoint, and find another cab. After we'd gone through several of these barriers I said to Sebastian, "I thought the checkpoints were mostly along the Green Line, or at least along the Fence."

He shook his head. "Nope. They're everywhere."

Yusif said, "One of our Palestinian teachers lives only ten kilometers from our headquarters in Nablus, but it takes him two or three hours to get through the checkpoints. If he can't get through, he has to walk five kilometers over the mountains carrying all his materials."

"But what's the point?"

Sebastian grinned. "Protecting the settlers, of course." He seemed to enjoy the constant look of shock on my face.

Along the way we passed several Israeli settlements, mostly on hilltops. Their identical white houses with red-tiled roofs were plunked down in perfect rows like Monopoly pieces in stark contrast to the variegated and organic Palestinian villages. Occasionally I saw groups of settlers walking among picturesque Palestinian olive groves with sleek automatic weapons slung over their shoulders like fashion accessories.

We were near the geographical center of the northern West Bank when we came across a massive blockage called the Huwara checkpoint.[1] We joined a line of pedestrians that snaked on for a quarter mile. Everyone was funneled toward a fenced-in pathway that resembled a cattle chute. Armed soldiers checked people's documents and rummaged through their bags and decided whether or not to let them through. A sniper tower draped in camouflage netting hovered above the scene.

Inch by inch, two hours later we presented our passports to the soldiers on duty and made it through. On the other side we caught a bus to Nablus. We'd gone only a few blocks when we were stopped at a "flying checkpoint," identifiable by an armored Hummer parked in the road and stopping cars to check IDs. Israeli soldiers ordered us off

---

1. Most major checkpoints are named after the village they are closest to.

our bus and sorted out half the passengers, choosing mostly young and middle-aged Palestinian men. The rest of us were allowed to get back on the bus. I looked at the men left behind as we pulled away. One of the Israeli soldiers said something to them over the Hummer's loud-speaker, then he broke into a short song in Hebrew that ended, "Ha ha ha ha ha!" The men's stoic faces didn't change.

Soon the full view of Nablus, nestled in its valley and built of indigenous white stone, opened up in front of us. But I was too distracted and depressed to notice much. We got off the bus in the center of town and walked toward the Old City. I asked Sebastian if we could visit a Turkish bath or a soap factory. I thought that might cheer me up. He shook his head. "Some of them have been destroyed by the Israeli army. I'm not sure which ones are working anymore." It hadn't even occurred to me that ancient tourist sites might have been affected by the violence. I kept my shocked disappointment to myself and just nodded.

As we neared the Old City, I began to see tattered posters featuring young Palestinian men carrying assault rifles. Yusif said they were fighters who'd been killed by the Israeli army. He pointed up and down one narrow Old City street and said, "They have gun battles in here almost every night. Everyone blocks the roads and takes up defensive positions in their houses to wait for the Israelis to come in. You can hear bullets flying all the way down these old passageways. There's nothing in the world quite like it." He sounded almost nostalgic.

We caught a cab to a house where several internationals lived, mostly Italians. They were busy preparing Iftar, the sunset meal that breaks each day's fast during Ramadan. I introduced myself and started slicing tomatoes and mashing chickpeas.

The call to prayer sounds five times a day in the Muslim world—at dawn, noon, mid-afternoon, sunset, and nightfall. It's sung by a muezzin and broadcast electronically from the mosques' minarets, reminding everyone that God is greater (*Allahu akbar*[2]), there's no god but

---

2. The *-u* at the end of *Allah* indicates that *Allah* is the subject of the sentence. This grammatical convention is rarely used in colloquial speech but is commonly used in Quranic or classical Arabic.

God (*La ilaha ila Allah*), and Mohammad is God's messenger (*Mohammad rasul Allah*). Each day's Ramadan fast begins at the dawn call and ends after the sunset call.

When the sunset call sounded that day, we gathered around our feast. On my first few days of fasting I had cheated a little and at least drunk tea or water. Today nothing at all had passed my lips. My body was starting to adjust and expect food around this time. As I ate, slowly and thankfully, at peace and among new friends, I felt like every cell in my body had had a two-week vacation in the Caribbean and was coming home lean, tanned, and relaxed to a hot meal and a massage. Every little neighborhood in my body tingled, wriggled, laughed, and broke into spontaneous applause.

Dan in Israel

I was due to meet Dan the Russian-Israeli at the Jerusalem central bus station the next evening. The Nablus-to-Jerusalem route, a little over forty miles as the crow flies, took most of the next day. I had to change cabs six times. At one "flying checkpoint" an Israeli soldier forced everyone out of our cab. We had to walk in the dark and cold for forty minutes carrying our luggage until we found another ride.

It was a happy relief to see Dan again after so much craziness. We caught up over dinner, then he drove us north to his apartment in Kfar Saba, an Israeli town just a few miles from Jayyous on the other side of the Green Line. Before I nodded off on his couch, he asked if I wanted to go to the canyon the next morning. I happily agreed. I didn't care which canyon, as long as we could get away from soldiers and Walls and politics for a while.

The next morning after breakfast he drove us toward the center of Kfar Saba. I said jokingly, "There's a canyon in the middle of Kfar Saba?"

"Yeah, a big one. It's really nice." I looked at him strangely. My guidebook hadn't said anything about Israeli cities with canyons in the middle of them.

We soon pulled into a desultory parking lot. After a security guard checked our trunk, we parked and headed toward what looked like a large shopping mall. I stopped short. "There's a canyon in that mall?"

"A what?" He furrowed his brow for a moment. Then he burst out laughing. "Sorry. *Kanyon* is Hebrew for 'mall.'"

"Ah." I was laughing, too. "But honestly, I was hoping for something a little more outdoorsy."

"Hmm . . . Maybe we can visit Haifa?"

Haifa is a seaside city north of Tel Aviv with a mixed Jewish and Arab population. After touring the town, we went swimming in the Mediterranean, camped on the beach, and shared a picnic of Israeli wine and Russian cheese. It was a perfect day, carefree and fun.

The next morning we drove to the Sea of Galilee and had breakfast at a café near the water. The "sea" is technically a lake, ten miles wide and still as a millpond, with the yellow-green hills of the Golan Heights towering solidly above it. I said to Dan, "This was seriously where the disciples thought they were going to drown in a giant storm?"

He laughed. "I know. I always thought it was like the Black Sea or something. But it's just this little lake." He shook his head. Nothing was what it seemed around here.

While we ate I told him a little about what I had seen in the West Bank—the Fences, the martyr posters in Nablus, the checkpoints and roadblocks. He listened with his usual openness, but at times he looked doubtful.

Finally I said, "Why don't you visit me in Jayyous? It's not far from where you live. I'll ask Yusif if it'll be a problem, but I don't think so. That way you can see it for yourself."

He looked even more doubtful. "Is it even possible with all the roadblocks?"

"You might have to wait until the Gates of Azzun are open. That's what they call the pile of rubble that blocks the road to Jayyous. But I think there's a way to go around it."

"If there's a way to go around, what's the point?"

I shrugged expansively. "Look, don't ask me. None of this makes any sense to me. I'm going to have to do a lot of research when I get home."

"Yeah . . ." He paused for a long moment. "Just . . . make sure you put all of this in context. Last year there was a suicide bombing practically every week, it was . . . unbelievable. The mall we went to yesterday was bombed last year. Three weeks ago a suicide bomber killed twenty people in a restaurant in Haifa. Just innocent people having a meal."

I sighed and looked out over the water. What I had seen in the West Bank was terrible, but there was another side to the story, after all. I tried to imagine the horror of people sitting around having a meal, and then all of a sudden—

I started and glanced around at the patrons in our little café. I was relieved not to see anyone with a suspiciously bulky midsection and an eerily calm expression on his face. But nothing could prepare me for what I'd feel a year later when two busloads of people weren't so lucky.

Ramadan Daze

Rania was overjoyed when I got back to Jayyous and asked if I could teach English with her during Ramadan. Our students were mostly fifteen-year-old girls with laughing eyes and perfectly sculpted eyebrows, sweet and funny and eager to learn. We held classes three times a week, two hours per session. I spent most of the rest of the long, hungry days sitting on the cushions in Rania's living room watching Arabic music videos.

Rania was thin but strong, her voice soft and girlish, and her gestures and inflections tended toward the melodramatic. Her English was adorably nonstandard, like a slightly faulty textbook that had picked up odd bits of slang. She often said things in Arabic first, then in English, which helped me tremendously in picking up the language. Her family had built their house and bought the lovely parlor furniture in better times, "before the Wall." Two of her brothers were policemen in the nearby city of Qalqilia, and another was in the Jordanian military. Her father was in Jordan running a small shop and sending money to his family in Jayyous.

Rania had tried studying to be a midwife, but she'd fainted at the sight of blood. Until the English teaching job came along, she said she'd felt like Cinderella, cooking and cleaning while her sisters studied and had fun. Rania's two oldest sisters were married, and her next-youngest was now studying to be a midwife. The youngest, Rasha, was only ten. Rania hoped to make enough money teaching English to put herself through college in psychology. But her mother, who seemed jealous of her smart and sweet-natured middle daughter, was making it difficult. Sometimes she forced Rania to clean the house instead of teaching English, and at the ripe age of twenty-three she was under pressure to get married.

As we watched TV, Rania's sisters and I played a game called *Helou mish helou*, which meant "Sweet not sweet" and referred to how attractive the singers on the music videos were. Our favorites were Nancy Ajram, a flirty, baby-faced Lebanese singer, and an Egyptian hunk with a honey silk voice named Amr Diab.

Some of the videos seemed oddly explicit for this conservative Muslim town. In one of them a raven-haired Egyptian woman named Ruby, wearing tight track pants and a sports bra, slowly pedaled a stationary bike in a highly suggestive manner. It was always incongruous to be watching scantily clad women gyrate away while we waited, starved and dehydrated, for our small-town muezzin to remind us that God was greater.

Rania's house was on the opposite end of town from my rooftop apartment, so I walked up and down Main Street several times a day. Aside from the fifty kids waving and shouting "Hallo!" from all directions, I'd always run into at least a dozen people I knew or who knew about me or who just thought I looked like I could use a cup of tea. Half of them invited me into their parlors and insisted I join their family for Iftar. Getting anywhere on time and making sure not to double-book myself for dinner became a serious problem. My saving grace was the cheerfully equivocal phrase *Insha'Allah* (God willing), which could mean anything from "I will be there unless I get run over by a car" to "I have absolutely no interest, thanks, but who knows? Maybe the five other invitations I have tonight will fall through."[3]

Each evening, families gathered at their dinner tables looking like broken puppets. As the call to prayer sounded and the food arrived, they slowly reanimated into chatting, good-natured human beings again. It was best to start with just soup, a date or two, and fruit juice to get a little blood sugar spike, and then let it spread over your body before starting in on the main course. In practice, though, huge masses of food were almost always piled on my plate immediately.

My favorite was *maqlouba* (upside down), a casserole of baked chicken, fried cauliflower, and eggplant embedded in a mound of rice plumped with broth and cinnamon and spices. After being removed from the oven it's flipped over onto a serving platter (hence the name), sprinkled with toasted slivered almonds and pine nuts, and served with fresh yogurt, vegetable soup infused with cardamom, and shepherd's salad.

After a few hours of digestion and conversation, the hostess would present us with tea, coffee, and fresh fruit, homemade *kunafa*, *harisa* (syrupy semolina cakes), or date cookies. It took me several days to wise up enough to ask Yusif to teach me a phrase that would prove critical to my digestive health: *Ana shabana* (I'm full).

Rania's family invited me to Iftar almost every night, but I managed to spend a few with the mayor's family, and Yusif invited me to Qais's house sometimes. Qais was usually away at school in Jenin, but his older brother Shadi[4] was one of Yusif's best friends, and it was easy to see why. Even taller than Qais, Shadi had an otherworldly aura of calm and kindness about him, and he always seemed to be concealing a cosmic joke behind his eyes. His family had the best porch in town under a thick grapevine canopy with a panoramic view all the way to the Mediterranean, where the lights of Tel Aviv shone against the darkening sea.

---

3. Older folks say something similar in Oklahoma: "God willin' and the creek don't rise."
4. Rhymes with "caddy."

One evening after Iftar, I joined a *nargila* circle on Amjad's porch and noticed a man who looked European and had a calm, luminous smile and a lovely accent. He was introduced as an Israeli named Ilan who was developing a plan to project videos from Palestine into public spaces in Israel. He said most people in Israel had no idea what was happening to the Palestinians. Many had stopped watching the news altogether because it was too depressing.

"And the news doesn't even tell half the story," he said, and everyone nodded knowingly.

Another time we were joined by a Japanese photographer who was marketing Palestinian olive oil in Japan and a Canadian who used to teach English in Saudi Arabia. I asked the Canadian what he thought of Saudi Arabia.

He smiled ruefully. "Twenty-three is the wrong age to be there hormonally."

Palestine is much more liberal than Saudi Arabia, of course. Women can drive, vote, and wear pants if they want. But here in the village, Palestinian women rarely joined groups that included men they didn't know well. It appeared as if the system of scarves and situational segregation was designed to protect women from men and men from their desires. It seemed excessive and unfair to me. But Palestinians could have judged and dismissed me, an American non-Muslim, for any number of reasons. Instead, they chose to suspend judgment and see the good. Until I knew a great deal more, I decided to return the favor.

I loved how people swept in, brought their richness to the moment, then went on their way. The usual accoutrements of identity—job, education, family, nationality—hardly seemed to matter. I appreciated how people treated me like an equal, or at least a promising student, and patiently explained things when I got confused. Amjad, the barrel-chested engineer, was like a big brother, gruff and humorous, always poking fun at me. His brother Amir was shy and quiet and barely spoke English. But when he did speak, what he said was usually worth listening to.

Of all the things I thought Palestine might be, I never imagined this colorful collection of characters with their open eyes and open faces. And I wouldn't have believed it if I hadn't seen it for myself. I felt like I was being let in on an important secret, something I wasn't supposed to know.

As the days passed, I learned that the usual response to *Keef halak?*[5] (How are you?) is *Al hamdulillah* (Thanks to God). Yusif said you were supposed to say it even if your dog had just died and your house had been bulldozed, because even in the worst situation you were supposed to remember that everything was a gift from God. I loved how it rolled off my tongue like a provincial greeting in Robin Hood's Nottingham, and it was lovely to be in a place where I could express my gratitude for life so openly. It reminded me of how I'd felt in the Sinai.

People who were unrelated, even strangers, often called each other brother, sister, aunt, or uncle. Older people, whether they'd visited Mecca or not, were commonly addressed by the honorific *Hajj* or *Hajja*. Nearly every day I learned a new poetic call-and-response—*Naeeman* after a haircut or shower to praise freshness and beauty, *Yislamu ideek* (bless your hands) when someone had done something kind for you, *Mabrook* to offer congratulations. If someone bids you good morning, the common response is *Sabah al noor*, morning of light.

Little by little Arabic began to sound more like a colorful, rocky waterfall and less like an alien, cacophonous jumble.

DAN IN PALESTINE

Dan finally agreed to visit Jayyous the following weekend. The Gates of Azzun were blocked, so Yusif and I had to meet him on a settler road and guide him through miles of rocky back roads. After a painstaking half-hour journey (which would have taken three minutes if the Gates of Azzun were open), we pulled onto Jayyous's Main Street.

---

5. *Keef halik?* if you are speaking to a female.

Dan felt uneasy driving in with his yellow-plated Israeli car, but Yusif assured him it wouldn't be a problem unless Israeli soldiers happened to invade. It was illegal under Israeli law for Israeli civilians to enter certain Palestinian areas, and it was frowned upon to visit any of them. Amjad's neighbor, a kindly older woman, hid Dan's car in her yard behind a privacy wall.

Yusif took us to a *nargila* circle on Qais's porch and introduced Dan, who was welcomed and offered a chair. One of the Palestinian men, who didn't speak English or Russian, spoke with Dan in Hebrew. His tone and posture weren't accusatory or angry, just very earnest, trying to get information across. Dan listened, blinking and nodding, taking it in. I saw the strain in his eyes and felt a deep admiration for him, following his openness into this vast unknown. After a while the Palestinian man smiled and said something politely. Dan answered in kind, and the man left.

Dan looked stunned. Sebastian had enjoyed the shock on my face when I first got here; I had to admit, part of me enjoyed seeing Dan's. It made me feel less alone.

Soon we moved to Amjad's porch, where Amjad and Dan chatted in English about their jobs. My mind began to drift while they chatted. I was absently watching Abu Amjad's cigarette, waiting for his ashes to break off like a calving glacier, when I recalled something disturbing I had seen earlier on Abu Nael's porch while watching Mohammad the Charmer sort olives from leaves. Mohammad had placed a plastic tub next to a large fan and was slowly pouring grain sacks full of olives into the tub. The leaves blew out into a cone-shaped pile and the olives thudded into the tub, ready to be washed and pressed into oil. Some of the sacks had UN WORLD FOOD PROGRAMME—PALESTINE printed on them.

"You know what I saw today?" I broke in. "Some of the sacks they were using to store olives in were from UN food donations. And I've seen people using donated *vegetable oil* to cook with. That's like . . . I don't know, like Russia donating wine to France."

"I know," Yusif said sadly. "There's a bounty here. It's just stolen."

"Why doesn't the UN *do* something instead of just giving hand-outs?"

Yusif chuckled softly. "That's a very good question, Pamela."

It was, in fact, a very naïve question, as I would find out in the years ahead.

Dan spent the night at Amjad's place. In the morning I showed him the Fence and how much land it isolated. He was speechless.

We drove out of the West Bank and were soon in Kfar Saba, another world. We watched *The Matrix Revolutions* in an air-conditioned theater and drank flavored lattes in a marble mall full of $200 sunglasses and low-slung jeans. The cognitive dissonance was wrenching.

On our way back into the West Bank, where Dan would drop me off at Azzun, I noticed a bumper sticker on a yellow-plated Israeli car in front of us. My eyes widened. I pointed it out to Dan, and he laughed incredulously.

The bumper sticker said: FREE TIBET.

THUNDERSTORM

I wandered over to Amjad's porch one night and found Yusif there alone. We lit up a *nargila* and watched a thunderstorm blow in from the Mediterranean, stalk across the coastal plains, and creep up through the olive groves until rain was falling in heavy sheets around our porch sanctuary. The nightfall call to prayer sounded amid deafening thunder cracks.

"I love Jayyous's muezzin," Yusif said dreamily. "He was one of the reasons I decided to stay here. I heard his voice from the minaret and just said, 'This is it.'" The muezzin's voice was high and clear and had a sweet, broken longing to it. The fact that this tremulous disembodied sound was just a guy down the street, and we could go find him and talk to him if we wanted, gave it an even more intense feeling of being a bridge between heaven and earth, between the unspoken and the day-to-day.

After the muezzin finished, Yusif drew on the *nargila* again. "What about you?" he asked as he exhaled a cloud of rose-scented smoke. "How come you followed us in here?"

"I don't know. It was just kind of an impulse."

He nodded. "I sensed you were on a quest when we met you in Amman." I laughed. Quest, indeed. When I was fifteen years old, I'd picked up a copy of Carl Sagan's *Cosmos*, which led to the collapse of my Bible-centric view of the world. Since then I'd prided myself on being the most skeptical of skeptics, the most left-brained of left-brainers. I studied physics in large part because it seemed like the least dogmatic subject, the furthest possible thing from faith.

But eventually I realized there were limits to scientific inquiry. Life, after all, wasn't a controlled experiment. It was just one long chaotic iteration of infinite potential, utterly unique in all of creation. Choosing how best to spend it would take more than the methods of science employed over the span of a lifetime. It fundamentally required a leap of faith in one direction or another, whether you realized you were taking it or not.

My initial, unconscious "faith" had been to organize my life around societal measures of success. That collapsed after I graduated from college. My new version of faith seemed to involve quieting down and trying to stay open to the world and to the vague impulses that quietly directed my actions and seemed to recognize truth better than I could. You could call the source of these impulses God, the Tao, the muse, Allah, the collective unconscious, or a by-product of evolution as it blindly followed the laws of subatomic interactions. But labeling it wouldn't get me any closer to understanding its nature or intentions, blind or otherwise.

Whatever it was, I was pleased with the results so far. Sitting under a thunderstorm on a porch in the West Bank with a seeker like Yusif was better than anything I could have thought up on my own, much less bought and paid for. I supposed I could only be grateful and hope the universe knew what it was doing. "I've just been following my nose," I said, "waiting for inspiration to strike."

"I think you're looking for light," he said matter-of-factly. "And you shouldn't worry. When you're following your destiny, the whole world conspires to help you."

I smiled. People certainly had been more helpful lately than I had any right or reason to expect. Nothing in my upbringing had prepared me for this level of kindness from strangers.

"But it's hard sometimes, letting go of the stories you think you know."

"It's true," he said. "Some say the battle with your ego is the toughest *jihad*."

I nodded as I watched the rain, soaking up the luck of being where I was. After a while I sighed. "But following your heart can be a pretty irresponsible business. All those people with all those expectations . . ."

He just looked at me and grinned.

Helicopters and Hellfire

We were walking through Jayyous's land a few days later when a helicopter flew low over the village. Yusif pointed out the two Hellfire missiles it was carrying and guessed it was heading to Jenin or Nablus to assassinate someone.

I froze. Sebastian had told me about the havoc wreaked in Nablus when Israeli helicopters and jets attacked in broad daylight, blowing up cars in the middle of busy roads, targeting suspected militants, and often killing innocent bystanders. A Japanese nurse had told me about treating kids in the Gaza Strip who'd been torn apart by shrapnel from Israeli missile strikes while on their way to school. But until now I had never actually seen an armed aircraft on its way to incinerate human flesh. My own flesh crawled and my mind raced. I wanted to say to Yusif, "Can't we call someone in Jenin or Nablus and warn them?" But if it was that easy, someone probably would have done it already. We couldn't do anything but watch it fly over.

On Amjad's porch that night, I sat silent and pensive. Sebastian and Yusif were talking about Ramallah, the de facto Palestinian capital since Israel annexed East Jerusalem, which Palestinians claim for their capital.

"How can they look out for the people?" Yusif was saying in disgust, referring to the Ramallah-based Palestinian Authority (PA). "The PA leaders don't have to live under the same occupation we're living under. They collaborate with the Israelis because it's the only way they can keep their positions of power. Some of them spend their weekends dancing and drinking with Israelis in West Jerusalem and Tel Aviv—sometimes literally sleeping with the enemy. You know, Pamela, some people think Fatah is worse than the Israelis." Fatah was Yasser Arafat's party, which dominated the PA. "Some people call them the 'second occupation.' At least with Hamas, if you give them money to give to poor people, the poor people actually get it. If you give it to Fatah, you'll be lucky if they get half."

I nodded numbly.

"You remember those guys we talked to in Qalqilia?" he went on. Sure, I remembered. Several days earlier we'd gone to Qalqilia, a city near Jayyous, to register Yusif's charity organization with the Palestinian Authority. The city and its forty thousand inhabitants are completely surrounded by the Wall, a twenty-five-foot concrete structure punctuated by sniper towers. The only gate is controlled by an Israeli checkpoint. The town had been turned into one giant prison. It was the most insane and dispiriting thing I had ever seen.

Yusif and I had walked down the shop-lined Main Street with its colorful racks of scarves fluttering in the breeze until we reached the PA office, where two shifty-looking men in ill-fitting suits offered us cups of bitter, lukewarm coffee. "They tried to sell me out," Yusif said.

"What does that mean?"

"Collaborators get bonuses from Israel if they tell them what people are up to. If the Israelis find out I'm setting up a charity organization for Palestinians on a tourist visa, they might deport me. They were only stopped by some higher-ups in the PA who knew me." He shook his head in disgust. "At least with Israeli soldiers, I can understand it. I used to be part of a militia in the Sudan, and we did some things I wasn't proud of. We were part of what caused the famines in '84. I finally realized how brainwashed I was, and I rejected Islam for a few years until I went on a quest to find out what it was really about. But at least I can empathize with that mentality. Palestinian collaborators? I just can't wrap my head around it."

I felt too tired and sad to listen anymore. I went back to my little apartment on Thaher's roof and went to sleep, wired and troubled.

When I awoke, I was alone on a small hilltop pasture. I noticed a helicopter flying low and carrying two missiles. When I blinked, it disappeared. My heart pounded in my ears as I strained to see or hear where it had gone. Suddenly it powered its engine and kicked up dust as it emerged from where it had been hiding under a rise in the land about two hundred yards away from me. It homed in on my position and started toward me menacingly. I turned and ran, delirious with fear, and ducked into a small whitewashed goat shed. I huddled in a corner, hoping desperately that there wouldn't be a deafening noise, a blinding light, a burning pain, and then oblivion from which there was no appeal. The world spun crazily. Death from the sky—the depersonalized destruction of someone's entire universe. Now maybe it had found me . . .

I awoke with a gasp, sweating and nauseous but overwhelmed by relief. I wanted to get some fresh air, but I was terrified a settler or soldier might see me on the roof and think I was a sniper. I imagined a little piece of metal slicing through my head, offhandedly consigning me to oblivion like so many in this region already had been. I decided to stay under my blankets.

THE NEXT MORNING I felt exhausted, as if the machine gun–like barrage of emotions and impressions had finally overloaded my circuits. But I felt ridiculous talking about it when everyone else had learned these terrible lessons long ago and was dealing with far worse now.

Soon little things started to get to me, like the kids shouting "Hallo! What's your name?" a thousand times a day. And the toilets rarely had paper, just a little plastic jug of water or a hose, which I had no idea how to use. How could I practice aiming without soaking my pants? Even if I learned to aim properly, how would I dry myself? I didn't dare ask because I was terrified someone might be solicitous enough to offer a demonstration.

Israel had reduced shipments of diesel to the West Bank, so there was a shortage of electricity in Jayyous. The village had refused to connect to the Israeli power grid because they didn't want the Israeli government to be able to coerce them by threatening to cut off the electricity. The villagers had pooled their money and bought a diesel generator instead. Unfortunately, Israel also controlled the West Bank's imports and exports, so Israel could stop or slow diesel shipments whenever they liked. Because of the current shortage, Jayyous had to shut its electricity off every evening at midnight. It wasn't so bad doing things by candlelight, but it was another depressing manifestation of Israel's total control over every facet of life.

I was also getting bored sitting around watching Arabic music videos all day. I had finished the books I brought with me, including *All Quiet on the Western Front*, which did absolutely nothing to improve my mood. And people didn't just say "Hi" when I passed them on the street. They'd ask, *"Ahlan, keef halik?"* (Hi, how are you?) *"Ila weyn?"* (To where?) *"Maa meen?"* (With whom?) And my favorite: *"Leish?"* (Why?) I knew they were only being polite, but I was starting to resent having people all up in my business all the time, especially when it was impossible to answer truthfully.

"How am I doing? I'm shattered, thanks. I'm dealing with emotional and intellectual shocks that everyone around me takes for granted, which makes the trauma I'm feeling seem naïve and trivial. I won't be able to talk about it when I get home, either, because no one will understand what I've been through. It'd be great if I could at least get a hug now and then, but we're in *Haraam*-town, where premarital necklines are forbidden. Everyone acts so relentlessly cheerful in the face of all this horror it's starting to drive me nuts. I feel like an ass because I can't deal with any of this except by feeling irritated, my blood sugar's low from fasting, and I don't know what's worse, the insomnia or the nightmares. How about you? How was your day?"

Al hamdulillah. That was all I could say.

SETTLEMENT

Near the end of Ramadan, Dan visited Jayyous again and joined us on Amjad's porch. Amjad was in the middle of a diatribe about his beloved aunt who lived in a nearby village.

"She is like a mother to me," he was saying. "She practically raised me and Amir. Then they built the settlement Ariel and closed all the roads, and I haven't seen her for three years. Three years! I have to use a settler road to get there, but I don't have Israeli license plates." He shook his head in disgust. Then a look of revelation crossed his face. He looked at Amir. Amir's eyes lit up too. They both looked at Dan.

Dan understood. He said, "I can drive you there, it's no problem."

An intense wave of guilt washed over me as Dan drove us along the settler road. I had dragged him into the West Bank without warning how upsetting it might be. And here he was being kind enough to help my Palestinian friends, which could get him into serious trouble with his own government if he got caught. If he did I would feel personally responsible, and terrible.

We dropped the brothers off at the roadblock near their aunt's village, and they walked across. We couldn't park Dan's car there because Israeli soldiers might find it and ask questions. I suggested we check out Ariel, the huge settlement built near the center of the northern West Bank, just to see what it was like. We drove up the massive hill Ariel was built on and passed a security gate and dozens of white houses with red-tiled roofs. We kept going until we found a pedestrian mall with open-air shops and restaurants and a few outdoor TVs.

It was an eerie feeling, being there. Ariel's expansion had been the reason Amjad's aunt's village was closed off and Amjad was forced to rely on the charity of a Russian immigrant to visit her. Settlements in general were the reason for most of the checkpoints, roadblocks, and license plate rules—and the devastating route of the Fence. And here were the settlers' lily-white kids smack in the middle of the West Bank wearing trendy clothes, watching Israeli news in Hebrew, eating kosher pizza, and arm wrestling with cute girls as if everything were perfectly normal. We sat on a picnic table and looked around in a kind of daze until it was time to drive back to the settler road and pick up the Palestinian brothers.

THE EID

I called Dan when it was nearing the end of Ramadan to see if we could hang out one last time before I headed back to Jordan. He said he could pick me up at the Gates of Azzun and drive me to the bus station in Jerusalem whenever I was ready.

"By the way," he said, "did I ever tell you what happened when I left the West Bank last time? The checkpoint near the Green Line had been moved, and I didn't notice. I drove straight through. Army Jeeps started chasing me with their lights flashing. Somehow I didn't notice that, either. Finally they put their sirens on and ordered me to pull over. When I got out of the car, they were all aiming their guns at me."

I felt the blood drain from my face. "What happened?"

I could tell he was still shaken up, but he just laughed and said, "I told them in Hebrew that I was Israeli. They were *very* relieved I didn't look like a terrorist."

My head dropped limply into my hands.

A SILVER SLIVER of moon signaled the end of Ramadan and the beginning of the Eid al Fitr, the three-day Festival of the Breaking of the Fast. Two neighborhood boys sang jubilant calls to prayer from the mosque's minaret, and I ate my weight in the signature dessert of the holiday, a syrupy pancake folded over sweet cheese called *qatayef*. Packs of kids set off fireworks to celebrate the holiday, which set my teeth on edge, and some of the boys got toy guns for their Eid presents. I'd played with plenty of guns as a kid in Oklahoma, both fake and real, and the guns of the Israeli soldiers literally ruled these kids' lives. It must have been empowering to get behind one now and then, even a fake one. Still, every time I saw a munchkin emerge from a side street carrying what looked like a rifle, my heart jumped into my throat.

If the hospitality gauntlet was intense during Ramadan, it was positively oppressive during the Eid. I couldn't walk ten feet without being invited into someone's doorway with a cry of "*Tfadaleh!*" and an invitation to a huge meal. The five-minute walk across town could easily take two hours. It was like walking through wet tar. I was torn between feeling utterly exhausted by Jayyous and knowing how painfully I would miss it as soon as I left.

I joined the men on Amjad's porch at the end of the first day of the Eid. Qais was back from Jenin, and Yusif and all the usual suspects were talking and joking and being outraged and delighted, sometimes both at the same time. Qais asked when I would leave. I told him I planned on leaving after the Eid was over. He asked if I would ever return.

"*Konechno*" (of course). As I said it, it occurred to me it might even be true.

The Last Picnic

On the last day of the Eid I made my rounds saying good-bye to everyone. It was impossible to see all the people I wanted to see because each family insisted I stay for lunch, or a snack, or dinner, or dessert, or coffee, or fruit, or all six. I saved Amjad, Yusif, and Qais for last because I wanted to spend as much time with them as possible.

I was ridiculously behind schedule by the time I got to Rania's house. After Rania and I said tearful good-byes, Rania's mother waved and said in Arabic, "We'll see you, yes?"

I put my hand over my heart. "Always."

She looked startled, and Rania laughed her girlish laugh. "Ah, Bamila, she does not know this word. For us it is a kind of . . . how you say . . . sanitary napkin."

"Ah." My face flushed. "Well, for us it is, too, but it's also a word. How do you say 'always' in Arabic?"

"*Daiman.*"

"Ah, *daiman!*" Rania's mother said. "Yes. Always. See you always." She laughed.

When I got to Amjad's place, I was overjoyed to see that Qais was already there watching TV in the living room. He stood up when he saw me. "Where have you been?" he asked. "I came here specially to see you."

As I fumbled for words in Russian to explain, I finally realized something. Until this moment I had merely noted that Qais was tall, dark, handsome, intelligent, funny, and kind. But there was nothing I could do about it. This was Jayyous, after all, and I was just passing through. But these thoughts had only masked feelings that were suddenly undeniable.

Amjad and Amir showed up and sat with us for a last evening of chatting together and watching the world go by. When it was time to go, I wasn't sure how to say good-bye to the brothers or express what my times on their porch had meant to me. As I opened my mouth to try, Amir asked, "How many brothers you have?"

"Um, just one," I answered, taken aback by the apparent non sequitur.

"No." His eyes smiled. "You have three." He looked at Amjad, and Amjad's eyes smiled too.

I took a deep breath and nodded. "*Maa al salaama, ya akhuy.*"

Qais and I walked toward his house for a last *nargila* together. Along the way we ran into the mayor and his son Mohammad the Charmer, who shook my hand and said all the warm, poetic good-byes I had learned in Arabic and some I didn't know. It was impossible to imagine I might never see these people again.

Yusif and Shadi were smoking on the porch together when we got to Qais's place. They were talking about a barbecue planned for the next day near a cave on Jayyous's land. The more they talked about it the better it sounded until I was practically fidgeting in my chair I wanted to go so badly. "It's really a shame you won't be there," Yusif said kindly.

"I know," I said miserably. "It's just that Dan is picking me up tomorrow to take me to Jerusalem so I can catch a bus to Jordan."

Qais, never one to be perturbed, said, "Invite him to come, too."

Yusif was staying at Qais and Shadi's house that night and arranged for me to join them. We set up foam mattresses on the living room floor, with Qais's positioned as far from mine as possible. (Yusif and Shadi took it upon themselves to be the *haraam* police.) The electricity went off at midnight, and we stayed up and talked by the light of an oil lamp for another hour. Qais reached over once to trim the wick and brushed his hand against mine. We met eyes and smiled. It was a maddening taste of what might be possible if only it weren't impossible.

In the morning Qais and Shadi, wearing white cotton undershirts, wet and combed their hair in the sink on the front porch with its little broken mirror like a scene out of a Norman Rockwell painting. Shadi and Yusif seasoned pieces of chicken and packed them in a bucket. Other folks brought tea and veggies, a small grill, and a *nargila*. Dan drove in and joined us, and we all caravanned out to a rare spot whose panorama was unsullied by the Fence or any settlements.

We made our way to a clearing with a soft, pretty view down into a valley. Shadi showed me a little cave where they'd stored provisions. Someone dragged out an old mattress, and one of Qais's cousins did amateur gymnastics on it. Qais told me he'd studied kickboxing in Russia, and he showed off some impressive spin kicks. The big boys threw one of Qais's nephews around like a football, and he laughed and laughed.

Qais told me his classes would start in Jenin the next day, and he'd have to leave before dawn to make it. "I was going to leave last night," he said. "But I couldn't miss this."

"When will you come back to Jayyous next?" I asked.

"It will be a long time, probably."

"Why?"

He half-smiled. "Because you won't be here."

Dinner was called soon. We feasted on grilled chicken and onions and tomatoes, bread and olive oil, hummus and olives and fresh yogurt and pickles and tea. We used bread to scoop the food and threw chicken bones and olive pits behind our heads with a careless feeling of infinite space and plenty. Qais and Dan, a Palestinian and an Israeli, chatted in perfect Russian—Qais with his dark, intelligent, slightly mischievous black eyes and Dan who'd come all the way to Israel from Russia and then been brave enough not only to venture into enemy territory but to find friends there.

After dinner we walked around and talked and picked wildflowers. I took a picture of Yusif, Qais, and Shadi with their arms slung around each other, smiling as freely as children against a backdrop of olive tree hills, feathery clouds, and a powder blue sky. I tried to capture the larger image of the day in my mind, a fleeting feeling of being flooded by good fortune, of stumbling into a place so exotic yet strangely homelike, witnessing for myself that even in the middle of one of the most protracted and ugly conflicts on earth, moments like this were still possible.

HOME AGAIN

My three weeks in Syria, Lebanon, and Turkey were a lovely blur infused with missing the Holy Land so badly it was an almost physical pain. When I got back to California, I felt desperate to share what I had learned and find out what it meant. Whenever Dan was hanging out with us in Jayyous, it seemed like the whole conflict should evaporate any second, shriveled and shamed by its own depraved pointlessness. Yet thousands of highly qualified people had been working on the problem for decades, with no end in sight. I wanted to understand why.

I got my first clue when I began talking with friends about what I had seen. Some were skeptical, which was understandable. Others refused to believe things I had seen with my own eyes. Several, who had never been anywhere near the Middle East, informed me that I was naïve and must have been brainwashed. More than one made vicious generalizations about Arabs and Muslims that they'd never dare make about any other race or religion. It was so bizarre to see friends turn into different people around this issue I almost began to question my own sanity.

Then I talked with Michel, my Lebanese ex-boyfriend, who had grown up in Beirut during the wars. I poured out my stories to him, and he smiled knowingly. When we were dating, he'd never talked about the conflicts he lived through. Now I understood why.

I also joined Arab and Muslim student groups on the Stanford campus, and they welcomed me as one of their own. It was such a relief to find people who understood what I'd felt and experienced, with no explanations necessary. But I also wanted to understand the mentality that lived on the other side of this strange psychological wall. I audited a class on the history of Zionism, attended Israeli film festivals, spoke with Jewish professors, and attended every lecture and read every book I could find.[6] I joined an Israel/Palestine dialogue group, and I had to research furiously to keep up. The deeper I dug, the deeper I saw there was to dig, right down to foundational questions of human nature itself. I'd never studied half as hard for anything when I was a student.

By spring there was no question I would go back to the Middle East as soon as I had enough money saved up to live there for six months or so. The longer I was away the more I missed the place, with its olive trees and ancient seas, sweet herb teas and night-blooming jasmine, dark jokes and devastating lessons. Things were *happening* in Palestine, while folks in America sat around arguing and intellectualizing about them.

I wasn't sure what I'd do once I got there. Yusif had left Jayyous, and the English teaching program had been discontinued. I was ready for something new anyway, probably in a city rather than a village. I just needed an excuse, a contact, something to lash my raft to while I figured out the lay of the land.

---

6. Zionism is a political movement, founded in the late 1800s, that supports Jewish self-determination in a Jewish national homeland. If you are new to this subject, visit www.pamolson.org and click "A Brief History of the Israeli-Palestinian Conflict" to read an overview of the Holy Land's history from the First Zionist Congress in 1897 to the second Intifada, which began in September 2000.

It arrived in the form of Dr. Mustafa Barghouthi, a Palestinian physician and politician with an MBA from Stanford. He gave a presentation on the campus in March that laid out the effects of the occupation clearly and brilliantly. When hostile audience members asked insulting or absurd questions, he kept his cool and handled them with reason and confidence—exactly the way I wished I could at the dialogue groups.

Dr. Barghouthi cofounded a political party, Al Mubadara (the Palestinian National Initiative), in 2002 as an alternative to the corruption of Fatah and the Islamism of Hamas. Half of Palestinians, he said, identified with neither Fatah nor Hamas. Al Mubadara was an attempt to build a reformist, inclusive party to fill that vacuum. It was committed to nonviolent resistance, providing public services, building international support for Palestinian human rights, developing genuine democracy, and negotiating peace with Israel based on international law.

If his methods worked, it would be thrilling to see them in action. If they didn't, I wanted to understand why. I didn't know what I could contribute, if anything. And it was easy to be liberal in California. Out in the real world of politics, violence, and implacable ideologies, my cozy view of the world—my belief in things like human rights, fair trials, and respect for other cultures—might break down, or the wrenching emotions of the place might destroy my ability to reason altogether. I hoped I'd be able to swallow my heart and stare down my assumptions and adjust. Either way, I wanted to know. The Holy Land was the most intriguing combination of colorful and friendly and devastating and insane. I couldn't imagine a better university of human nature.

Dr. Barghouthi did a little meet-and-greet at the end of his presentation. When it was my turn to shake his hand I said, "I'm thinking of moving to Palestine this summer, and I might like to volunteer with Al Mubadara."

He smiled kindly. "Take one of my business cards. It has the number of my office in Ramallah on it."

I took one and held onto it like a first-class ticket.

CHAPTER 4

Ramallah—
Palestine has its own Beer?

It is difficult to imagine how dull the world would be if our ancestors
had used free time simply for passive entertainment, instead of
finding in it an opportunity to explore beauty and knowledge.

—Mihaly Csikszentmihalyi, *Finding Flow*

"What are you doing in Israel?"

It was mid-June 2004, and I was at Israel's Ben Gurion Airport after a red-eye from San Francisco to Heathrow, an eight-hour stopover in London, and a second red-eye to Tel Aviv. It was two o'clock in the morning.

Bleary-eyed, I told the woman at Israeli passport control I was just a tourist. She frowned at the Syrian and Lebanese stamps in my passport and asked me to step aside. After everyone else had gone through, she moved me to a bench near a security office and told me to wait. Several other people came and went while I was held, my baggage and documents confiscated. I'd been expecting this kind of treatment, so I sat quietly and read my stepdad's ancient paperback of *Catch-22*.

After two hours passed with no word from anyone, my patience began to wear thin. I caught the attention of one of the guards and asked her what the problem was.

"Just wait," she answered.

"Is it my baggage? Can I help in any way?"

"Just wait."

"It's been two hours already."

"Just wait."

Twenty minutes later, another guard appeared.

"What was the nature of your visit to Syria?" she asked.

"Just as a tourist."

"And where did you visit?"

"Damascus, Palmyra, and Aleppo."

"And do you know anyone there?"

"A friend of mine has family there."

"Did they ask you to deliver anything to friends or family members here?"

"Yes, they gave me some bulky belts and mysterious tubes and canisters and asked me to deliver them to the Gaza Strip. Can you point me in the right direction, please?" Actually I said, "No."

Another twenty minutes, another guard. "And how much time did you spend in Egypt?"

"About a month."

"What did you do there?"

When the fourth woman approached and asked the same endless list of insinuating questions, I said, "Look, I already told someone else all this information."

"You told the police, but I am security. I don't know what you told them."

"Why don't you ask them?"

"It is not helping for you to be upset. Just do what I say and we can finish."

After two more hours, I was finally cleared for passage. Exhausted but relieved, I grabbed my documents and passed through the gates toward baggage claim only to be stopped by yet another security guard who asked for my passport again.

"I am head of security," she announced, "and I want to ask you a few questions. What is the nature of your visit to Israel?"

Half an hour later I was free at last, and Dan was kind enough to pick me up and take me to his apartment on his way to work. I collapsed on his couch until dinnertime, when we shared a meal and caught up properly.

The next day I called Qais from Dan's phone. The connection was bad, and I was afraid he wouldn't have any idea who I was. I sputtered a few half-Arabic, half-Russian greetings and asked if he remembered me.

"Of course," he said warmly in Russian. "I recognized your voice." He spoke as if it had only been a few days since we'd parted instead of half a year.

Silver-tongued as ever, I thought with a smile. "Listen, I'll be in Ramallah for six months or so. Hopefully I can visit you in Jenin at some point."

"I am sorry," he said regretfully, and my heart fell. "I do not live in Jenin. My university is in a town outside of Jenin, and I am living in a village near there."

"Oh, that's OK," I said, brightening again. Jenin was hardly the point.

RAMALLAH

By now my parents were used to my shenanigans—going off to California for college, studying in Moscow, working for a summer in China, traveling solo in Europe, backpacking in the Middle East. I knew how much they worried about me, and ever since Moscow I'd been writing long and detailed letters as a way to bring them along and ease their fears. But Israel and Palestine had almost been a bridge too far. We came up with an unspoken compromise: I would write even more often, and they would pray for my safety.

For months I'd been looking forward to a new life in Ramallah in an idealized, abstract way. But now that I was sitting in Dan's
apartment with a phone in one hand and a business card in the other
and nothing to say except, "Hey, I saw Dr. Barghouthi speak one
time and decided to come halfway around the world to see if he,
you know, needed any help or anything . . ." Suddenly the whole
plan began to seem a little half-baked. But it was too late for second
thoughts. I took a deep breath, dialed the number on the card, and
hoped for the best.

A woman's voice answered: *"Allo?"* I introduced myself and told
her why I was calling.

"Oh." She seemed surprised. "Have you sent us your CV?" I hadn't
thought of that. "All right, dear, why don't you do that? And then, let's
see . . . Can you come by our office in Ramallah on Saturday at two for
an interview? Ask for Muzna—that's me. We'll see you then, OK?"

I hung up with a feeling of profound relief. Now at least one person in Ramallah knew I was coming.

On Saturday I said good-bye to Dan and caught a cab to the
Qalandia checkpoint between Jerusalem and Ramallah. Ramallah is
only twelve miles north of Jerusalem, but it took nearly an hour to get
there. The road to Qalandia was a ruined mess. The foundation for the
Wall, a thick concrete barrier twenty-five feet high, was being laid
along the center of the road, right through the middle of a Palestinian neighborhood.[1] The street was lined with shops, which were dusty
from the construction and already looked half abandoned.

Finally we reached the Qalandia checkpoint. The massive complex had two sections, one for vehicles and another for pedestrians. A
line of cars stretched as far as I could see on the other side of the checkpoint, pointing south. The pedestrian crossing was a dingy covered
walkway crowded with hundreds of Palestinians being herded into
lines and searched and questioned by Israeli soldiers. A few impromptu

---

1. When the Wall is finished, it will stretch more than four hundred miles, or twice
   the length of the Green Line. It will be four times as long and twice as high as the
   Berlin Wall.

stalls selling roasted nuts, socks, and toys were scattered along the lanes, and young boys wandered from car to car selling packets of gum.

The land around the checkpoint was blasted bare and littered with dusty trash snagged on bales of razor wire. The mammoth, encroaching Wall and its sniper towers dominated the scene. More than six hundred checkpoints and roadblocks, big and small, saturate the West Bank, which has an area only slightly larger than the state of Delaware. Qalandia, the main crossing point between the West Bank and Israel,[2] is the biggest and busiest.

People trapped in this netherworld tried to look nonchalant, as if they were merely waiting in line at a grocery store, chatting with neighbors and scolding or soothing their children . . . until they got near the soldiers, at which point they would compose themselves into emotionlessness as they stepped through a metal detector and quietly submitted to being questioned and having their documents checked and their baggage rummaged through. If they talked back, looked suspicious, didn't have the right permit, or were simply unlucky, they might be detained, body-searched, or forced to abandon their journey or attempt to bypass the checkpoint by some obscure, circuitous route. It was astounding that any semblance of normal life continued to push and struggle around such a massive, humiliating obstruction.

The Israeli army wasn't checking people on their way into the West Bank, however, and I walked through in a matter of minutes and caught a cab to the center of Ramallah.

Ramallah's Main Street was lined with restaurants, money changers, *shawerma* stands, shoe stores, coffee shops, and colorful awnings and signs in Arabic and English. A dress shop called Heliopolis displayed extravagant ball gowns and bridesmaids' dresses in its windows, and I was surprised to see a perfume ad in the window of a cosmetics boutique featuring a scantily clad Elizabeth Hurley. Several posters plastered on the walls depicted people who had recently died or been killed. Unlike in Nablus, they were mostly civilians. One featured

---

2. The checkpoint is actually several miles north of East Jerusalem and serves to isolate East Jerusalem from the rest of the West Bank.

a bright-looking, smiling ten-year-old boy, and others mourned the passing of famed Palestinian intellectual Professor Edward Said.

Soon I came upon a traffic circle with a thirty-foot-tall birdcage-like steel structure in the middle. It supported a few Palestinian flags and was surrounded at every compass point by carved stone lions whose grandeur was marred by the tattered political posters stuck to them. This was Al Manara,[3] I would later learn, the central traffic circle of Ramallah.

It was a pleasantly warm day, and I sat on one of the birdcage's lower rungs to read and people-watch. An imposing Arab Bank building bounded the circle on the east along with billboards selling Coca Cola and Snickers. Knockoffs of name brand luggage spilled out of a shop to the west, and a man sitting on a chair next to it sold charcoal renderings of Arab leaders and American music stars. To the south a busy street led to another traffic circle, and to the north was a row of tall, thin palm trees. Street vendors sold fruit, nuts, bread, and small plastic cups of coffee out of wooden carts.

The sidewalks were thick with pedestrians, a distinctly more modern-looking crowd than the one in Jayyous. Many women didn't wear headscarves, and some wore fashionable Western clothing. The young men wore mostly jeans and T-shirts, and the professional class wore suits and carried briefcases. The oldest doddered along with canes and wore traditional white tunics, grey suits and *keffiyas,* or embroidered black robes and white *hijab.* It was strange to think all this would soon be the familiar backdrop of a new life. I felt a bit lost without Yusif there to introduce me to everyone, but I remembered how easy it had been to make friends in Jayyous. The future was excitingly blank.

I hunted down Dr. Barghouthi's office with the help of a stranger. A receptionist directed me to Muzna's office. Muzna was in her late twenties, slim and regal, with large expressive eyes and dark shoulder-length hair.

---

3. *Manara* means "watchtower" or "lighthouse" in Arabic.

"Hi!" she said brightly as I entered. "Did you get through the checkpoint all right?" I had assumed the sweet, musical lilt in her voice over the phone had been a secretarial affectation, but she spoke the same way in person. "For now what we need is someone to help finish a new Al Mubadara website and update and edit press releases, pamphlets, and informational folders, that kind of thing. How does this sound?"

We agreed I would start once I got settled in and oriented. I asked where she was from, and she told me her family were refugees from Haifa, the coastal city in what is now northern Israel. She'd grown up in Morocco and spoke fluent French. Her family had moved to the West Bank in the early 1990s when hopes of peace were in the air.

Before I left she said, "There will be a big demonstration this afternoon. It's part of fifty-six days of nonviolent demonstrations to commemorate the fifty-sixth anniversary of the Nakba. You should join us."

By late afternoon the streets were swarming with protestors marching down Main Street and chanting slogans. Some were carrying signs and flags, mostly the Palestinian flag or the yellow Al Mubadara flag, its logo an oval-shaped drawing of a crowd of diverse men and women clustered in front of a Palestinian flag. No foreign journalists were on hand that I could see, and few from the Arab world.

After the crowd dispersed, I found Muzna and asked if I should try to find a hotel. I'd never had trouble finding a place to stay in the Middle East. Even if there was no room at the inn, I was fairly confident a manger of some sort could be arranged.

Muzna introduced me to a blonde British girl named Emily who worked in the office next to ours, and she invited me to spend the night in her guest room. As we were walking to her house, I asked if she knew of any rooms for rent in the area.

"Actually, a room just opened up in a house near here. A woman from Gaza named Yasmine lives there. I can take you by there if you want to check it out, it's not far."

I accepted gratefully, and she directed me to a squat stone house a few blocks from the Al Mubadara office. I stepped in the door expecting to meet a prim, emaciated young woman in a *hijab*. Instead I came face-to-face with a plump girl with pouty lips, severely plucked eyebrows, and black ringlets that erupted from her head in all directions. She was wearing a thin nightgown and had her hand on her hip, which was cocked to one side. I could feel her appraising this pink newcomer with an eye that had seen everything—twice.

I apparently passed muster, because after chatting for a while she offered me the room for $120 per month—half the average rent in Ramallah. My room had no bed, just a lumpy mattress on the floor, and the small, windowless living room with its echoing tile floor had no couch or TV. The kitchen had a sink, a stove, a toaster oven, a refrigerator, a small pantry, a rickety card table, and a single chair with orange cushions and wooden armrests that looked like it had been manufactured in the early 1970s. It was clearly a case of "You get what you pay for," but I was glad to save the money.

My first day and I already had a job and a house. The depth of my relief was overwhelming.

THE MUQATAA

I had tea in my new kitchen the next morning and then set out to explore the neighborhood. The houses were built of heavy cut stone and shared a unified style of flat roofs, ample porches and balconies, and yards or gardens with pine, palm, or deciduous trees. Windowsills overflowed with bougainvillea, green and fuchsia against the creamy white stones.

Ramallah is built along the ridges of connected hilltops, like a supersized version of Jayyous. To the west of the gently curving road leading to Main Street, the land dropped vertiginously into space forming a steep, rocky valley before rising again to form more voluptuous terraced hills. I could just see Tel Aviv outlined against the blue Mediterranean thirty-five miles to the northwest. A mile or so due north I could see Arafat's compound, known as the Muqataa, on another hill. It was built in 1920 by the British, who administered

Palestine after capturing the territory from the Ottoman Empire at the end of World War I. Now it was the headquarters of the Palestinian Authority. One end of it looked like a giant hand had crunched it up and scattered the pieces—remnants of Israel's bombardments in 2002. I walked to Al Manara, then followed the road to the north to see the Muqataa up close.

High walls around the compound hid most of the damage, but through the gates I could see acres of twisted wreckage and crushed cars. Yasser Arafat (also known as Abu Ammar) was in there somewhere. He had apparently picked his handsomest men to guard his front gates. I greeted one of them in Arabic, and he answered in polite English. Everyone seemed to speak English in Ramallah.

Arafat's political party, Fatah, dominated the Palestinian Authority. Arafat had been placed under house arrest by Israel in 2002 following a wave of suicide bombings in Israel, even though Hamas and Islamic Jihad had done most of the bombings.[4] If he ever left his shattered compound, he risked arrest or assassination. Little did I know how soon he would take his final exit, or what the consequences would be.

OFFICE LIFE

It was strange to be sitting in front of a computer, editing documents or having lunch and chatting with coworkers like in any other office, and then have a report come in about another violent death a few miles away, another operation, incursion, arrest raid, or assassination, another checkpoint closed or olive grove razed, and my stomach would turn to water. Twenty Palestinians were killed in the first week of July alone. Eleven of them were children. One was ten, killed by Israeli

---

4. *Fatah* means "opening" or "beginning" but can also mean "victory" or "conquest." It is the backwards acronym for Haraka al Tahrir al Falastini, the "Palestinian Liberation Movement." *Hamas* means "zeal" in Arabic and is the Arabic acronym for Haraka al Muqawama al Islamiya, the "Islamic Resistance Movement." It was founded in 1987 at the beginning of the first Intifada. Islamic Jihad is much smaller and less powerful than either Hamas or Fatah, and it lacks Hamas's wide social network and welfare programs.

helicopter fire; one was nine, killed by a tank shell; one was four, killed by Israeli gunfire. Their deaths barely made the news. Events like this had become commonplace.

The story that hit me hardest involved a professor, Dr. Khaled Salah, who got his PhD at the University of California, Davis, and turned down a lucrative Silicon Valley job to teach electrical engineering at Al Najah University in Nablus.[5] A wanted militant ran into his apartment complex one night seeking cover from Israeli soldiers. The soldiers attacked the building using tanks, guns, and helicopters. When the onslaught ended and the militant was presumed dead, the soldiers shouted over loudspeakers for everyone to evacuate the building. They threatened to demolish the building, crushing anyone who remained inside.

The professor, his wife, and their three children tried to comply, but the door had been damaged and wouldn't open. Dr. Salah went to his bedroom window, held up his hands, and shouted that he was a professor, a person of peace, and he needed help opening his door.

Shots rang out, and he collapsed on the floor. The professor was killed instantly. His son Mohammed—a sixteen-year-old who loved British soccer and wanted to be a pharmacist—was hit in the mouth. He lay bleeding in front of his mother, sister, and eleven-year-old brother. By the time the soldiers allowed them to leave and seek medical help, he was dead.

Maybe it was because Dr. Salah's field was electrical engineering, which I had considered studying, or because he and his son were killed in front of their family, or because he went to university in California and probably spent his vacations in the same national parks I did, but I felt their deaths in my guts all week. I read detailed reports about their night of horror—the family huddled on the floor while the glare and boom of rockets reverberated through their home, the sounds of glass breaking and pipes bursting, the red laser beams of sniper scopes tracing lines across their walls, the smell of broken perfume bottles in the

---

5. *Najah* is Arabic for "success."

bedroom. And the image of a newly widowed mother watching her son bleed to death while all she had to staunch the flow of blood was a wad of paper towels.

The clearest account I found was in an article by Gideon Levy of *Haaretz*, Israel's main center-left newspaper.[6] The American papers were strangely silent about it, given that Dr. Salah and his wife were U.S. residents and two of their children were American citizens.

Other than the terrible news surrounding us, I enjoyed the work and the people I worked with. Dr. Barghouthi walked among us like a leader and an equal at the same time. He often said the traditional phrase *Yatik al afiyeh* (God give you strength in your endeavors) as he passed by, like people in Jayyous did. His employees referred to him fondly as Dr. Mustafa or just Al Doktoor (The Doctor). In addition to cofounding Al Mubadara in 2002 with Professor Edward Said, Dr. Haidar Abdel-Shafi, and Ibrahim Dakkak,[7] he was also director of the Health Development Information and Policy Institute (HDIP), a health policy think tank, and president of the Union of Palestinian Medical Relief Committees (UPMRC). One of Al Mubadara's core principles was that a viable state had to be built on a robust civil society, including a self-reliant network of educational, medical, cultural, environmental, and legal nongovernmental organizations (NGOs); Dr. Barghouthi had certainly done his part.

The office vibe was laid-back but professional. The album *Life for Rent* by the British singer Dido was popular in Ramallah, and at the end of the day someone in the Administration office was usually playing either that or Bill Withers's *Ain't No Sunshine*. Maps of settlements

---

6. Gideon Levy, "Death in a Cemetery," *Haaretz*, July 26, 2004.

7. Dr. Abdel-Shafi was a physician trained in Beirut and the United States and the founder and director of the Palestinian Red Crescent Society in Gaza. He was an independent nationalist linked with the secular left who enjoyed the rare confidence of all competing factions due to his singular lack of corruption. He was also among the first Palestinians to call for the acceptance of Israel alongside a Palestinian state. Mr. Dakkak is an engineer and economist with ties to the Israeli peace camp.

Author's Note: Visit www.pamolson.org and click "Chapter Companions" to find links to the full text of each article cited in this book.

and the Fence/Wall were tacked up on the office walls, along with posters of blindfolded detainees and bulldozed homes with the caption, "Collective Punishment is a War Crime." Comics were posted on the bulletin board in the lobby. One was labeled "The Palestinian Daily Olympics" (a reference to the upcoming Summer Olympics in Athens) and showed Palestinians pole vaulting over walls, running from Israeli soldiers, and shot-putting rocks at tanks.

Another comic had President George W. Bush surrounded by two advisers. The first says, "They've broken a number of UN resolutions and the UN has failed to act . . . They've killed thousands of their local population and invaded a neighboring country . . . They torture suspects and assassinate opponents . . . And we've confirmed they secretly developed nuclear weapons."

Bush says, "That does it! Bomb Baghdad!"

The second adviser says, "Uh . . . Sir, this is a briefing on Israel."[8]

SANGRIA'S

Muzna invited me to join her for drinks one day after work at a place called Sangria's. We walked to Al Manara and turned right toward another traffic circle called Duwar al Sa'a (Clock Circle). There had apparently been a clock in the circle at some point, but now only a white stone column rose from a fenced-in circle of shrubbery. A massive candy shop, *shawerma* stands, office buildings, an optometrist's clinic, and trees surrounded the unmarked monument. We turned right again and walked down a street I'd never seen before. The view opened up to a valley full of trees and white stone houses. We walked downhill until we arrived at a row of elegant buildings made of tawny hand-cut stone. We turned into one marked with a small wooden sign carved with the word "Sangria's."

---

8. Israel has never admitted to possessing nuclear weapons, but an Israeli nuclear technician named Mordechai Vanunu came forward in 1986 and confirmed that Israel had secretly produced nuclear warheads. By not admitting to its nuclear program, Israel skirts a U.S. ban on funding countries that proliferate weapons of mass destruction.

An empty foyer led to an outdoor corridor that opened onto the most enchanting beer garden I had ever seen, built on a grassy hillside enclosed by stone walls overhung with flowering vines. The tables on the upper terraces were shaded by large canvas umbrellas, and the lower tables sat under leafy trees hung with strings of lights. A grass hut in the center served as a bar. Waiters in maroon Polo shirts were busy distributing olive oil candles to each table under a clear, darkening sky. The crowd was young and stylish, the women dressed in club clothes, with almost no headscarves in sight.

We found a table and I ordered Turkish coffee and a *nargila*. Muzna ordered a beer called Taybeh. "Where's the beer from?" I asked.

"From here," Muzna said. "Taybeh is a Christian village east of Ramallah. They have a brewery."

"Really?" I was surprised. I had assumed it was foreign, or possibly Israeli. "Can I try yours?" She handed over her frosty longneck, and I took a sip. It was medium-bodied, refreshing, with just the right amount of hops. "Wow," I said. "That's good beer." Muzna smiled.

Just then a goofy Happy Birthday song came on over the loudspeakers at ear-splitting volume in Egyptian-accented Arabic. Two waiters emerged carrying cakes with giant sparklers spewing fire out the top. The birthday party had ordered enough cake for everyone on the patio, and after the birthday girl made her wish and the sparklers burned themselves out, the waiters sliced it up and handed out pieces. I happily accepted a plate, but when Muzna was offered one, she shook her head and said in Arabic, "No, thanks."

The waiter raised his eyebrows and asked chidingly, "*Leish?*" (Why?) I laughed out loud. It was good to be back in the Middle East.

INVASION PARTY

Yasmine invited an even mix of foreigners and Palestinians to our house one evening. It was a going-away party for a Norwegian woman who was taking a new job in the southern West Bank city of Hebron. The weather was perfect, and we congregated in our little overgrown front yard under a fig tree to drink Taybeh beer and eat barbecue chicken pizza from a nearby restaurant called Angelo's.

Yasmine and I were talking to an Irishman named Sean who worked for an NGO that specialized in human rights law and a Spaniard named Guillermo whose head was slightly oversized for his body, which made him look coltish and young. Sean said his favorite Arabic colloquialism was *"Bukra fi al mishmish"* (Tomorrow there will be an apricot). Apricot season is very short, so it's used the way we say, "When hell freezes over."

A Palestinian guy piped in, "Don't even dream."

Yasmine said, "By the way, did you know all our books are written in Egypt, published in Lebanon, and read in Iraq?" I laughed, but she said, "No, I'm serious, it's been true for two hundred years. All the thinkers are in Egypt, but they don't have democracy. So everything gets published in Beirut. But they are too busy to read. In Iraq, everyone is so smart, so that's where they read the books." I couldn't help but wonder how much reading Iraqis had done lately.

I wandered inside a bit later and found a French diplomat and a German economist playing bottle caps on a mat in the living room. I struck up a conversation with an American guy who was watching them. He'd lived in Palestine for five years, two of them in Gaza City. "Gaza was great," he said, "but the whole experience was very disillusioning."

"How so?"

"Well, I worked for the U.S. Agency for International Development, and they did things like build wells for the Gazans. Then Israel would destroy them using weapons paid for by U.S. foreign aid. Then USAID would rebuild the wells. Our tax dollars at work, eh?" He shook his head. "I've seen so much stuff, I didn't think I could get mad anymore. But the Wall makes me very angry."

We were still talking about the Wall when we heard a sudden commotion. I glanced up in time to see Yasmine ushering guests into the house as if an unexpected thunderstorm had broken out. Behind her an Israeli army Jeep, its yellow lights flashing, pulled up next to our house. Yasmine shut the door once everyone was inside. Soon we began hearing muffled explosions. Our guests took it in stride for the most part, vainly making guesses as to how far away each explosion was and what kind of damage it might have done.

I was terrified. Israeli soldiers had just killed a professor and his son in Nablus with no repercussions. Dr. Salah had been joking around with his family, assuring them everyone would be OK, minutes before he and his son were killed. If the Israeli army bombed our house, they could probably blame faulty top-secret intelligence, or claim a wanted man was hiding among us, and that would be that. For all I knew there might actually be a wanted man in a neighbor's house, and he might get flushed out and try to seek shelter in ours.

The American man turned to me. "This is odd. Incursions like this are pretty rare in Ramallah these days."

"Why?"

"Well, this is where the centers of power are located, and most of the press and ex-pats. The foreign aid money flows through Ramallah, so it attracts the most qualified and connected people. If business is good here, it gives us less incentive to rock the boat."

The army Jeep stayed next to our house for hours, blocking access to the main road. I stayed up with our trapped guests as long as I could, then I went to my room and tried to figure out where I could put my bed so it would have the slimmest profile in case a bullet happened to slice through a window. I soon gave up because I was too scared to do anything but pass the windows quickly and lay down on my bed as flat as I could. I awoke several times in a cold sweat, groggy with dreams, half-expecting the house to blow up at any moment.

The Jeep was gone the next morning, and so were our guests. When I got to work, I learned six people had been arrested, three of whom worked for the Palestinian Red Crescent Society. All were taken to unknown places. Arafat's compound was surrounded again. Someone said two houses were demolished, several doors were blown down, and two children were injured. Details were sketchy because a curfew had been in place during the incursion, which meant anyone who ventured outdoors risked being shot on sight.

YASMINE

One day I came home from work and found Yasmine in the kitchen wearing all black, her eyes puffy. Alarmed, I asked her what was the matter.

"The brother of a friend of mine was killed in Gaza last night." She shook her head. "His mother and wife back in Gaza are destroyed. His brother lives here, and he still has to work in his restaurant. I was helping him today."

"I'm so sorry."

She held up her hand as if to wave it off. I put cinnamon tea on to boil and said, "I don't understand how you deal with this. I've only been here two weeks and I'm already starting to feel overwhelmed."

She sighed. "*Habibti*,[9] I was grazed by a bullet for the first time when I was seven years old. Some kids were throwing stones near my neighborhood in Gaza, and Israeli soldiers were shooting at them. The soldiers were always coming into our house and beating my father in front of us during the first Intifada,[10] when I was just learning what the world was about. I thought it was always about soldiers and beatings and killings and checkpoints."

I shook my head. "But how do you deal with it?"

"I don't know. You just do. You'll get used to it, *habibti*. Or you'll leave. That's it."

"Do you think you'll stay in Palestine?" I asked. "I mean, raise kids here?"

"Of course. This is my home. I don't want my children to see what I have seen, but at the same time, my experiences have made me stronger." She shrugged.

---

9. *Habibti* is the feminine of *habibi*, which means "my beloved." Depending on the intonation, it can literally mean "my beloved" or be used the way Americans say "sweetie" or "hon."

10. The first Intifada was a collective uprising of Palestinians against repressive Israeli policies. It began in 1987 and ended in 1993 with the signing of the Oslo Accords. More than 1,100 Palestinians and 150 Israelis were killed, and tens of thousands of Palestinians were injured or arrested. It was a public relations disaster for Israel because videos were shown around the world of Palestinians armed only with flags and slingshots facing down Israeli tanks, and of Israeli soldiers beating Palestinian children.

"Is your family Muslim or Christian?" I'd never asked before. It had never come up.

She looked at me strangely. "We are Communists."

I blinked. "Communists?"

"Yes."

"Really? I mean, are a lot of Palestinians Communist?"

"Not a huge number these days,[11] but many of our leaders and intellectuals have been Communists. It wasn't easy for my family in Gaza, though. One time these extremist assholes tried to throw acid in my sister's face because she refused to wear the *hijab*. Ugh, morons." Her face twisted. "And it's getting worse here, too. Before the second Intifada,[12] maybe one-quarter of the women wore *hijab* in Ramallah. Now three-quarters do. This is what happens when things get bad. People turn to religion when everything else turns to *khara*."

Khara is the impolite Arabic word for "excrement."

"Do you think the second Intifada will accomplish anything?"

She scoffed. "This isn't a real Intifada. All we do is sit on our hands while they kill us and take our land, and every once in a while some asshole does a suicide bombing. It's bullshit. If this were a real Intifada, everyone would be involved, and they would have some principles, and there would be Israeli soldiers marching down the streets of Ramallah every day."

Some of her words surprised me, but I didn't feel qualified to have this discussion yet, so I changed the subject and asked about the roommate I had replaced.

"She was a Jewish woman who worked with an international peace movement."

---

11. During the Cold War the Arab world was aligned with the Soviet Union, which brought many Communists and Socialists to prominence in the Arab world. The fall of the Soviet Union left them with little international support or ideological credibility, but some are still known and respected as intellectuals, musicians, and tireless builders of civil society, as well as a non-Fatah alternative to Hamas for Christians and atheists.

12. The second Intifada began in the fall of 2000 and was ongoing as of the time of this conversation. It was a far more devastating and militarized conflict than the first Intifada. The word *Intifada* means "shaking off."

"Really?" I asked weakly. Beer, Communists, Jews . . . These were not the kinds of things I had expected to find in Ramallah.

"Yeah, why not?" She seemed amused. "One of my best friends in Ramallah is an Israeli woman who is married to a Palestinian man. She's raising two kids here. It is tough for her, because it is illegal under Israeli law for an Israeli to live in Ramallah. Sometimes she gets in trouble with the soldiers when she goes to protest the Wall or whatever."

"Do a lot of Israelis come here and protest the Wall?"

"Not a huge number, but some."

We chatted a while longer until she looked at her watch and said, "There's a movie on tonight at the Qasaba. *Mystic River*, I think. You want to go?"

The Qasaba Theater was a block off the Clock Circle in the opposite direction from Sangria's, a venerable old cinematheque whose unassuming Art Deco façade hid a foyer of patterned marble and a spacious theater. We bought tickets at the box office and took our seats. When the movie was over, we grabbed a bag of roasted nuts at the shop next door and headed home. On our way to the Clock Circle, we heard a commotion and saw an Israeli army Jeep blocking our path. Teenaged boys were running toward it with stones in their hands.

Yasmine turned me around. "Don't go that way, ugh, I hate when they do that. Don't they know some of the soldiers aren't right in the head? They get scared and they just shoot."

Her tough act didn't quite conceal the tremors of fear and anger in her voice. I took her cue and feigned nonchalance while my cold sweat dried in the evening air as we walked home.

I'D NEVER BOUGHT a cell phone in the States because I resented the overpriced year-long contracts they made everyone sign. But here it was pay-as-you-go, and I figured I should get one in case I ended up lost or injured or in jail. Yasmine found me in the kitchen one evening staring at my new phone as if it were some kind of incomprehensible technology from *Star Trek*.

"Can you show me how to use this?" I asked.

She looked at me strangely. "Don't you have cell phones in America?"

Once I got the hang of it, I texted Qais to let him know my new number. He texted back that he missed me. Glowing, I replied that I hoped I'd see him in Jayyous or Jenin soon. He texted back a four-line poem in Arabic. I showed it to Yasmine and asked her to translate.

She squinted and said tonelessly, "Night of love, O absent one, um . . . O sugar melted with honey." She rolled her eyes. "I hope only to be in your thoughts, I hope that, uh . . . in this I don't fail." She sighed and handed it back to me.

RAMALLAH INTERNATIONAL FILM FESTIVAL

Posters had been advertising the first annual Ramallah International Film Festival for weeks, and Yasmine managed to get us tickets for opening night in mid-July. The venue was the new Ramallah Cultural Palace, a state-of-the-art complex on a hilltop in western Ramallah. The marble foyer was posh and cavernous, and the crème de la crème of Ramallah were there, dressed up as if for a gala. It was a historic event, a hard-won chance for Palestinian artists and filmmakers to reach out to the world and assert their cultural identity.

We settled into plush seats and watched the opening speeches. Then two men played a beautiful, haunting oud (lute) duet while the names of the more than five hundred Palestinian children killed so far in the second Intifada shimmered across the movie screen in muted silver. The list seemed endless. Each name represented a future lost, a family bereft, an unweighable, uncountable tragedy.

It had been a depressing week, with constant reports of violence and destruction. Too many casual conversations involved the weather, work, and how many people had been killed in Gaza the night before. By the end of the duet, I felt choked and despondent.

Then the *dabka* started, a traditional Palestinian folk dance, with children in colorful costumes dancing and leaping, whole and alive. When two boys ran out carrying Palestinian flags and held them aloft over a radiant little girl flashing a peace sign, the energy in the room rose to a warm and excited pitch. The applause at the end was like nothing I'd heard before, as if it were not just for the *dabka* but for life itself.

Finally the feature film, *The Motorcycle Diaries*, began. After intermission, just as the story was getting interesting, the film stalled and then bubbled and melted before our eyes. Everyone looked hopefully at the projector room. Soon an embarrassed-looking woman in a smart pantsuit emerged and announced that the proper projector, sent in from Europe, had not been allowed past the Israeli checkpoint. They'd had to find another one hastily, and it wasn't quite the right size for the film. As they'd feared, it had overheated.

"But, *insha'Allah*, the film will be shown in its entirety tomorrow."

Cops and Robbers

The festival went on for a week of world-class cinema, including *Monsoon Wedding, City of God, Hable con Ella (Talk to Her)*, and *Bloody Sunday*, along with several Palestinian films.

One evening Yasmine and I watched a double feature of Palestinian documentaries at the Sakakini Cultural Center, which is housed in an elegant stone mansion with arched windows and vaulted ceilings. A screen had been set up in its charming courtyard. During one of the movies, a burst of gunfire erupted on film. As if in answer, real gunfire sounded on the other side of the nearest hill. Three ambulances streaked past. People craned their necks, then shrugged and continued enjoying the films. I followed suit, though it felt strange.

Yasmine and I headed to Sangria's afterward. We sat at the thatched-roofed bar in the middle of the beer garden to wait for a table to open up. When the bartender gave me my drink, he said, "*Sahtein.*" I smiled, unsure of what to say. He hesitated, then turned away.

Yasmine rolled her eyes. "*Ala qalbak,*" she said to him, then she turned to me. "You have to say that, *habibti*, it's what people say to be polite."

"What does it mean?"

"*Sahtein* means, like, 'double good health.' And *ala qalbak* means 'to your heart.'" I smiled. There was poetry even in the city.

One of the documentaries we'd just seen had been about a woman from Hebron who didn't visit the doctor at all during her first pregnancy because she was afraid of the Israeli checkpoint that stood between her and the clinic. When she went into labor, her husband tried to drive her to the clinic. As they passed the checkpoint, a soldier shot her husband through the neck and killed him. The soldiers then pulled her out of the car and forced her to give birth in the street. The baby survived but the mother, a young, pretty widow, was a psychologically destroyed nervous wreck. She said she only wanted to secure her daughter and then die.[13]

After we found a free table and sat down, I said disgustedly to Yasmine, "Why don't they show these films at the UN?"

Yasmine answered with the longest, clearest, most genuine laugh I'd ever heard from her. "I hate to say this," she said when she finally composed herself, "because it is so insulting, but . . . don't be so naïve. They know all of this shit. Everything."

"Why don't they do something?"

"What can they do? America has veto power, and America is allied with Israel."[14]

I sighed in frustration. When I talked to people in America about the situation here, many accused me of being cynical or melodramatic. And here was Yasmine telling me I was hopelessly naïve. I felt stuck in the middle between blindness and despair.

She went on, "Did you hear about the bank robbery in February? Israeli soldiers just walked into a bank in Ramallah and held the

---

13. According to the UN and the Palestinian Ministry of Health, sixty-one women were forced to give birth at checkpoints between September 2000 and December 2004. Thirty-six of their babies died as a result.

14. The United States has used its Security Council veto to block at least forty-two UN resolutions that attempted to curb Israel's violations of international law. It would take me a few more years and a stint in Washington to understand the dynamics behind America's "special relationship" with Israel.

employees hostage and stole $8 million. Nobody stops them from doing these things."[15]

I said weakly, "Wasn't there any outrage in the international community?"

"Don't you read the papers?" she said. "France 'condemned this illegal action.' They are always helping us out. Don't be so cynical."

Later a comic came out in a Palestinian newspaper that showed an Israeli soldier pointing his rifle at a Palestinian bank teller. The bank teller was holding his hands up with a look of resignation on his face. The soldier was saying, "If you don't like it, you can go to the Hague." This was a reference to the recent Advisory Opinion handed down by the International Court of Justice (ICJ) in the Hague. The court ruled that any part of the Wall built on occupied Palestinian land was "contrary to international law" and that Israel was "under obligation to . . . cease forthwith the works of construction of the wall being built in the Occupied Palestinian Territory, including in and around East Jerusalem, to dismantle forthwith the structure therein situated . . . [and] make reparation for all damage caused by the construction of the wall."

The Opinion passed 14-1, with the American judge the sole dissenter. I had thought of it as a great victory. Most Palestinians received the news with equanimity at best. Sadly, it looked like they were right. The Israeli government ignored the ruling, and no country applied any measures to enforce it.

Yasmine said, "Look, we have international laws all over the place, and none of them get implemented unless America wants them to. So to be very honest, Pamela . . ." She arched her eyebrows in a kidding-on-the-square kind of way. "You can stick your international laws in your international ass."

---

15. The Israeli army claimed the money was being used to fund militant groups. Former Israeli justice minister Yossi Beilin told *Haaretz* he doubted the government could prove the money was earmarked for militant groups. Yuval Steinitz, a lawmaker from the ruling right-wing Likud Party, retorted, "We are in a war against the Palestinians and the Palestinian Authority, it is not about proof." See: "Israeli Troops Raid Ramallah Banks," *The Washington Post*/Associated Press, February 25, 2004.

COLD WAR AND PEACE

Now that I was settled in Ramallah, it was time to start planning visits to Jayyous and Amman to catch up with old friends. I asked Yasmine one evening, "Will it be hard to get to Jayyous from here?"

She said dryly, "For you, no."

I winced. I'd forgotten she was a virtual prisoner in Ramallah. Like all Palestinian cities, Ramallah is surrounded by checkpoints, and Yasmine didn't have an ID that would let her pass any of them freely. To have any hope of getting through she'd have to go through an all-day ordeal to apply for a permit from Israel that would probably be denied. Even if it was granted, it could be revoked at any time for any reason. She'd once lost an entire year of college because Israel wouldn't give her a permit to reenter the West Bank after she visited her family in Gaza.

She sighed wistfully. "When I was studying at Bir Zeit,[16] my friends and I used to drive to Nablus in the middle of the night just to get some *kunafa*. Those were good days."

"Now it's possible, huh."

She scowled. "Now it's all crap."

At sunset, I walked to the curving street with the steep valley view and found a low wall to sit on and watch the twilight show. After a while I looked down and noticed a family standing under the wall and looking up at me. "*Marhaba,*" I said.

They greeted me in Arabic. They were the first people I met in Ramallah who didn't speak English, and when I asked the mother what her work was, I didn't understand her answer. She pointed to her *hijab* and trailed her hand along it. I still didn't understand, so she invited me down and showed me her hairdressing salon. Then she motioned for me to sit on her porch. Nearly a dozen kids crowded around excitedly. They were a good-looking family, especially the flirty four-year-old Mustafa. As I chatted with them in my halting

---

16. Bir Zeit University, established in the 1920s and located north of Ramallah, is the most prestigious center of higher learning in Palestine.

Arabic I was embarrassed to realize that, although I knew words like *national, organization, director, busy, report, meeting,* and *ministry,* I didn't know the words for *grandmother, child,* or even *family.* I spent several days afterward filling in those blanks.

Dinner was placed on the table, and the family insisted I stay and eat with them. While we were eating the oldest son, Jamil, who seemed sharp and healthy but was small for his age of seventeen, pulled up his shirt and showed me an immense scar. It looked like someone years ago had run him partway through with a dull blade and sliced down from his heart to his waistline. I guessed it was from surgery, but he made a gesture like aiming an M16 and said, "Israeli soldiers." He pointed to another scar on the meaty part of his calf, an entry and exit wound side by side. He held up seven fingers.

"Seven bullets hit you? When?" *When* in English sounds like "where" in Arabic, and he pointed to his backyard. It was on a hillside, which gave it a magnificent view—and also made it an easy target. I could barely believe he was still alive.

After dinner they walked me back to the road and made me promise to come back soon. When I got home, Yasmine was making coffee for a visiting friend. "He is a Capitalist," she informed me, but apparently she forgave him for it. He was an older gentleman who worked in the newspaper business, and he had excellent taste in *nargila* tobacco.

Occasionally they would launch into a discussion in Arabic and I'd be left to my thoughts while we smoked on the porch. I began to wonder what percentage of the seven bullets that hit Jamil was my responsibility. I could have learned about all this much sooner. I could have protested or refused to pay taxes. Somehow, without my knowledge or consent, I'd let this happen.

Yasmine asked me what I was thinking about, and I told her.

"*Habibti,* it's not just America," she said. "Did you know France is one of the largest arms traders with Israel?"

She was right, of course. This conflict was a particularly intractable example of a much more fundamental disorder. Was it a problem with human nature, I wondered, or just a massive, temporary failure of imagination? Institutionalized injustices like slavery, Jim Crow, and Apartheid had once been mainstream, but the arc of history had curved away from them. And who could have guessed, when a fractured Europe was massacring itself in the depths of World War II, that two generations later there'd be a European *Union*? Why shouldn't something similar be possible in the Middle East?

CHAPTER 5

Suddenly a Journalist

*When I look up, I see people cashing in. I don't see heaven
or saints or angels. I see people cashing in on every decent
impulse and every human tragedy.*

—Joseph Heller, *Catch-22*

I made my way to Jayyous one morning near the end of July. The drive
was beautiful, past rolling hills, tilled valleys, blue skies, and villages
crowned with soaring white minarets. The Mediterranean climate has
a dry season that lasts through the summer and fall until cool winter rains bring forth an explosion of green grass and wildflowers in
the spring. Wells, springs, irrigation systems, and the skillful hands of
farmers turn large areas of the West Bank rich and green even through
the dry season, laying the groundwork for the bounteous fall harvest.
The natural stone outcroppings of most of the hills have been fashioned
into agricultural terraces planted with olive trees whose hardy roots
allow them to flourish for centuries in the stony soil.

Bir Zeit, with its famous university, is the first village north of
Ramallah. Beyond that lies the Atara checkpoint, its clunky sniper
tower commanding a hill once graced by a beautiful stone mansion,
now in ruins. The next major checkpoint, Zaatara, controls access to
the northern West Bank, including Nablus. Along the way we passed

several lines of cars stopped at "flying checkpoints" and dozens of pre-fabricated settlements perched on commandeered hilltops. Most of the road signs pointed to settlements in Hebrew, English, and Arabic, though the Arabic was often blacked out with spray paint. A few pointed to Nablus, known in Israel by its Biblical name "Shechem." Nothing at all indicated the names of the Palestinian villages passing by, as if they didn't exist.

It was blazingly hot by the time I arrived at Rania's green metal front door in Jayyous. I rang the bell and heard Rania shout from the kitchen upstairs, "*Meen?*" (Who's there?)

"It's Bamila," I said.

"Oh!" She ran down the stairs and threw open the door, and we laughed and hugged. Her natural radiance was infused with a level of confidence I hadn't seen before. She took off her *hijab* once we were inside, and I could see she'd had highlights done in her hair. "I just got back from Jordan, where my oldest brother got married," she explained. "And Bamila, I have good news. I am going to university!"

I was astonished. She had talked about this often, but so many things stood in her way. "*Mabrook!*" (Congratulations!) "Which university?"

"Al Quds Open University in Qalqilia. With God's help, I am studying psychology. But Bamila," her face fell. "Probably I cannot continue. I spent everything I had on this semester, and I don't have a job since Yusif left. I have nothing." I asked how much a semester cost.

"Tuition is $400." I nodded. I had come very close to not being able to afford Stanford. It had taken months of begging the financial aid office and scrambling for loans and scholarships until we just managed to piece it together. I vividly remembered the frustration and fear of those months, and I hated the thought of someone as bright and motivated as Rania being denied an education altogether for the sake of a few hundred dollars.

I asked her how things were in Jayyous compared to last year. She leaned in and put her hand on my knee. "Bamila, it is bad. Many people are losing their land behind the Wall, and the land is all they have. I know three families who go through the garbage of their neighbors after everyone is asleep. This is a big shame. I gave one of them fifteen shekels last week to buy bread and hummus, but . . ." She shrugged helplessly.

We chatted for a while over tea until she gasped and said, "*Ya Bamila*, I promised the neighbors I would visit them! You will come with me?" We joined two middle-aged women and five daughters on their porch next door and helped them shell almonds from the trees in their yard. They urged me to try one. To my surprise, it tasted almost as sweet as marzipan. I had no words to explain, so I just made a really enthusiastic face. The women smiled proudly and the daughters giggled to see a grown, bare-headed woman wearing straggly traveling clothes and getting all excited about an almond. They were used to Palestinian women, who are paragons of decorum.

When we got back to Rania's house, she told me to gather my things because we'd be sleeping at her uncle's house that night.

"Why can't we sleep here?" I asked.

She sighed in her tragicomic way. "Before we could, but . . . one time when my youngest sister and I were sleeping in the house alone, the Jewish[1] came in the middle of the night. They banged on the door and shouted with very high voices. They were in our house for one hour and a half, looking for things." She must have seen the look of horror on my face, because she said soothingly, "We were not afraid, because we had nothing. We are simple people." I was terrified for them, though, ex post facto.

So we slept in her uncle's house. He'd had three-quarters of his olive trees isolated by the Wall and was raising three children on the money he could make selling chickens out of a coop attached to their house. The smells and sounds of the chickens saturated everything. His wife, a pretty, dark-haired woman who seemed too young to be a mother of three, fixed us a dinner of fried potatoes, homemade ketchup,

---

1. Palestinians, especially villagers, often refer to Israelis as *al Yehud* ("the Jews," although they tend to translate it to English as "the Jewish") or simply *jeish* ("army"). The Arabic word for "Israelis," *al Isra'iliyin*, is cumbersome in colloquial speech.

bread, and three small pieces of fried cheese floating in vegetable oil, a meal whose poverty in the face of a guest made me want to cry.

I set out to visit Amjad the next day. Walking down Main Street with the kids shouting "Hallo!" from all directions felt like a happy homecoming. I recognized many of them, including Qais's nephew from the picnic and a tiny girl with curly sun-bleached hair and berry brown skin who was always playing under the flowering vine that marked the turnoff to the mayor's house. I called her Mary Sunshine because she radiated joy so intensely from her sparkling black eyes. "*Marhaba!*" she squealed with a fluttering wave even though she was only twelve feet from me, and I laughed and waved back.

Amjad was alone when I arrived, and he welcomed me warmly and asked how Dan was doing. I caught him up on the news and asked where Amir and Abu Amjad were.

"My brother and father sleep on the land now because it is too hard crossing the Wall every day," he replied. "They come home once a week."

"Rania told me things are getting worse here."

"Yes, the situation is very bad. One of my friends fought for months to get to his greenhouses. Then he had to throw out all of his tomatoes because he couldn't make enough money to cover the cost of getting them to the market. Many citrus trees have died for lack of water. Some people can't get their seedlings or fertilizer past the Wall. It is very bad."

I was so downhearted to hear all this it took me a while to notice he looked slightly uncomfortable as we spoke. A year earlier, Yusif had told me that Amjad would soon be looking for a wife. He was known in the village for his piety, and being alone in his house with a foreign girl probably wasn't the best idea. As soon as I realized this, I made an excuse and took my leave. He looked relieved but said, "Nice to see you, and you are welcome anytime."

I walked to Qais's place next feeling equal parts nervous and excited. Unlike Rania, he was expecting me. When I arrived at the turnoff to his family's driveway, he materialized from the darkness and opened the gate. He took my hand and said, "May I?" I nodded, and he leaned in to kiss both my cheeks.[2] He was taller than I remembered, and more handsome.

He said, "You are thinner than you were before. Also I think more beautiful."

I smiled and followed him to his porch, and we sat in the dim light of the moon and talked in our strange mix of Arabic, Russian, and English. His brother Bilal was visiting from Sweden, and he soon joined us. He spoke Swedish as well as English and Arabic, and he had a smirking but generous confidence that was exceedingly charming. Other friends and neighbors arrived one by one, and soon we had a full-fledged *nargila* circle going. Everyone spoke English except for a bearded cousin who refused to shake my hand for religious reasons. We spoke in English sometimes for my benefit and Arabic sometimes for his, and people translated particularly good jokes or comments.

A man who'd spent years working in Saudi Arabia spoke the best English and told the best jokes. He said proudly, "I have Jordanian citizenship. But even if Jordan gave me a house and land for free, I wouldn't take it. Why? Because Jayyous is the best."

Qais muttered in Arabic, "Miserable Jayyous," and everyone chuckled.

The man turned to me. "Listen, before American people came here, I thought all of them were like Bush. All of them hate Arabs. All of them are like cowboys, kill everyone. But now, I know. There are good people, and many of them don't agree. Some even come here to help us with their own time. We appreciate this very much."

I nodded in agreement. It took a minute to realize he was directing some of his appreciation at me. I opened my mouth to protest. I was the guest here, the one welcomed so warmly into their homeland to work with great people in Ramallah, to travel to beautiful places

---

2. A kiss on both cheeks is a normal greeting in Palestine, including between males and females.

like Jayyous, to learn about things I found fascinating, and to evolve my worldview over a *nargila* with charming people like him. If anyone should be grateful, it was obvious it should be me.

Then I had a strange thought: *Maybe if you do it right, concepts like "selfishness" and "selflessness" collapse like virtual particles into meaninglessness—or into pure energy. After all, how can it be selfless to try to learn about and improve the very world in which you're living?* Before I could organize these thoughts into anything resembling a coherent sentence, the conversation had long since moved on.

After the crowd tapered off, Bilal and Qais invited me up to their roof for a barbecue. The roof had a gorgeous view over dark valleys, lit-up villages, and the bronze coin of the harvest moon hugging the eastern horizon. Bilal, who was twenty-eight, introduced me to his new wife, Marwa, who was eighteen. He whispered to me in English, "She is very young, so there might be difficulties due to differences of temperament." He shook his head. "This is what girls do here, after school get married."

I looked at her, so young and fresh-faced, with her fingers still dyed with henna from her wedding. She looked happy and comfortable with her new family. She was lucky to have married into this one. Rania had told me that women were generally allowed to turn down any man they didn't want to marry. But economic and social pressures could make the choice less than free. I hoped Rania would be able to finish her education before the pressure to marry became overwhelming.

I shared a *nargila* with one of Qais's dozens of cousins while Qais teased and wrestled with his adoring nieces and nephews. Palestinian girls are almost as free and boisterous as boys until puberty, when they're expected to don the headscarf and act like ladies.

We soon gathered around a white plastic dinner table for the feast, talking and joking and laughing, until we heard gunshots in the middle distance. We froze and listened intently. If it was Israeli soldiers shooting at cans or something, we didn't want to let it interrupt our dinner. But if it was a real problem, it felt awkward and callous to ignore it. Each time we heard a shot, we became still and waited to hear what came next—a scream, return fire, whatever. If we heard nothing, we would resume eating like nothing had happened.

A flare was shot into the sky during dessert. We watched it lazily circle down in its helical path, shining red. I wasn't sure what flares were for, but I had a sense they were used to light up an area that an army planned to bomb. No one seemed to expect a bomb, so I relaxed somewhat. Qais said a burning flare had almost landed on their roof once.

Bilal turned in around eleven o'clock. After Qais said good-bye to him, he said sadly to me in Russian, "This is the last time I will see my brother for a long time. I'm leaving for university tomorrow, and the day after that Bilal will go back to Sweden." I was honored that he had invited me to share this night and meet his brother, and I felt sad to think how fractured his family was. Maybe after Qais finished university, he'd be forced to leave the country to look for work, too.

When it was nearly midnight and the electricity was about to shut off, I said good-bye to everyone. Qais walked me to Main Street. He apologized that he couldn't walk me home. He had to get to his exams early the next morning, and not long ago he'd been out on the street when Israeli soldiers invaded and took away several young men seemingly at random.

"It was very *uzhas*," he said. *Uzhas* is Russian for "horrible."

"That's OK, it's not far," I said. Then I turned to face him. "It's been really nice to see you again."

"Yes, it has been very nice. I will be back from Jenin in a few days. Will you be here?"

"I'll be here for a week before I head to Jordan."

"I will see you?" We looked at each other for a long moment. I wished he would kiss me, but I knew it was an impossible thing to expect in the middle of a public street. I smiled and said, "*Insha'Allah*." But I was already counting the hours until I would see him again.

The electricity cut out while I was walking home. The lights of the village silently winked off, and the deserted streets became impenetrably dark. As the scent of jasmine filled my lungs and starlight filled my eyes, I smiled with my whole body.

GRAPEVINES AND SEA BREEZES

I found an open room at the International House, a small home on Jayyous's Main Street that rented rooms to peace activists, where I could stay for the rest of the week. Three delegates sent by the World Council of Churches were living there. The program had been launched following a call by churches in Jerusalem for an international presence to monitor human rights violations and support nonviolent resistance in the Palestinian territories.

I was reading on the porch one day when a skinny girl in braids stopped by and tried to strike up a conversation. She knew only a few words of English, but we managed to have a friendly if rudimentary chat until another girl ran up and exclaimed, "*Jeish!*"

The first girl's eyes widened. I looked at her quizzically. She pantomimed pointing an M16 and shrugged apologetically. They both ran off.

Just then an Israeli army Jeep raced past the house much faster than was safe on the narrow street. A Swedish woman joined me on the porch. "There's been a lot of activity lately," she said. "The youth have been protesting against the Wall, and there hasn't been a day without soldiers in the village since I've been here. Sometimes they come in the middle of the day and randomly throw tear gas canisters. People were showing us their scars when we got here."

"How are things at the Wall?" I asked.

"It's getting worse and worse. We tried to go to the land with the farmers today. They all had permits, but the soldiers were three hours late opening the gate. They said they couldn't find the keys. When they finally opened it, the internationals weren't allowed through. We protested, and a soldier said he would call the DCO.[3] But they never came. After a few hours, we walked back here."

Just then the army Jeep roared back past the house. The Swedish girl said brightly, "Well, I guess they had their daily peek!"

I spent the next few days meeting and catching up with old and

---

3. The District Coordination Office was established under the Oslo Accords of 1993. The offices are responsible for coordinating security and humanitarian cooperation between Israelis and Palestinians.

new friends, helping Mohammad the Charmer and his equally charming fiancée pick out fixtures for their new house, and visiting one of their cousins who had just finished medical school in Tunisia.

I also met Sharif Omar, known as Abu Azzam, the largest landowner in Jayyous and a long-time leader of the Land Defense Committee for the Qalqilia region. He's a jolly farmer, an ex-Communist with greying temples who never tires of talking about his land and its olive, citrus, almond, guava, apricot, and loquat trees and its mangos, grapes, and avocados. He is also well-connected with the Israeli left, and he's testified about the Wall's effects at the International Court of Justice and published an article in *USA Today*.[4]

We sat in the shade of a lime tree on his land beyond the Wall to chat over a plate of fresh fruit. He confirmed that more and more permits were being denied, usually for unspecified "security" reasons that rarely made sense. One of his sons was given permission to travel to Haifa in Israel to pick up goods for a company he ran in Ramallah, for example, yet he was denied a permit to access his father's land in Jayyous. More ominously, Abu Azzam said the Israeli authorities were using an Ottoman land law that said any privately held land not cultivated for three consecutive years could be confiscated by the state.[5] Abu Azzam said he'd seen land taken by Israel whose only "proof" of noncultivation was aerial photographs taken at a time when there were no crops in the ground. Then there was a British Mandate law that said land covered by more than 50 percent stones could be acquired by the state as not suitable for agriculture.

Abu Azzam said, "They once tried to confiscate my land by claiming it was unfit for agriculture!" He looked around at his abundant orchards and gardens, seeming almost gleeful at the irony. I didn't laugh. Abu Azzam was more than sixty years old, and all he wanted

4. Sharif Omar, "Israel's Wall Hems in Livelihoods—and Dreams," *USA Today*, August 17, 2003.

5. See: "Land Grab: Israel's Settlement Policy in the West Bank," B'Tselem, May 2002. B'Tselem, the Israeli Information Center for Human Rights in the Occupied Territories, is a well-respected Israeli NGO that works tirelessly to expose human rights violations (www.btselem.org).

was to enjoy his golden years in his own personal Garden of Eden. Israel wanted to deny him that, not because of anything he'd done but because his land was desirable and he was not.

After we made it back through the gate, mercifully without problems, Abu Azzam laughed and said, "Did you see how the soldiers respected us? You should come with us every day. You are the best passport for us."

ONE LATE AFTERNOON I ran into Qais on the street. He was just back from Jenin and looked devastatingly handsome in a pressed light grey shirt and dark grey tie. We greeted each other with big smiles, and he invited me to come to his porch at ten.

We were joined by his cousin Karim, a wiry mechanic with wild grey eyes and bulging arm muscles. He didn't speak a word of English, but we found enough to joke about in the Arabic I could speak. Qais showed me a few old text messages and jokes on his cell phone, and I showed him some pictures from Oklahoma. Qais looked at them with intense interest. When he saw a graduation photo of me wearing a blue and white shirt, he slipped it into his front pocket.

"It's never leaving here," he said. Then he pointed to his heart. "Or here." I rolled my eyes and smiled. The discourse in this part of the world is so flowery and effusive, it's difficult sometimes for a Westerner to know which lavish praise is routine and which is personal. But even if it is handed out fairly indiscriminately, I had to admit I enjoyed it.

Karim got bored around midnight and headed off to bed. Qais and I remained on the porch talking softly, trying not to wake anyone. A sea breeze blew through the grapevines overhead as the coastline shone far below. It was the first time we had ever been alone together, the first time we could hold each other's hands. Finally, naturally, our lips came together.

Few men get the first kiss just right, with the perfect mix of warmth and restraint that takes all the anticipation leading up to it and builds on it perfectly. The last person I expected to be a master of it was a Palestinian farmer's son. We talked and laughed, kissed and shared sweet green grapes off the vine until long after the electricity shut off.

I WANDERED OVER to Qais's house the next evening after extracting myself from the black hole of last-day-in-Jayyous hospitality. I was able to see him only briefly on his porch in a big *nargila* circle. When the crowd thinned, Qais walked me to Main Street.

He turned to me, looking contrite and harassed, and said, "I am very sorry, but I can't see you anymore tonight. I hope I will see you when you come back from Jordan?"

I'd been expecting this. I knew how important it was, in a tightly knit religious community, to be from a "good" family, untarnished by vice or scandal. My hometown in Oklahoma wasn't quite as strict as Jayyous, but it had the same basic pseudo-Victorian structure. Qais's family was known for being devout, and for him to spend time alone with a foreign woman out of wedlock was flirting with scandal. Whatever our relationship turned out to be, it would have to be a secret.

"My father has sacrificed everything for us," Qais explained, searching my face for understanding. "I don't care what the village thinks, but I don't want to disappoint him."

I smiled ruefully, indicating that I understood. My motto of late was a quote by H.L. Mencken: "We are here and it is now. Further than that, all knowledge is moonshine." Here and now I loved spending time with Qais, even if it might not be very often or very easy. If at some future date the costs started outweighing the benefits . . . Well, that was for a future version of myself to contend with.

AMMAN AGAIN

I made my way to the Jordanian border the next day and shared a taxi to Amman with an Israeli businessman. He seemed at ease, as if he traveled to Jordan all the time. He stopped us along the way to treat the driver and me to *kunafa*. While we were eating, I asked the driver where he was from. "Beit Shean," he replied.

The Israeli man's fork paused halfway to his mouth. Beit Shean is now part of Israel. More than half the population of Jordan are Palestinian refugees, driven from their homes in 1948 or 1967. Nearly every cab I took in Jordan, every shopkeeper I talked to, when I asked where they were from, they would give a small smile and name a place they were not allowed to go to. In California I'd met refugees who'd never been to the Holy Land at all. When I talked about visiting their hometowns, their eyes lit up or misted over with a look that seemed to stretch over horizons of memories I couldn't begin to fathom. The magnitude of this patient suffering, multiplied by decades and by millions, was overwhelming to me.

The driver didn't say it bitterly, though, only matter-of-factly. After a moment's pause, we went on talking as before.

When I got to the Al Sarayya Hotel, I found Fayez, the man who had introduced me to Yusif and Sebastian a year earlier. He was in his office, as lanky, silver-haired, and full of jokes as ever. We greeted each other warmly and caught up over his famous coffee, a tiny liquid confection, rich and strong and infused with Christmassy cardamom.

"So, how is Palestine?" he asked with a smile. I shared my impressions so far. I knew by now that he was a Palestinian refugee, and after a while I thought to ask, "By the way, where is your family from?"

"You know Ben Gurion Airport?"

"Sure, that's where I flew in."

He nodded with a sad half-smile. "My village used to be there."

I SPENT A week with a friend named Laila whom I had met in one of the Muslim student groups at Stanford. She was a petite woman with long, straight, strawberry-blonde hair, almond eyes, a Jordanian father and an American mother. She toured me around her family's horse riding club in the gorgeous hill country north of Amman. The land was awash in fruit trees, olive groves, grapevines, and gardens. Laila's father was fond of saying, "Many people read the Bible, but only a few get to live in it!" I joined her family when they hosted a children's day at the riding club. The kids, mostly Palestinian refugee orphans but also two African boys and a little Chinese girl, were a delight, sweet and funny and excited about everything.

A few days later Laila's sisters and I were watching the Opening Ceremonies of the Athens Olympics in their spacious living room in affluent West Amman. It was thrilling to see the Palestinian and Iraqi Olympic teams receive the biggest cheers of anyone other than the Greeks. During a lull, Laila's sister mentioned that one of her friend's parents let their underage kids drink in the house.

Laila said indignantly, "They let sixteen-year-olds drink?"

Her sister shrugged. "They're Christians."

"O-o-o-oh," Laila said, as if that explained everything. I almost spit my hot cocoa out laughing. I wished I could explain how funny it was, coming from the Bible Belt of America, to be in a country where Christians are considered the licentious ones.

When the call to prayer sounded, Laila and her sisters invited me to join them in prayer. Laila pulled out a decorative prayer rug for each of us and showed me how to stand with my hands in front of me, bow, drop to my knees, and gently touch my forehead to the ground while reciting words and phrases in Arabic. The ritual reminded me surprisingly of yoga. It was soothing to think that for a few minutes five times a day, every practicing Muslim had no worries—just a mind, a body, and a spirit with no earthly distractions.

The family invited me to lunch with one of Iraq's most famous equestrian coaches and his family the next day. We had *mansaf*, a traditional Bedouin dish of goat meat cooked over rice with a savory yogurt sauce and toasted slivered almonds, eaten with crêpe-like flatbread. The Iraqi family was working with Laila's father at their horse riding club. The equestrian scene in Iraq was devastated by the long periods of anarchy following the American invasion. Many horses were stolen, and many people had been driven off their properties. They wanted to rebuild the program in Iraq as soon as they could, but conditions were still too dangerous. Laila and I chatted with the three pretty young daughters about everything but the war. The girls' eyes, solemn and wary, made it clear what a feeble pretense it was.

It was crushing to feel the deep sense of helplessness among people. Giving refugee kids a fun day or hosting an Iraqi family were absolutely worthwhile. But things got worse so much faster than anyone could keep up. The Palestinian refugee question still wasn't solved, and now Jordan and Syria were being overwhelmed by Iraqi refugees.

At the end of the week, I thanked Laila's family for their superb hospitality, and they dropped me off at a restaurant called Al Fardous on the outskirts of Amman. I was scheduled to meet with another Jordanian friend, a Palestinian refugee named Ibrahim who was on vacation from his economics PhD at Stanford.

We found each other and a table in the restaurant's greenery-draped courtyard. I told him how struck I was by the wealth in Laila's end of Amman, with its mansions and Mecca Mall, its KFCs and charming but overpriced cafés. It's a world away from the older, poorer, but always friendly and interesting downtown area where the Al Sarayya was located.

He smiled. "Look at us here in Jordan. We have no oil, no natural resources, but we are very educated, and some of us are very rich. How do we have all this? Every time there is a war, or a refugee problem, the refugees go to Jordan—from Iraq, from Palestine—and Jordan gets money from the West to keep them, to deal with them, to accept them and be quiet about them. Not out loud, but secretly, the Jordanian government supported the war in Iraq. So did the Egyptian government. And they both made separate peace deals with Israel without demanding justice for Palestinians. The Americans pay both of them to keep quiet about Palestinian rights."

After Israel, it turns out, Jordan has the most per capita American foreign aid in the world; Egypt is second to Israel in absolute terms. Both Egypt and Jordan began receiving their checks after signing peace agreements with Israel that ignored the question of Palestine.

This was the first I'd heard of it, but soon I saw the implications everywhere. Each time the governments of Egypt and Jordan remained silent when Iraqi cities were bombed or Palestinians were killed, the populations of Egypt and Jordan seethed. But the autocratic regimes treat dissenters harshly, often using American weapons, training, and political cover. This is why politics is often driven into the mosque—the only place citizens are allowed to gather—squeezing many ordinary people between corrupt client regimes and Islamist opposition.[6]

I MADE MY way to the Pasha Palace Hammam (Turkish bath) the next day, where I enjoyed a sauna, pool, exfoliation, scrubbing, and divinely inspired massage in an old Arabian palace for less than $20. The main steam room had the customary tiny, round stained-glass windows in the central dome that broke the sun into colorful beams as it cut through the steam. I left as soft and relaxed as a baby in a blanket.

I went to Fayez's office to hang out one last time before returning to the West Bank. Al Jazeera was playing as usual and activists, journalists, and Iraqi drivers were coming and going and congregating. A report came on about a bungled Palestinian bombing attack that killed two Palestinian bystanders at the Qalandia checkpoint, which I would soon be crossing. My chest immediately tightened up again. Still, I missed Ramallah and felt impatient to get back to my friends and routine and my little stone house.

THE ALLENBY BRIDGE crossing, on the border between Jordan and the West Bank, is halfway between Amman and Jerusalem. Like all access points to the West Bank, it's controlled by Israel. The Jordanian half of the crossing was a breeze, and my interrogator on the Israeli side was a cute Russian girl who seemed more interested in what I had been doing in Russia than what I was doing in Israel. When she finally got around to questioning me I told her, as usual, that I was a tourist, and—even

---

6. In the early 1950s, for example, the democratic government of Iran voted to nationalize Iran's oil resources. That government was overthrown in a coup orchestrated by British and American agents and replaced by the autocratic Shah, who restored foreign control of Iran's oil. The Shah's dictatorship was supported by the United States and Britain—right up until it was overthrown in 1979 by the Islamic Revolution.

though my passport revealed that I had spent time in at least four Arab countries—I didn't speak any Arabic or know any Arabs. She gave me a standard three-month tourist visa with a sweet and sincere smile.

I walked to the cavernous waiting area, where scores of Palestinians were milling around waiting or having their bags unpacked and rifled through. I was surprised to see Dr. Barghouthi among them. I opened my mouth to say hello then quickly closed it again, reminding myself I wasn't supposed to know *any* Arabs, much less a Palestinian political leader. He saw me, though, and walked toward me with his hand extended.

"Ahlan, ya Pamela, keef halik?" he asked warmly.

"Fine," I mumbled, and looked down and walked away.

Home Sweet Ramallah

I apologized for my rudeness the next day at the office, and Dr. Barghouthi laughed and apologized for his politeness. He told me that while I'd been gone, the Palestinian Prisoners Society had announced an open-ended hunger strike. They accused Israel of "robbing us of all our rights, treading on our dignity and treating us like animals."[7] They demanded that Israeli guards stop conducting gratuitous strip searches; allow more frequent contact with prisoners' families (organizers said 40 percent of inmates were denied any visits at all); improve sanitary conditions, access to public telephones, and medical care; allow prisoners to pursue their education by registering at Palestinian and foreign universities; reduce prison crowding; and stop beating detainees en route to courts. The Israeli government responded

---

7. Most Palestinian prisoners, whose numbers hover between seven thousand and eleven thousand, are held for political rather than criminal reasons. Many are community leaders or minors accused of throwing stones. Peaceful protest is often grounds enough to be detained. About 10 percent are held under "administrative detention," which means they haven't been charged with any crime at all. Various human rights groups claim that Israeli military courts violate international standards of fair trials by denying access to lawyers, using confidential evidence, and giving briefings in Hebrew without translation. See, for example: Martin Asser, "Palestinians Languish in Israeli Jails," BBC, August 8, 2003.

by imposing further restrictions on the hunger strikers, holding barbecues outside their cells, and depriving them of water and salt.

Forty percent of the male population of Palestine has been through the Israeli prison system since 1967, so this is an issue that leaves no one untouched. Hundreds of children and scores of women are also held at any given time. Around 4,000 out of 7,500 prisoners were participating in the strike, and impassioned vigils and marches were held all over the West Bank in solidarity, including one in Ramallah that afternoon.

It was heartening to see young people peacefully marching for something they believed in. But, as in previous demonstrations, no one in the international media was paying any attention.

Yasmine and I went on a long walk around town at the end of the week. We stopped along the way to play basketball on an outdoor court. Hassan was there, the IT guy from our office, one of those tall, good-looking nerds with a bone-dry sense of humor who knew too many lines from *The Simpsons*. He wasn't a bad basketball player, either. It felt brilliant to be on the court sweating and moving and passing and shooting. I learned how to call for the ball and talk a little trash in Arabic, and my senses came alive and into focus for the first time in ages.

When the game broke up, Yasmine and I walked toward the old part of town, where the homes look like small stone castles, then through the trendy part of town, where the expansive Art Deco houses are made of smooth white stone with blue-tinted glass and wrought iron accents. The tawny hills surrounding the city are striped with ancient, crumbling retainer walls and punctuated here and there by a *qasr*, a small hand-wrought stone dwelling. Farmers used to camp in them while working on their lands far from home.

Soon a crescent moon shone faintly in a sky all the pastel shades of a child's dream of heaven. The hills and their white houses blushed rose as the sun sank into the horizon. Distant towns were tiny and toylike on the far horizons, and the weight of ancient hills lent a sense of immensity.

We could see the village of Bir Zeit twinkling on a forested hill-top to the north. I'd recently visited the university, which reminded me of Stanford with its elegant light-colored stone buildings, big central plaza, and sharply dressed students. During both Intifadas Bir Zeit had been shut down several times by the Israeli authorities. Professors taught in secret in their homes so classes could carry on.

I asked Yasmine, "What does *bir zeit* mean?"

"*Bir* is like, when you dig a hole and line it with stones. It's usually for water. And *zeit* is because they used to store olive oil in them."

"Oh, you mean a cistern." My eyes widened. "Jesus! Cisterns full of olive oil?"

"Yeah, yeah, it's normal. Olive oil used to be cheaper than water. I mean, before the problems, the refugees, the settlements . . ." She shrugged. "Now they use them all for water."

The thought of olive oil literally flowing like water out of this land enchanted me beyond all reason. As we turned to walk home I was infused with a sensation I'd never felt before, as if I had arrived in just the right place on earth at exactly the right time. Suddenly I couldn't imagine living anywhere but Palestine, close to olive trees and white stone houses and Bible hills turning blue as the sun set over a sea we couldn't walk to and touch without crossing Walls and checkpoints. Life here was hard and lonely and confusing, but it was also full and exciting, cynical and funny, and often lovely beyond description. For the first time since I'd arrived in Ramallah I wasn't looking forward or back anymore. I was just here, now, and happy.

DEAD SEA STROLL

It was a big party on the bus. The Palestinians sang and danced and clapped and drummed in the back while the German volunteers sat in front looking prim and slightly alarmed. We were on our way to the Dead Sea on an outing organized for volunteers who worked at HDIP, Medical Relief, and Ramallah's Youth Center.

Everyone quieted down when we neared a checkpoint, though,

and behaved like good little natives. There was no mood for antagonism on a light-hearted day like this.

The Dead Sea beach we visited was on West Bank land, but it was operated by an Israeli settlement. We ignored this for the day and enjoyed a nice chat with the proprietress, who had a clear German accent. When a Palestinian man who had spent time in Germany asked where in Germany she was from, she said emphatically, "I am *Israeli* now."

The shining blue Dead Sea sparkled under a hot, brittle sky, and the views of the Jordanian mountains were almost as nice as the views of slim young men smearing each other with cleansing Dead Sea mud. The minerals sucked everything out of our cells and pores, and after we rinsed and rehydrated, our skin felt like baby silk. We swam and barbecued, kicked a soccer ball around, and had a great time.

On the way home I sat next to a guy named Ahmed who wore wire-rimmed glasses and a blue-and-white-striped Polo shirt. We struck up a conversation, and he mentioned that he'd recently been awarded a scholarship to study in England. He introduced me to his friend, also named Ahmed, who was from Jenin and attended Bir Zeit University. The first Ahmed was a clean-cut kid, boyish and enthusiastic, while Ahmed 2 was the sharp-eyed, cynical type.

They invited me for coffee when we got back to Ramallah. Talk turned inevitably from music and sports to the occupation. The first Ahmed told me a soldier had once asked him for his ID. Just to be a punk, he said he didn't have one. The soldier reached into Ahmed's pocket and pulled his ID out. Ahmed said, "Oh, that's right, I forgot. My ID is with you." The soldier said, "Come with me." They made him get into an armored vehicle and started beating him on the face and shoulder with their rifle butts. They drove him to a remote location, told him to "be careful," and let him go.

Ahmed 2, not to be outdone, said, "You know the Surda checkpoint between Ramallah and Bir Zeit? One time I was late for university and it was raining hard, and there was a long line of cars at the checkpoint. I decided to try my luck on foot. I asked the soldier if I could cross and get to school. He said, 'You can cross, but you can't use the road. You have to walk beside the road in the mud.' I asked why. He said, 'You don't deserve to walk in the street.'

"So I thought to myself: Either I can walk in the mud, or I can turn back, or I can say something. Finally I said to him, 'You know, when Germany occupied Warsaw, they treated you badly just because you were Jews. Now you are doing the same thing to us.'"

Ahmed 2 laughed at the memory. "He was very angry. He started yelling, 'This checkpoint is closed! Nobody can pass!' More than five hundred people were stranded. They asked me, 'What did you say to him?' I said, 'Nothing.'" He affected a comically innocent expression.

I shook my head. The past of nearly every Palestinian I met was a litany of beatings, detentions, humiliations, or worse at the hands of the Israeli army. A military occupation is one of those classic asymmetric power relationships that's ripe for abuse even in the best of times. An Israeli ex-soldier named Liran Furer had recently written a book called *Checkpoint Syndrome*. Furer, "a creative, sensitive graduate of the Thelma Yellin High School of the Arts," wrote about how he "became an animal at the checkpoint, a violent sadist who beat up Palestinians because they didn't show him the proper courtesy, who shot out tires of cars because their owners were playing the radio too loud, who abused a retarded teenage boy lying handcuffed on the floor of the Jeep . . ."[8] He said it was nothing unusual.

In 1971, the Stanford psychology department ran a study known as the Stanford Prison Experiment. To study the psychology of prison life, Professor Philip Zimbardo randomly divided twenty-four college students into groups of "guards" and "prisoners" and placed them in a simulated prison scenario. Within days the "guards" turned to abuse to control the "prisoners," stripping them, hooding them, and sexually humiliating them. Four of the "prisoners" suffered emotional breakdowns. Though it was intended to run for two weeks, the experiment was cut short after six days.

---

8. Gideon Levy, "Twilight Zone: I Punched an Arab in the Face," *Haaretz*, November 21, 2003.

"Human behavior is much more under the control of situational forces than most of us recognize or want to acknowledge," Zimbardo wrote years later in an attempt to explain the Abu Ghraib scandal. "In a situation that implicitly gives permission for suspending moral values, many of us can be morphed into creatures alien to our usual natures. My research and that of my colleagues has catalogued the conditions for stirring the crucible of human nature in negative directions. Some of the necessary ingredients are: diffusion of responsibility, anonymity, dehumanization, peers who model harmful behavior, bystanders who do not intervene, and a setting of power differentials."[9]

Here it was being played out in real time on a massive scale with no one in a white lab coat to tell them when to stop.

ARABIAN IDOL

A few nights later the Ahmeds invited me to Zarour, an Arabic restaurant in an old building with broad arches of sand-colored stone. Ammar Hassan, a handsome Palestinian from a town near Nablus called Salfit, had made it to the final round of *SuperStar*, the Middle Eastern version of *American Idol*. His rival was a cute, skinny, spiky-haired Libyan. A projector had been set up on the veranda, and we ordered appetizers and chatted while we waited for it to start.

As the first singer took the stage, the projector screen clicked off. We looked at each other in confusion. The waiters began officiously dismantling the video setup and buffet table. People started leaving, and we got up to leave, too. On the way out we saw a pile of tires burning in the street. I asked Ahmed 2 what was happening.

"I think some Palestinian gunmen are going around shutting down parties."

Another guy in our party, the one who had paid for everything, said archly, "All the bad ideas come out of the refugee camps."

9. Philip Zimbardo, "Power Turns Good Soldiers into 'Bad Apples,'" *The Boston Globe*, May 8, 2004. For more on the Stanford Prison Experiment, visit prisonexp.org.

When I got home I asked Yasmine what was going on. She said angrily, "There are people starving in prison just so they can be treated like human beings, and people are worried about this stupid singer. The prisoners call for our support, and what kind of support is this?"

Well, I thought, *what kind of support is terrorizing your own people?* But I could understand their frustration. The poor and imprisoned had less to lose when it came to resisting the occupation, while the middle and upper classes had more invested in the status quo, however undesirable it was. I remembered how, when I was in Jayyous, the elites of Ramallah had seemed like cheaters, if not collaborators, for living so large while people suffered so badly. I imagined this lifestyle looked similarly obscene from the refugee camps surrounding Ramallah.

From what I could see in Ramallah, though, most people were just trying to eke as much happiness out of life as possible, albeit with more resources at their disposal. Ironically, since I was an outsider, I could interact with more layers of Palestinian society than most Palestinians could. It was confusing to have a foot in so many different worlds and to empathize with all of them even when they contradicted each other.

BETHLEHEM'S WALLS

Dr. Barghouthi and half a dozen HDIP employees went on a fact-finding mission to the Bethlehem district a few days later, and they invited me to join them.

Bethlehem is surrounded to the north by two hilltop settlements called Gilo and Har Homa, to the southwest by the Etzion Bloc of settlements, and to the southeast by smaller settlements. The Wall was being built to surround Bethlehem on three sides, severing it from most of its farmland and from its sister holy city, Jerusalem. We made a long detour through a dry canyon called Wadi Nar (Valley of Fire) to bypass Jerusalem and the maddening bottleneck at the Qalandia checkpoint.

As we neared Bethlehem, we passed the twenty-five-foot-high concrete barrier standing in space like a postmodern nihilist sculpture, heavily foreshortened, a distant line that swerved up into an incontrovertible grey fact on the ground, inching its way inevitably toward the birthplace of Jesus Christ. Such a heavy, angular abomination was absurdly out of place in this soft, old, rolling landscape. As we passed it I had an odd sensation in my stomach, as if I was looking bald, unapologetic insanity straight in the face.

We drove to Bethlehem's City Hall and spoke with a local councilman over coffee. He loaded up with us and pointed the way to a nearby village called Nahalin. The village is surrounded on all sides by Etzion Bloc settlements, and the biggest, Betar Illit, is expanding onto its land. We drove to a site where an Israeli bulldozer was flattening land that belonged to an old man in a white *keffiya*. We watched as the man marched toward the bulldozer and started throwing fist-sized rocks at it. The stones bounced harmlessly off the bulldozer's bulletproof windows. The driver opened the door and got out. The man in the *keffiya* put his rock down and shouted, "This is my land!"

The driver, who looked Palestinian-Israeli, said, "It's not my problem. I'm just doing a job."

A chill of familiarity rolled down my spine. The Nuremburg defense.

The farmer reminded me of my grandfather. I thought of my grandparents' ranch in Stigler with its vegetable garden, its little plum grove, and the chicken coop where we gathered eggs in the afternoons, the huge grey barn where we played hide-and-seek, the pasture with its cows and fish pond and giant oak tree, and the creek where we swung on vines and built forts and bridges. I tried to imagine my grandfather watching his land being bulldozed illegally by people who knew nothing about his family's history on the land. And the only pathetic, symbolic weapon at his disposal being a broken-off chunk of his own devastated property.

After a few minutes of arguing, the driver turned his bulldozer around and trundled back up to a settler road. But there was no doubt he or someone else would be back the next day.

We drove to another man's land, a site where settlement construction had constricted and polluted a spring. The owner said his channels used to have cold, clear water running through them; there was nothing but a fetid trickle now. He flicked a shriveled cluster of grapes off one of his rotting vines and said disgustedly in Arabic, "Not even one." On his face was a mottled combination of fury and bitter helplessness. The Palestinian Authority couldn't protect him. The international community ignored him. He had no legal way to oppose what was happening to him.

We traveled next to Wadi Rahhal[10] on bumpy, washed-out roads. The land on one side of the road, expropriated for a settlement, was green and thriving. The land on the other side was dusty and barren. Construction of a new settlement was just beginning on a forested hilltop to our right. It looked like something out of colonial Africa—people of European descent living on islands of red-roofed suburbia on land belonging to someone else surrounded by "buffer zones," barbed wire, and guard towers, with bulletproof bus services running between them on Israeli-only roads. The sense of entitlement, or at best thoughtlessness, necessary to live in such a place was breathtaking.

"The trip to Bethlehem from these villages used to take three minutes on good roads," the councilman told us. "Now it takes at least twenty minutes on these terrible roads and costs up to ten times as much. Do you know what that means? It means many villagers cannot afford to go to school or university. Some students move to Bethlehem for school, but many can't afford this, either. Thousands of students have been forced to drop out."

When we arrived at Wadi Rahhal's City Hall, Muzna and I waited in the lobby while Dr. Barghouthi and the Bethlehem councilman spoke with the mayor. A woman offered us sticky fruit drinks. After she and Muzna had chatted at length, I asked what they were talking about.

"This woman's sister was seven months pregnant with twins when soldiers stopped her at a checkpoint and threw a tear gas canister into her car," Muzna said. "She had a miscarriage and both babies died."

---

10. The village's name means "Valley of Travelers." A massive Israeli settlement called Efrat has been built directly adjacent to it.

I glanced at the woman, shocked that this was the story she'd been telling. She had told it in a glazed, matter-of-fact way, as if she feared one slip of emotion might bust the whole dam. I wondered if anyone who stayed here long enough would develop the same manner of speech, the same psychological scar tissue.

The next town we visited was Battir. I was so struck by its beauty I asked someone to write its name in Arabic so I'd remember to come back some day and stay longer. It was built into a steep, green hillside, and some of its buildings were carved in part from the living rock of the mountain. A spring ran from the center of town into a narrow valley, where the water was captured in a reservoir and allocated to farmers according to law and custom.

Muzna told me the route of the Wall in this area was going to cut both Battir and Nahalin off from the West Bank entirely, trapping them between the Wall and the Green Line in a settlement-encrusted area called the "Seam Zone."[11] Israel's West Bank military commander, Major General Moshe Kaplinski, had declared the Seam Zone a closed military zone in October of 2003. The only people eligible to enter it freely, without having to apply for a permit, are citizens and residents of Israel and any person eligible for automatic Israeli citizenship—i.e., any Jewish person in the world. Palestinians living in villages trapped in the Seam Zone might soon face the absurdity of having to apply for permits to remain in their own homes. They wouldn't be allowed to visit Israel without a permit, either. They'd be ghettoized even more profoundly than the people of Qalqilia are, with no universities or hospitals and far fewer job prospects.

Back in Bethlehem, Dr. Barghouthi gave a speech at a tent in solidarity with the hunger-striking prisoners. The tent was filled with mothers clutching framed eight-by-ten portraits of their sons. Muzna

---

11. The "Seam Zone" is the name given by Israel to all Palestinian land isolated by the Wall (other than the land around East Jerusalem, which Israel illegally annexed—see the maps on pp. 297 and 299). The finished Wall will isolate 9 percent of the West Bank's land. Restrictions on access to the Jordan Valley isolate another 28.5 percent. See the map on p. 298.

and I took the opportunity to sneak off and grab a *shawerma* from a street vendor. Neither of us had eaten all day, and we tore into the charred lamb wrapped in chewy flatbread with pickles and tahini as we walked to a clinic to drink coffee and wait for Dr. Barghouthi. Along the way I noticed a huge building that had been smacked down into an almost comically sad, saggy pile. Its floors had collapsed onto each other like pancakes.

"What building is—was—that?" I asked. I was surprised how easy it was to make light of such a terrible thing. It didn't change anything whether I made light or not, and it gave me a false, giddy sense of toughness—an illusion of control when things were clearly out of control and I had no idea how to react to them.

"That was Bethlehem's municipality building," Muzna explained. "Israel bombed it in 2002 along with the security centers and prisons. They did this in almost all the cities." She was talking about Operation Defensive Shield, Israel's military offensive in the spring of 2002. Its stated goal had been to stop the rash of suicide bombings that began during the second Intifada. Five hundred Palestinians and twenty-nine Israeli soldiers were killed in the operation. Hundreds of millions of dollars of damage was done to Palestinian homes, businesses, schools, government buildings, and cultural centers.

HDIP had a display in its foyer commemorating the operation's impact. It showed photographs of the Al Mubadara and HDIP offices after they'd been invaded. Israeli soldiers stole or destroyed hard drives and paper archives, smashed computers, poured coffee into copy and fax machines, broke swivel chairs and piled them on desks, and left graffiti on the wall that said in Hebrew, "THANKS FOR THE HOSPITALITY." A few twisted hard drives were on display along with shards of shrapnel and photographs of unarmed men lying bleeding in the middle of Ramallah's Main Street. Several other NGOs and cultural centers, as well as most of the key institutions of the Palestinian Authority, had been similarly sacked or destroyed.

In the clinic Muzna and I talked with a cheerful middle-aged nurse. She told us that while we'd been visiting the villages, Israeli soldiers had raided a hospital in Bethlehem looking for wanted men. I tried to imagine the horror and chaos of a military raid in a hospital, with guns and shouting and terrified patients and helpless doctors and nurses. I was too overstimulated to be angry or sad; I felt shocked and tired.

It was dark by the time we left Bethlehem. Israeli soldiers stopped us at a checkpoint on the way out. One soldier opened our door and took the men's IDs, but not the women's, so he didn't know I was American. He asked, "Which one of you is from Jerusalem?"

Abu Ali, our slim and affable driver, said it was he.

"You are Israeli?" the soldier said.

Abu Ali affected a comically blank look of polite confusion, as if the soldier had casually suggested he was from Neptune. I suppressed nervous laughter.

"You are Israeli," the soldier said again.

Israel annexed East Jerusalem and much of the land surrounding it in 1980 in violation of international law. The Israeli government gave the Palestinians living there blue ID cards, which obliges them to pay Israeli taxes and gives them certain privileges like insurance and greater freedom of movement without granting them Israeli citizenship. It leaves them open to several kinds of discrimination and abuse, including inferior public services and the fact that their IDs can be revoked at any time without warning.[12] It's a way to keep blue-ID holders quiet about the annexation and settlement of their land. Those who step out of line can find themselves "deported" behind the Wall.

This soldier was trying to force a man whose city was already occupied and maltreated to renounce his Palestinian identity in front of his coworkers. There was no telling what might happen if Abu Ali refused to play along. Plenty of people had been beaten, or worse, for less.

"*Qudsi, Qudsi,*" Dr. Barghouthi said diplomatically, breaking the

---

12. Nir Hasson, "Israel Stripped Thousands of Jerusalem Arabs of Residency in 2008," *Haaretz*, December 2, 2009.

tense silence. *Al Quds* means "The Holy City." *Qudsi* is Arabic for "Jerusalemite."

The soldier ignored him. "You are Israeli," he repeated to Abu Ali.

"From Al Quds," Abu Ali said.

"You are Israeli."

Abu Ali just looked at him.

The soldier narrowed his eyes threateningly. "You. Are. Israeli."

Abu Ali blinked. Then he shrugged. "*Tayyib.*"

The soldier understood the word to mean "OK," but the rest of us knew he was saying, "You can say what you like, it makes no difference to me. I just want to get home."

The soldier finally handed his ID back and let us go. We drove on, saying nothing and avoiding eye contact. Before long we reached the Qalandia checkpoint. As we pulled up to the end of a long line of vehicles, a woman approached our car, which was marked as a medical vehicle, and asked if we could take her sister, who was having stomach pains, to the hospital in Ramallah. We said sure. They both got in.

As we crept closer to the checkpoint, we heard gunshots to our left and saw a pile of burning tires. We shouted to another car to ask what was going on, and they told us teenagers were demonstrating and throwing stones at soldiers. The shooting was a hundred yards away and we weren't in the line of fire, but that could change in an instant. My stomach began spinning.

A portly kid of sixteen or seventeen soon hobbled to our car, his hand pressed against his bleeding back. Someone helped him in. He must have been hit by a rubber-coated steel bullet; if it had been a live bullet, he wouldn't have been walking. He sat across from me muttering, "*Yaba, yaba, ya Allah, ya Allah.*" After a while he gathered enough presence of mind to call his dad on his cell phone and tell him what had happened. Then we let in another kid of fifteen or sixteen. I saw a gash in his jeans where a rubber-coated bullet had penetrated. Blood was seeping out from under his hand, which he held over the wound until one of us bandaged it up. He looked alert but uninterested, as if all of this were old hat to him.

After interminably inching along, we finally passed the check-point and made our way to the hospital in Ramallah.

Dr. Barghouthi caught my eye. "You've seen a lot today," he said.

I nodded, numb and exhausted.

IT TOOK A few days for my feelings to develop from tired shock into sad rage. *Is there nothing,* I wondered, *that can make a dent in this fearful and ignorant, uncompassionate and unreflective world order that allows these things to happen? Maybe I should chain myself to the Wall and go on hunger strike until—*

Until what? The Wall was torn down? The settlements were dismantled? There was peace on Earth, good will toward men? Even if I had the guts to do something like that, which I doubted, the progression of events was entirely predictable. I would be arrested, then I would be deported. The thousands of hunger-striking prisoners probably wouldn't even get their meager demands met. Israeli Minister for Internal Security Tzahi Hanegbi said, "They can strike for a day, a month, until death. We will ward off this strike and it will be as if it never happened."[13] And he was probably right.

Dante said, "The hottest places in hell are reserved for those who in times of great moral crises maintain their neutrality." On the other hand, the road to hell was paved with platitudes unthinkingly applied. I was worried that living with integrity in a world as messed up as this one might mean poverty, prison, or early death. But I was even more worried I might unwittingly become a part of the problem. It's very easy to confuse righteousness and self-righteousness. Trying to "help" when I wasn't sure what the hell I was doing might be far worse than doing nothing at all. Passions were all over the place here, and nothing was getting better.

Someday, I desperately hoped, things would come into a kind of focus. Someday I'd have enough of a grasp on things to know where my place was—where I could be most genuinely dangerous to the forces

---

13. "Israel Turns up Heat on Prisoners," BBC, August 16, 2004.

that supported injustice. But as many times as I went over it in my mind, I couldn't think of anything better for me to do, for now, than keep learning and observing. It hurt to wait. It felt morally remiss and maddeningly passive. But I had to remind myself that I was just getting started. I had so much to learn, and this was part of it—this feeling of shock, of anger, of helplessness. This was what it looked like to be on the powerless butt-end of a major power's national security strategy.

Goons. Hired Goons.

One Thursday afternoon I was sitting in Al Karameh Café,[14] the little cake-and-cappuccino shop across from my office, when the brother of a friend from Jayyous named Khaled spotted me and joined me at my table. He was in his mid-thirties, an edgy but jovial chain-smoker whose English was almost as bad as my Arabic. He worked for the Palestinian Authority in some kind of security capacity that was never clear to me. He spoke with obvious pride about the Grand Park, a swanky hotel on the edge of town where Palestinian Authority bigwigs liked to hang out. He pronounced it "Grond Bark" and edged it into every sentence he could. As we were parting, he invited me to join him there later.

The PA was, from most accounts I'd heard, disorganized, ineffective, and corrupt. It was rumored that Prime Minister Ahmed Qurei, a dour man who looked like Yoda's grumpy uncle, had sold concrete to Israel to build the Wall. Whether this were true or not, it spoke volumes that no one would be surprised if it were. But roughly one-third of the population depended on the PA for their livelihood. Many worked as "police," which often amounted to little more than a "workfare" program to keep families afloat and reward Fatah loyalists. Even Palestinians who weren't financially dependent on Fatah had little to fall back on politically except Hamas, and many considered them an even less attractive option.

---

14. *Karameh* means "honor" or "dignity" in Arabic. It is also the name of a battle that was a major moral victory for combined Palestinian and Jordanian forces against the Israeli army in 1968.

I'd never met any PA elites before, and I was curious how this "other half" lived, so I accepted Khaled's invitation. I went home to change and tell Yasmine where I was headed. As I walked out the door I said, "If I don't come home tonight, call the police!"

She smirked. It was a joke, of course. There are no police to protect you from the police.

The hotel had the cut-stone-and-marble refinement I had begun to expect from the Levantine gentry. We walked through the lobby to a garden patio out back that overlooked an elegant swimming pool. The crowd was well dressed and subdued and had a wariness in their eyes that made me feel slightly defensive in a way I hadn't felt anywhere else in the West Bank.

Khaled looked around until he found someone he knew. He walked over and introduced me to a portly, shiny-faced man in an expensive-looking suit. The man looked me up and down once, seemed unimpressed, and went back to delicately eating his expensive meal. He and Khaled spoke in Arabic for a few minutes until they were interrupted by a commotion behind us.

Khaled looked back, and his eyes widened. Through the plate glass doors we could see the concierge taking the suit jacket of an important-looking man with a medium build, a wide jaw, and thick, curling lips. He was surrounded by eight or ten shifty-looking men carrying a mismatched collection of automatic weapons. Khaled whispered excitedly, "Do you know who that is? Mohammed Dahlan!"

I didn't know who that was, but I nodded as if I did. Khaled got up from his chair and walked toward the man as he emerged onto the patio. He spoke to Dahlan briefly in the same tone and posture as if he were addressing the pope and kissed Dahlan's hand. Dahlan gave him a popely acknowledgment and walked on, his cartoonishly heavily-armed bodyguards glancing around nervously as they trailed after him.

When I got home I asked Yasmine who Mohammed Dahlan was. She said, "Dahlan is the head of the Fatah security services. Everybody knows he works with the CIA. Israel and America give him money and arms, and he intimidates critics of Fatah and especially people from Hamas. A lot of people want him dead."

As head of the Palestinian Preventive Security Services, I found out later, he was implicated in financial scandals and human rights abuses. He worked with both the United States and Israel to crack down on terrorism, and he was accused of suppressing legitimate dissent and opposition as well. He'd arrested thousands of Palestinians, some of whom he allegedly tortured. He would later be instrumental in a disastrous failed coup attempt against Hamas in the Gaza Strip in 2007 that was, according to journalist David Rose, sponsored by the CIA.[15]

Suddenly I felt foolish for accepting that invitation from the hapless Khaled, an easily impressed man who never thought to ask where the money came from, or didn't care.

I CALLED QAIS a few nights later. We'd spoken several times since I got back from Amman, and he always said he missed me and asked when I'd be coming to Jayyous. This time he sounded upset, probably because I'd been going to the Dead Sea and Bir Zeit and Bethlehem, everywhere but Jayyous or Jenin to see him.

"I want to see you," I said. "I really do. Things have just been crazy. And it takes so much time to get there. I have to switch from buses whose schedules aren't posted to service taxis[16] that might take forever to fill up, never mind the flying checkpoints. And then I get to see you for only a couple of hours on your porch. Why don't you come to Ramallah?"

"I'm working on my father's land a lot lately," he said. "It is very hard for me to get away. I wish you could be here."

I sighed. I missed him terribly, and it would be fun to spend time with him in the fields. But people would wonder why I'd come all the

---

15. David Rose, "The Gaza Bombshell," *Vanity Fair*, April 2008.
16. Service taxis are affordable communal cabs with fixed destinations that leave only after they fill up so that passengers can split the cost.

way to Jayyous just to work on his dad's land, and we wouldn't get a minute alone together. One evening in Jayyous wouldn't be worth all the trouble, and any more would take me away too long from my full life in Ramallah.

We had a sweet conversation, though, like old friends even though we'd seen so little of each other. *Maybe*, I thought, *there's nothing there after all. Maybe he's just another passing phantom for me to pin my frail hopes on, someone affectionate and attractive as a counter to all the cold madness in the world. And maybe he just likes the idea of a foreign girl.*

But how would I know unless we could finally spend some quality time together?

An Offer I Couldn't Refuse

A few nights later I was getting ready to step into the shower when my phone rang. It was Muzna.

"Hi, dear! Listen, you know the *Palestine Monitor*, right?"

"Yup." It was the English-language news source across the hall from the HDIP and Al Mubadara offices. Dr. Barghouthi was the managing editor. Its updates, reports, and fact sheets were near the top of most of the Google searches I'd done when I was in California researching the conflict.

"The head writer and editor is stepping down next month," Muzna said. "Dr. Mustafa told me to let you know you can have the job if you want it. The pay is $900 a month plus a free apartment and health insurance."

"Oh . . . thanks," I said haltingly. "Listen, I'll need to think about it for a little while."

"Sure, dear, no problem."

I hung up and threw the phone across the room as if it were a poisonous snake. A *job*? Forty hours a week in an *office*? Where I'd have to *ask permission* if I wanted to go to Jayyous or Jordan for a week or a month? And I could forget about going home for Christmas. I'd have to stay in Ramallah for at least another year. And what about the olive harvest! I'd been looking forward to it all year . . .

After a few minutes, I stopped hyperventilating and started thinking. First of all, had I really come here just to avoid unpleasant responsibilities and enjoy picnics under olive trees? Surely not, although part of me apparently thought I had. Second, I was already researching and writing stories and articles about the situation in Palestine, sending them to a long list of family, friends, friends-of-friends, and fellow travelers, and posting them on my website. If I took this job I could do it in a more focused and disciplined way, have a worldwide audience, and get paid for it. It'd be nice to put "international journalist" on my résumé next to "bartender." And after living on nothing for so long, I'd feel like a drug czar on $900 a month.

The clincher was that if I didn't take the job, I *would* have to leave at Christmas. And what on earth would I do then? Where could I go that would compare to the West Bank?

I took a deep breath and called Muzna back.

"Actually, sure, that sounds great. When do I start?"

CHAPTER 6

Bombings, Weddings, and a Kidnapping

*When you are sorrowful look again in your heart,
and you shall see that in truth you are weeping
for that which has been your delight.*

—Khalil Gibran, *The Prophet*

At the end of August, I was chatting with some coworkers at the office when Muzna received a text message on her phone. Her face changed as she read it. She looked up and said tonelessly, "There's been a bombing."

It was the first suicide bombing since I'd moved to Ramallah—the first, in fact, since March. We were all apprehensive as we waited to find out how many had been killed, where, and by whom. And what Israel's response might be.

I called Dan to make sure he was all right. He said tiredly, "We've been waiting for something like this ever since Yassin was assassinated."

Sheikh Ahmed Yassin, the spiritual leader of Hamas, was a paraplegic, white-bearded old man in flowing white robes. Like most Gazans he was a refugee, driven out of his home in 1948. When the first Intifada broke out in 1987, Yassin and other members of the Palestinian wing of the Muslim Brotherhood[1] cofounded Hamas, which called for the establishment of an Islamic state in all of historic Palestine.

Hamas was initially tolerated and even encouraged by Israel as a counterweight to the secular nationalists of the Palestine Liberation Organization (PLO).[2] They were allowed to set up a wide network of schools, clinics, and charitable organizations that increased their power base and popularity. They carried out their first violent attack in 1989 targeting soldiers and settlements.

Then in 1994 Baruch Goldstein, an American-Israeli settler, opened fire on Palestinian worshipers in a mosque in Hebron during the holy month of Ramadan, killing 29 and wounding 125. The settlers in Hebron refused to denounce the massacre. On the contrary, they erected a monument in Goldstein's honor.

The PLO called on Israel to evacuate the settlers from Hebron or at least bring international peacekeepers in to protect the Palestinians. Instead, the Israeli army enforced a closure on the Palestinian areas of the West Bank to prevent reprisal attacks and shot dozens of Palestinians who defied the curfew, some of whom were trying to get to hospitals to donate blood for injured victims. After that Hamas began targeting civilians inside Israel to "show the Israelis they could not get away without a price for killing our people," according to Yassin.

Aside from being morally indefensible, the tactic was disastrous for the image of the Palestinian struggle. And every dead Israeli civilian drove the Israeli public further to the right—toward believing no peace was possible because there was "no partner for peace."

Yassin had rejected the Oslo Accords of 1993[3] and was initially marginalized by the hopes surrounding the peace process. But he

1. The Muslim Brotherhood is an Islamic political opposition movement founded in Egypt.
2. The PLO was founded in 1964 and is widely recognized as the sole legitimate representative of the Palestinian people. It has enjoyed observer status at the United Nations since 1974 and is composed of several Palestinian political factions including Fatah, the PFLP, and the DFLP.
3. The Oslo Accords were signed by Israel and the Palestinian Authority in 1993. They raised many hopes that peace was around the corner. But the peace process gradually unraveled and came to an end in September 2000, when the second Intifada erupted.

gained popularity as talks broke down, settlements went up, and Israeli soldiers and settlers continued to kill Palestinian civilians with few or no repercussions. Israel's devastation of PA institutions during Operation Defensive Shield in 2002 left Palestinians further dependent on Hamas's social services.

In March of 2004—six months prior to this bombing—a Hamas suicide bomber from Gaza had killed ten Israelis in the port city of Ashdod. It was a retaliation for two weeks of Israeli incursions that had killed twenty-six Palestinians in Gaza. Eight days later, in the small hours of the morning, an Israeli helicopter fired three Hellfire missiles at Sheikh Yassin as he was being wheeled out of a Gaza City mosque after predawn prayers. He and two bodyguards were killed along with five bystanders. Yassin's successor, Dr. Abdel Aziz Rantisi, was assassinated a few days later.

The assassinations were condemned around the world and by some in Israel because it was clear they would only lead to further radicalization and violence.[4] Even Palestinians who didn't support Hamas were appalled. Hamas had vowed revenge, as they always did when their leaders were targeted. The attacks today appeared to be it. Hamas in Hebron claimed responsibility—two bombings within minutes of each other on two city buses in Beersheba in southern Israel that killed sixteen Israelis and wounded dozens.

I said grimly to Dan, "I guess now it's the Palestinians' turn to wait for the retaliation for this retaliation."

An American friend sent me an article with profiles of the Israeli victims. Part of me didn't want to read it. I was having enough trouble absorbing the impact of the constant Palestinian casualties. But I knew that the moment I declined to mourn for the innocents killed on the other side, I would effectively become a part of the problem.

With a heavy heart I clicked the link, read the article, saw the pictures, and was physically sickened. Most of the victims were immigrants like Dan who'd come to Israel looking for a better life. They

---

4. See, for example: Roane Carey and Adam Shatz, "Israel Plays with Fire," *The Nation*, March 25, 2004. Extrajudicial assassinations, or "targeted killings," are a frequent tactic of the Israeli army.

probably didn't know much about the political situation. A three-year-old boy. A woman who'd immigrated from Tbilisi, Georgia, to be with her family. A young man from Azerbaijan who'd just finished his degree in biotech. A Ukrainian biology teacher. A woman from the Black Sea region of Russia whose son was a cellist. Sixteen unique, striving lives all in one moment, gone.

The international news was blanketed with headlines about how this savage attack had shattered a six-month "lull" in the violence. It was true that since the last suicide bombing only three Israeli civilians, eight settlers, and eighteen soldiers had been killed by Palestinians. Those were low numbers compared to similar periods over the previous two years. But in the same six-month period, more than 350 Palestinians, including 90 children, had been killed by Israeli soldiers and settlers. The press was conspicuously silent about that.

THE PRISONERS' HUNGER strike was broken two days later. Some prisoners reportedly lost half their body weight. One mother fasting in solidarity with her imprisoned son died. A spokesman for the Israeli prisons authority claimed, "Israel has not caved in to any demand of the prisoners and nothing is being discussed." Other sources close to the Palestinian prisoners said some demands had been met. It was hard to know who was telling the truth.

When I was reading *Haaretz*'s account of the end of the hunger strike, I noticed one of the advertisements on the page read, "Make your point: Why haven't the Palestinians turned to nonviolence? Click to send your response." Last I checked, hunger-striking was textbook nonviolent resistance. A better question might have been, "Why does the world demand nonviolence from Palestinians and then totally ignore them unless they do something violent?"

CHECKPOINT WEDDING

Rania invited me to her older brother's wedding the next weekend. His fiancée was from a village called Anabta near the city of

Tulkarem, twenty miles north of Jayyous. Its lands are closer to the green Galilee than the arid hills of Jerusalem and covered with greenhouses, cultivated fields, olive, fig, citrus, and almond trees, and pine forests.

The women trooped to the salon first. The traditional dress code goes out the window during weddings. Straightened and curled, highlighted and trimmed, swept up and falling down, painted and glittered, short skirts and spaghetti straps, for one day everyone looks Lebanese. Even the little girls put on makeup and tiny white dresses, and the salon was a zoo of kids and primping.

"See how we do like this, even under this situation?" Rania said dreamily. "Imagine if there was no occupation! Palestine would be like paradise."

The ceremony took place in Anabta's community center courtyard. While things were still being set up, the kids took over the dance floor. One little girl with a halo of curly black hair got up on the bride and groom's stage to dance. The grown-ups made her come down, but instead of walking down the steps, she danced her way down them like a Broadway star, as if the stairs were part of the act. I would have given anything for a video camera. The thought of it cheered me up for days.

The bride, whose name, Jamila, means "beautiful" in Arabic, was radiant. The groom, a portly man in his late twenties, had lost a lot of weight with the work he'd put into building their new house. The couple sat on the stage like figurines on a cake while people danced and took pictures. They cut the cake together with a traditional sword and passed pieces around to the guests. Sweets were thrown into the crowd every now and then to keep the kids' attention. Finally the bride's gold was handed over with great ceremony by the groom's mother—bracelets and necklaces and medallions, the traditional backup savings system in the Arab world.

When the ceremony was over, the immediate family stayed in the village for a small private party. The rest of the weary guests loaded into four chartered vans for the trip back to Jayyous.

We were almost home when our caravan was stopped at a dark and dusty checkpoint. The women, keyed up from the wedding, started singing and clapping as a soldier walked toward our window. As he got closer, they got louder. The soldier hesitated. The men told the women to pipe down. The soldier, a thick young man with a congested voice, cautiously approached the driver's window.

"This checkpoint is closed," he said. "Go back."

A collective groan of dismay arose from our van. Home was so achingly close, and we were so ready to get out of our nice clothes and into pajamas and soft beds. Someone turned to me and said, "Can you do anything?" I doubted I could, but I got out and asked the thick soldier if he spoke English.

"*Ivrit*" (Hebrew), he said indignantly.

"*Russky?*" I asked hopefully. He pointed at a vague skinny boy leaning against a concrete roadblock and toying with his M16. I walked over and asked if he spoke Russian.

"*Da. Ti Russkaya?*"

"*Nyet, Amerikanskaya.*"

He looked confused. I told him I had studied in Moscow.

"Really?" he said, perking up. "I'm from Moscow."

It was clear from the way he said it that he missed home and wished he was anywhere in the world but a checkpoint in the West Bank in the middle of the night. But I had other things on my mind. "Listen," I said, "there are fifty people here, and we just want to go home. There was a wedding in Tulkarem, but they have no place to sleep there. Only in Jayyous."

He looked away. "*Nelzya*" (It's forbidden).

"I know, but there are fifty wedding guests here. We have nowhere else to go. We only want to go home and sleep. There was a party in Tulkarem, you see . . ."

After several minutes of going back and forth he finally asked, "Where will you sleep?"

"Jayyous."

"What are you doing there?"

"Teaching English." It was the most simple, harmless answer I could think of.

"English, huh." He thought for a few long moments. Finally he made a small motion with his hand. We could go.

Once we were out of earshot of the soldiers, the wedding guests cheered. But I felt ill and disgusted. If I hadn't been here, those bored kids would have had the power to spoil this festive occasion for no reason. I kept thinking I'd get used to this kind of thing, but it felt like a slap in the face every time.

THE NEXT MORNING I pulled Rania aside to tell her some good news. I'd written several friends about her story; one friend's father, who lived in the United Arab Emirates, had written back and offered to pay her tuition for the next semester.

Rania gasped. "I won't have to quit! Bamila, maybe even I can graduate! But . . ." her face fell, "I don't know if I can pay it back."

"No, Rania, it's a gift." She gasped again, and I laughed, embarrassed. It was crazy to think I had that much power simply by sending an email. "Don't worry," I said. "I wouldn't have been able to go to college if people hadn't helped me out, either."

It was my last day in Jayyous. Strangely, Qais hadn't been in touch at all since I'd texted him that I was in town for the weekend. I didn't know if he was in Jayyous or Jenin. Luckily I ran into his brother Shadi on the street, and he invited me to come to their place that evening.

When I arrived, Qais greeted me at the gate wearing a *jalabiya*, a traditional light robe with gold and navy blue stripes. He looked unbearably cute, like a little boy in a nightgown.

"*Marhaba!*" he said with his winning smile.

"Why didn't you return my calls?" I asked more sharply than I intended.

"Oh, I am sorry about that. Shadi was borrowing my phone. His is broken."

Just then my phone beeped. It was Yasmine texting to ask how things were going with Qais.

Qais asked me something in Russian while I was reading the text. "*Shto khochesh?*" I asked distractedly. (What do you want?)

He answered with a warm half-smile that gently mocked my sulky mood, "*Potselovat tebya.*" (To kiss you.)

I looked up at him and smiled despite myself. "Look, you see how difficult this is," I said teasingly. "Maybe impossible. And maybe if you don't come see me in Ramallah soon, I'll find somebody else."

He looked genuinely hurt. "It is *nelzya* to say words like 'impossible,'" he said quietly.

I sighed. "I was only joking." The truth was, the more time I spent with him, the crazier I was about him. But that only made it harder to sustain so much emotion only to see him on his porch once a month. "Things will be so much more relaxed in Ramallah. I can show you my favorite places, introduce you to my friends." I smiled. "My roommate's heard all about you."

He smiled, too. "I would like that. But it is difficult for me. Classes start next week, and I have to work on my dad's land whenever I have time off." He sighed heavily. "But I will try."

Disappeared

A few days later, he called.

"I'm coming to Ramallah on Saturday morning, *insha'Allah.*"

My eyes widened. "*Seriozna?*" (Seriously?) The coming weekend would be his last before classes started again, and he wanted to spend it with me. Maybe there was hope for us after all.

He laughed. "Yes. *Insha'Allah.*"

He called again on Saturday morning and said he was on the bus and would arrive in forty minutes if there were no checkpoints. I happily began cleaning the house, buzzing with energy, humming with possibilities. By the time I finished and looked at a clock, I was startled to realize nearly two hours had passed.

I called Qais's number. He rejected the call.

Feeling some mixture of alarm and irritation, I texted, *Bolshoi checkpoint?*

Several minutes later, he texted back: *They booked my ID and the bus went i dont know wat wil happen. I am stopped with some bodyelse. Dont try to cal. I wil cal wen they leave me. My kissing to u.*

My blood runs cold. This is how it starts. The soldiers take them off their bus, off the street, out of their house, and they disappear, maybe for hours, maybe for days, maybe for years. Palestinians can be held in Israeli jails for up to three months without charge or trial, a practice known as "administrative detention." The three-month sentences can be renewed indefinitely. I've heard stories of innocent people being held for years in Israeli prisons, of people being destroyed by the experience. No warrant. No charge. No phone call.

This isn't arrest in any sense I recognize. This is government-sponsored kidnapping.

If the soldiers are just harassing him, he'll call in a couple of hours. If they're taking him for days or months, I'll have to sit here as dreadful minutes drag into unbearable hours waiting for his call, my imagination getting worse as time goes on. I can't concentrate enough to do anything but stare at my silent phone. By the time four hours have passed, I am a basket case.

Shadi calls at four in the afternoon and says he's been trying to call his brother all day with no luck. He asks me if Qais reached Ramallah. "No," I say. "He was stopped at a checkpoint. Soldiers took him off his bus."

Shadi is silent for a moment. "Please call me if you hear anything."

"I will. Same to you, OK?"

Yasmine shows up half an hour later with a cheeseburger and fries from the Checkers on Main Street. I haven't eaten all day. She splits her food with me. I numbly choke it down.

She says reassuringly, "Don't worry, *habibti*, they do this all the time. One time they took me off my bus at a checkpoint and made me stand in the sun for ten hours."

"Why?"

She scoffed. "There is no reason. They just do this to humiliate us. He is not politically active is he? He is just a student. Maximum they will beat him and throw him in prison for a few days."

I hope to God she's right. But even that is more than I can bear imagining. He's never been in prison before. If they keep him more than two days, he'll miss the beginning of class. Even if he misses a single hour of his life, a day with his family, a week of class, it's more than I can bear. Anything worse is beyond imagination, but I imagine it all the same.

Once while we were sitting on his porch in Jayyous, Qais told me about a cousin who'd been in prison for two months in unsanitary conditions and was suffering from terrible hemorrhoids and back pains, neither of which he'd suffered before. I think of Qais sitting next to me on the porch, whole and perfect, telling me about his poor cousin. Now maybe it is his turn.

The worst part is that even if they let him go and don't hurt him, for every friend and mother and sister and daughter who's ever felt what I am feeling (and much, much worse), the fears of some are justified. Some loved ones never come back, or spend years of their lives being broken, caged, tortured,[5] starved, injured, and sickened, their dreams curtailed by the year, their hopes ground down into the most basic things they'd taken for granted before: respect, decent food, seeing their family. Never mind what they want to study, what lessons they want to teach their kids, where they want to travel, or how they want to arrange their garden.

I call Shadi, but he still hasn't heard anything. He sounds as worried as I am. I call a friend named Mohammad Othman, a wiry peace activist from Jayyous who travels the world educating people about the situation in Palestine.[6] We meet in a coffee house on Main Street.

---

5. Torture in Israeli jails has been documented by respected human rights organizations such as Amnesty International, Human Rights Watch, and B'Tselem. According to Human Rights Watch, prisoners reported "sleep deprivation, hooding, prolonged standing or sitting in unnatural positions, threats, beatings and violent whiplashing of the head . . . Applied in combination, these methods often amount to torture." Prisoners also reported being given rotten food and inadequate medical care, being interrogated for ten or more hours a day, and threats against their friends or family members, among many other types of abuse.

6. In 2009 Mohammad Othman would be arrested on his way home from Norway, where his testimony helped convince Norway's Finance Ministry to divest from the Israeli security firm Elbit Systems because its surveillance system was one of the main com-

"My brother was arrested one time while he was eating falafel in a restaurant," he says. "The official report said he was throwing stones. But many witnesses, including Israelis, said he was not. I called a lawyer and human rights groups, and he was released after six days."

"Six days! Surely they won't keep Qais for six days . . ."

"And my best friend, who is also not political, was arrested eight days ago. He is still missing. We think he is in the Shin Bet interrogation facility in Petah Tikvah.[7] I hope not. I've heard stories about the Shin Bet torturing and fatiguing prisoners to the point that they will admit to killing Yitzhak Rabin[8] if only they can be left alone."

My mind and stomach are spinning. I'm reminded of a time when I was fifteen and my mom asked me if I knew how to drive a stick shift.

"Sure," I said confidently.

"How do you know how to drive a stick shift," she asked, "if you've never tried?"

"I read a book about it." They all laughed at me. Sure enough, when I tried to drive my brother's little Honda Civic, I nearly dropped the engine out of the bottom of the car.

It's the same difference, it turns out, between reading a thousand human rights violations reports and then having someone you personally care about disappear.

My body feels like I've been crying all day, but I'm too wrung out to cry. Yasmine and Mohammad seem almost embarrassed by how sensitive I am. In so many words they tell me to grow up. These things happen. If you want to live in Palestine and not be a complete greenhorn *ajnabiya*,[9] you've got to put a little starch in your spine.

---

ponents of the Wall. "We do not wish to fund companies that so directly contribute to violations of international humanitarian law," said Finance Minister Kristin Halvorsen. Mohammad was jailed for three and a half months without charge or trial.

7. The Shin Bet (also known as "Shabak") is Israel's internal security and intelligence service. Petah Tikvah is a city in Israel.

8. Israeli Prime Minister Yitzhak Rabin was assassinated in 1995 by a radical right-wing Israeli Orthodox Jew who opposed the Oslo Accords.

9. The word means "foreigner," but it often carries a tinge of pity with it because Europeans and Americans can't help but look a little soft and pink and bewildered on their first wide-eyed visit to the other end of the guns.

I can't stand the thought of going to bed without knowing where he is or what's being done to him. But I don't know what else to do. I lie in bed with my phone next to me until unconsciousness overtakes me.

I wake up in the morning, and the nightmare continues. I go to the office for something to do besides stare at my silent phone. I start writing the story of my weekend, trying to capture some of the feelings while they are still raw. It is impossible.

At half past seven, thirty-two hours after Qais disappeared, my phone rings. I see his name on my phone. My stomach seizes. Maybe it's his family telling me that—

"*Privyet.*" (Hi.) It's his voice, full of sardonic exasperation. Warm tears of relief stream over my fingers and onto my phone. The only utterances I can manage sound clumsy and inarticulate.

"Qais, are you OK? What happened?"

He spoke in an indignant stream of Russian so fast I couldn't understand it all, but I gathered that they had "checked his ID" for a few hours. "Who am I, Bin Laden, or what?" he asked me. Then they tied his hands, blindfolded him, and told him to get into an army Jeep. He asked why. They said, "Just go."

They took him to a settlement, tied him to a chair, and interrogated him about every aspect of his life. He had no idea if he would be in there for hours or years. They repeated questions incessantly. They terrorized and tormented a completely innocent person for thirty-two hours, not to mention his friends and family, and ruined all of our weekends. And there's no one to appeal to. They are the law.

After we said good night and hung up, I felt like a thread of unbearable tension holding me up sickeningly by the armpits had been cut. I was left fallen in a dazed heap in an old landscape of everyday concerns that now seemed unfamiliar and strange.

I just had to catch a taxi. Go home. Brush my teeth. Wake up the next morning, go to work, check my email. Life goes on. It keeps going on and on, with or without you. You ride the wave called "normal life" because it seems easier. Every now and then, though, you catch a glimpse of just how mad it all really is.

OSAMA THE COMMIE

"This is my friend Osama," Yasmine said a few days later. "He is also a Communist." And he came bearing gifts: a six-pack of Taybeh beer. With his compact figure, black goatee, and cynical, visionary eyes, he was on the tail end of being reminiscent of a young Arab Trotsky. I shook his hand, and we settled into the kitchen for a chat.

Osama worked for the Palestinian Agricultural Relief Committees (PARC), an NGO that works with farmers to reclaim rocky ground, build terraces and retainer walls, and construct agricultural roads, which become crucial links between towns when Israel shuts down the main roads. PARC also promotes organic and sustainable farming techniques in lectures and workshops. Many Palestinian NGOs are affiliated with political parties, and PARC is a stronghold of the Palestinian People's Party (PPP). When I told Osama whom I worked with, a shadow passed over his face. Dr. Barghouthi, I later learned, had been head of the PPP until 2002, when he left it to found Al Mubadara. The Communists never quite forgave him for rising to prominence among their ranks and then defecting.

I told Osama about Qais being taken that weekend. I couldn't seem to get across how drained and horrified and worried I'd been. He looked at me in mild confusion, as if I were a grown woman complaining about a scraped knee. "The first time I was in jail was when I was fourteen," he said. "They took me for three months."

"How did they treat you?"

"They tortured us, of course. They'd do things like make us lean back in a chair for six or eight hours, and if you raised up, they'd hit you. Sometimes they tied our neck and hands and feet together, so you are left hunched over, and if you fall asleep, you hang yourself. And of course they beat us. When I saw the pictures from Abu Ghraib, I laughed. This is nothing new for us. No one comes out of Israeli prison without mental or health problems." He turned his arm over and showed me a scaly patch above his elbow. "I developed psoriasis in prison. It's been more than ten years, and I still have to take medication for it." He saw the sick look on my face and added, "But

I enjoyed it. Really. It's just part of growing up here, of becoming a man. It makes you more tough. Ready for anything."

We drank our beers in silence for a while. Then he said quietly, "It's OK for young people. But it's hard on the mothers."

"I know! I was thinking about that. Imagine raising a son for nineteen, twenty, twenty-one years, and then . . ." Osama snapped his fingers lightly, and a nauseous chill ran up my spine.

Yasmine had told me Osama was from Qalqilia. I asked him how people in his hometown were dealing with being surrounded by the Wall.

"Qalqilia used to be a very nice town," he said fondly. "But we are very poor now. We used to feel the sea breezes, and Israelis would come and shop in our markets. It gave us great hope. We could see there was a partner for peace. Now all we see is a thirty-foot concrete Wall, and behind the Wall we can only imagine people who hate us and want to imprison and kill us. We can't even watch the sunset anymore. This is not right, Pamela. It is not the way to peace."

"Do you think nonviolent resistance has any chance of working?"

"Just to exist here is nonviolent resistance. Helping farmers when the occupation is trying to turn them into beggars and refugees is nonviolent resistance. Demonstrating, hunger striking, and educating ourselves, it is all nonviolent resistance. But it is not enough. Nothing gets better. It only gets worse. There are more settlements every day. People are killed every day. Nobody stops the Israelis from doing this. So we have to fight. Anyone will do this."[10]

"But don't you think suicide bombing is wrong?"

He shook his head. "It is not an interesting question whether suicide bombing is wrong. Of course it is wrong. The question is, what causes a person to do that? After all, it is not a natural thing to do. But maybe if someone kills a man's family, he goes crazy. I can tell you this: If anyone touches my brothers, I will do it. It's simple. If I feel pain, you will feel pain."

---

10. In 1998 Gideon Levy, an Israeli journalist for *Haaretz*, asked then–Israeli Prime Minister Ehud Barak what he would do if he were born Palestinian. Barak answered, "I'd eventually join one of the terrorist organizations."

I considered this. For him it wasn't about religion—he was an atheist. It wasn't even a political calculation. It was like Sheikh Ahmed Yassin had said: *You can't kill our people without paying a price. If I feel pain, you will feel pain. If you take hope and security from me, I will take it from you, too.* The conflict was feeding on itself like an avalanche with each side "telling" the other they would pay a price for killing. The price was always to kill more.

Years later I'd read an article in *The New York Times* that explained why starting such a cycle was so easy and ending it so hard even in the absence of any ill will. "First, because our senses point outward, we can observe other people's actions but not our own. Second, because mental life is a private affair, we can observe our own thoughts but not the thoughts of others."[11]

Thus we see the wrongs others do but not the reasons, while we see the reasons for our own bad behavior but we don't feel the consequences. It leads to all kinds of spirals, from squabbling siblings in the backseat of a minivan to the Troubles in Northern Ireland. With the Wall and closures and increasing separation in the Holy Land, it was becoming ever easier for each side to see the other as a faceless, evil force, not as a group of human beings with hopes and dreams and stories and fundamental human rights.

"But . . ." Osama raised his eyebrows. "You can tell your government that if they don't like suicide bombings, there is a very easy way to stop them. All they have to do is give us the same tanks, Apaches, and F16s that they give to the Israelis, and we will promise never to suicide bomb again. We will be just *exactly* as humane as the Israelis."

I shook my head. He went on, "You know, I heard someone on CNN say Palestinians hate Israelis because of propaganda in our textbooks. First of all, when I was a kid our textbooks were Jordanian. We learned more about Petra and Amman than Jerusalem. Either way, we don't need textbooks to teach us how to feel about Israelis. Let me

---

11. The research explaining these human dynamics was first brought to my attention in an article by Daniel Gilbert, "He Who Cast the First Stone Probably Didn't," *The New York Times*, July 24, 2006.

tell you who taught us to feel this way. I was eight or nine years old, in Qalqilia. It was the Eid al Fitr, the feast holiday, and my sister and I had just bought new clothes. We were walking home, very happy. Two Israeli soldiers stopped us. They said, 'What you are doing?' We said, 'Nothing, we are just walking. We bought new clothes.' 'Let me see them.' 'OK.' They took our clothes. It had just rained, and there were small pools on the ground. They put our clothes in the mud and moved them around until they were covered. Then they laughed and said, 'OK, you can go.' This kind of thing, Pamela. This is one of my earliest memories.

"But look, I don't hate the Israelis. I have friends in the Israeli Communist Party. If the soldiers and settlers will leave us alone, and leave our land alone, no one can kill an Israeli. It would simply be a crime."

I hoped this was true. There was only one way to test it, and it didn't seem forthcoming any time soon. "Or the Palestinians can all just move to Jordan," I said jokingly.[12]

He smiled indulgently. "When I am in Jordan, the shackles come off. I can go anywhere I want. No soldiers, no checkpoints. I can't even imagine the freedom. But I am like a machine, a robot. In the West Bank, I am in prison always, but I feel like my soul is in me. I am home."

"You know," I said, then hesitated. I wasn't sure if he would take me seriously. "When I left the West Bank the first time, I felt that way, too. Like I *had* to come back."

He nodded as if it were a matter of course. "Many people feel this way. When I go to the Church of the Nativity or the Al Aqsa Mosque and feel the stones, I can feel this is a special place. It's like the middle of the world. Millions of people come here, and if you stay, you are not a foreigner very long. You start to belong."

Long after midnight, Osama asked if he could stay over in our spare room. I fell asleep and dreamed I was visiting a friend. After a while she took me to a house with other friends, and once I was

---

12. A common refrain of the Israeli far-right wing is that Palestinians don't need a state in the West Bank and Gaza because they have a state called Jordan, already full of Palestinian refugees, that they can go to instead.

distracted she quietly disappeared. Soon the new friends spirited me to yet another house and disappeared. Then it happened again. I finally realized I was in a network of safe houses that, one after another, stopped being safe. I had to be passed on and on. Someone was always seeking us, chasing us, and everyone was trying to protect soft, innocent me.

I woke up in the middle of the night thinking, *Maybe Osama is hiding out here, and the soldiers really will come after him.* My stomach tingled with half-conscious terror. But what could I do? I turned over and went back to sleep.

SHOOT 'EM UP

I officially started my job at the *Palestine Monitor* in mid-September. Immediately it was like drinking from a fire hose. On my first day, three men were killed while they were driving down a street in Jenin by a missile fired from an Israeli Apache helicopter. They were members of Al Aqsa Martyrs Brigades, an armed offshoot of Fatah.

Two days later, Israeli soldiers shot and killed five men in a house in Nablus. Most of them were members of the Al Aqsa Brigades. Four of the five were shot in the head at close range, medical examiners said. As the Israeli soldiers retreated under fire, one of their bullets hit an eleven-year-old girl in the face and killed her.

According to Reuters, "Hours later, Israeli special forces backed up by helicopter gunships killed four Palestinians—a militant, a policeman, and two civilians—at a car repair shop in the northern city of Jenin . . . They had earlier said all four dead were militants."[13]

On Friday an Israeli soldier killed a nineteen-year-old Palestinian woman in Nablus. She was shot in the heart as she stood on the roof of her house calling her brothers to come inside and away from Israeli soldiers who were patrolling the area.

A ten-year-old girl had been shot in the head on September 7 by

---

13. Wael al Ahmad, "Violence Erupts in Nablus," Reuters, September 16, 2004.

an Israeli soldier while she sat at her desk in a UN elementary girls' school in the Khan Younis Refugee Camp in Gaza. The bullet entered under her eye and exited the back of her head. She died two weeks later. The UN wrote a press release saying it was the third such incident in eighteen months, and that "the kind of live firing into refugee camps that is so indiscriminate that it makes classrooms dangerous for ten-year-old children is totally unacceptable."

On the same day, Israeli helicopters bombed a Hamas community center in Gaza City, killing fourteen men. The Palestinian Authority condemned the attack, and Hamas responded by firing five Qassam rockets[14] and a mortar shell that damaged a settlement bus stop.

Every morning a colleague called the families of Palestinian victims, eyewitnesses, and/or hospitals, and I read reports by human rights organizations, investigative journalists, foreign presses, and the UN. I recorded each victim's name, age, hometown, status as a civilian or combatant, place of death, cause of death, location of fatal injury, and who had killed him or her. Respected sources usually confirmed the Palestinian version of events and contradicted official Israeli army statements. But most of the reports were buried so deeply few Westerners would ever see them.

Israeli soldiers invaded Ramallah during my second week on the job. We saw the armored Jeeps from our office window tearing around the streets like teenagers on four-wheelers. They almost hit a guy in a blue car who was desperately trying to get out of their way. Main Street retracted and closed itself off like a frightened coral, transforming instantly from a vibrant commercial street into a ghost town. Hostility bristled like electricity behind every hastily closed door and window. Someone ran out of a doorway near our office and hurled a large stone at the convoy. It hit one of the Jeeps square in the back end. The Jeep slammed on its brakes. The man ran away. A British colleague muttered, "Nice shot!"

---

14. Qassam rockets are unguided homemade missiles used by Palestinian fighters against Israeli civilian and military targets. Since 2000, about twenty Israelis have been killed by them. Source: Israeli Ministry of Foreign Affairs.

The soldiers went into an Internet café and arrested six people. After they left, people gathered at Al Manara to protest the invasion, though I wasn't sure to whom they were protesting. No journalists were there, and the Palestinian Authority could do nothing when Israel chose to invade. Maybe they were protesting their own helplessness.

Not long afterward, the Al Aqsa Martyrs Brigades committed their first and only suicide bombing of the year in retaliation for the assassinations of their men. A female suicide bomber killed two Israeli border policemen and injured seventeen other Israelis at the French Hill junction hitchhiking post in East Jerusalem.

At the end of the week, feeling exhausted, I went with Yasmine to a place called Almonds, a cozy dance club near Sangria's. It felt amazing to forget everything for a while and just dance. I'd never heard anything as infectiously, shoulder-shakingly danceable as Arabic pop music. People kept buying my drinks (including an ex of Yasmine's, though I wasn't sober enough at the time to notice her ire), and I chatted with cute Palestinians and fascinating foreigners on the balcony outside with its little potted palm trees.

A few days later the Israeli army invaded Jenin with thirty tanks backed up by aircraft. With my heart in my throat I called Qais to make sure he was OK.

"I'm fine," he said in a soothing tone. "Don't worry. It's normal."

I rested my forehead wearily on my arm. *Sweetie, it's not normal.* "Anyway," I said, "I'm coming to Jayyous next Friday to help with the olives. Will you be there?"

"If you will be there, I will be there. I *must* be there."

My face, still resting on my arm, expanded into a smile.

ZEITOUN

I had accepted the *Palestine Monitor* job only on the condition that someone would cover for me for a week during the olive (*zeitoun*) harvest. The best time was the first week of October after the Jewish

High Holidays were over (during which travel in the West Bank was restricted) and just before Ramadan began.

By the time I arrived in Jayyous I was too late to cross the Wall, so I wandered through the groves on the Jayyous side until a family waved me over. I introduced myself as Bamila.

One of the daughters giggled. *"Bomaleh?"*

Bomaleh means something like "grapefruit" in Arabic. The girls eventually learned a better approximation of my name, but the mother called me Grapefruit all day as we picked olives together.

They invited me back to their house after we finished the trees. We watched *The Professionals* on MBC2[15] starring Burt Lancaster and Jack Palance and dined on *maqlouba*, the baked chicken and rice dish I love so much. When the movie was over, I thanked them for the lovely meal and walked to Qais's house. He greeted me warmly and we sat on his porch under the grapevines and talked about Russia for a while.

"You know, the Wall was built while I was in Russia," he said. "You see that hill over there? You can see all of Jayyous from there. My cousins and I used to go there every day after school. It's a very nice place, with the best views and breezes. When I arrived from Russia, I called my cousin from Jericho and said, 'Get everything ready to go to our place!' He told me that was impossible. I asked why. He said, 'You will find out soon enough.'

"I slept on the roof that night. It was dark, so I couldn't see anything. But in the morning . . ." He saw everything. The roads, the Fence, the razor wire, the blasted hillsides and bulldozed "buffer zones." The barrier between him and his birthright, or what was left of it. "I saw it, and the tears fell down. It was a very sad moment for me." He paused. "Sometimes the Jeeps stay there now."

He tried not to sound bitter. But having your childhood illegally bulldozed into a military base in full view of a silently compliant world is a bitter pill.

I couldn't think of anything to say. He was toying with his *hawiya*,

---

15. MBC2 is a Saudi-owned channel based in Dubai that plays American movies subtitled in Arabic.

his Israel-issued ID card. I asked if I could look at it. It was slightly bigger than a credit card and was encased in a green plastic cover. A menorah was stamped on the front, a symbol of the Israeli government's authority. His information was written in Hebrew and Arabic next to a mug shot taken when he was sixteen. He looked so young and cute in the picture. But he must have known this document would thereafter define the boundaries of where he could go without obtaining permission from an Israeli soldier.

He said distantly, "I often think of good times that will never come again. In Russia, I was so young and thoughtless . . ."

"Qais, for God's sake, you're only twenty-one."

"I know. And I don't want to leave home again. But here in Palestine you can't plan your life. You can't plan anything. Unemployment is so bad. So bad, even when people are very educated. At least . . ." He laughed bitterly.

"What?"

"Before I went to Russia I thought about studying in Iraq instead."

Qais's father invited me to join them for dinner on the porch that evening. He was a devout farmer with a grey-white beard who looked rather Amish and had a simple, direct, kindly way of dealing with the world. He'd never gone to college, but he made sure all of his sons were well educated. Two were living abroad, Bilal in Sweden and Majed in the United Arab Emirates. It was impossible to measure what he had sacrificed to set his sons so far ahead of himself.

Qais's soft-spoken mother had a sweet round face, soft dark eyes, and an air of peaceful melancholy. She made her own flatbread, which had a grainy, earthy consistency. They gently reminded me to say *Bismillah al Rahman al Rahim* (In the name of God, the Merciful and Compassionate) at the beginning of each meal, and *Al hamdulillah* at the end, in the same patient tone Qais used when he corrected my Russian grammar. I knew they were looking out for my body and soul in their own way, and I appreciated it.

Qais went to bed early because he had to get up before dawn to travel to Jenin. I stayed and chatted with Shadi and Marwa, Bilal's wife, who was staying in Jayyous until her Swedish travel documents came through. Shadi talked about the jokes and pranks he and Marwa played on each other while they harvested. He said as if in explanation, "We have no power in the situation of occupation to do anything. We just have to live. We have to keep laughing and joking. Otherwise . . ."

He looked at me earnestly. I knew exactly what he meant.

When we parted at the gate he shook my hand and said in Arabic, "Go safely, good night, God with you . . ." His words and smile lingered like a warm blanket in the starry air as I walked back to the International House.

I WOKE UP at six the next morning and found a family who offered to take me out past the Wall on their tractor. As I passed the gate, a young Israeli soldier took my documents and demanded, "Where are you from? What are you doing here?"

I wanted to say right back, "Where are you from? What are you doing here?" I figured I had as much right to question him on Jayyous land as he had to question me.

Alas, he had a gun. I answered, "America. Pickin' olives."

"This is your job?"

"No. Just for fun."

"It's very dangerous for you to be here, you know."

"Really? Why?"

He seemed surprised and embarrassed by the question. "Uh . . . well . . . Many people have been killed," he answered lamely.

"Really? Why?" I wanted to ask again, but I just nodded as if I appreciated the news flash and walked on, chuckling at his clumsy attempt to frighten me.

The bumpy tractor ride took us through some of Jayyous's prettiest land. Olive groves, greenhouses, citrus trees, and the sparkling dawn sky passed by. The mayor had invited me to harvest with his family that day. I didn't remember exactly where his land was, but I figured I could ask around and find it easily enough. I'd somehow forgotten that the land isolated by the Wall encompassed more than ten square kilometers.

When the tractor stopped, the driver asked if I wanted to help his family harvest.

"Oh, no, sorry. I'd love to, but I'm supposed to meet up with the mayor's family."

"Abu Nael? His land is next to the gate, four kilos back. Why didn't you tell us?"

I walked back east facing the rising sun on gravel and dirt roads that passed near the Israeli settlement of Zufin.[16] The road was covered with the tracks of donkey carts, tractors, Jeeps, and armored Hummers. When I found myself on a small ridge not far from the Wall, I asked a young couple if they knew where Abu Nael's land was.

The man yelled, "Abu Nael!"

A voice from the trees answered, "*Na'am*?" (Yes?)

"There," said the man. I walked toward the voice and found Abu Nael, his wife Umm Nael, and three of their sons, Nael, Hael, and Thaher. They welcomed me, and I got to work.

Nael, the mayor's oldest son, was in his mid-thirties with a neatly trimmed Groucho Marx moustache and wire-rimmed glasses, and he spoke the most perfect English of anyone I'd met in Jayyous. He'd gotten his master's degree in business in India and now worked for a bank in Ramallah. I asked him about India.

He said fondly, "India is so great. You can pass from one state to the other and the weather is different, the food is different, the language is different . . ."

"And no checkpoints," I joked, but he didn't smile.

"Yes." He seemed almost surprised. "Things are very bad here." He stood lost in thought for a moment. "You know, in the old days, before the Wall, the whole family used to come out and the kids would join in after school. We'd have barbecues and hand-pick everything together, little by little, in no particular hurry." He

---

16. Also transliterated as Tzufim, Tsofin, Zufim, etc., Zufin was founded in 1989 and has two hundred housing units and a population of one thousand who live within an easy commute to Tel Aviv. Its built-up area covers two hundred dunams (fifty acres) of Jayyous's land, but its "jurisdictional area" is ten times larger.

shook his head. "There's no mood for that now. We just want to get the olives and get out."

Every few minutes Thaher would yell from whatever tree he was in, "*Heyyyy, ya ammmmmmmi!*" He was greeting a favorite uncle, Abu Dia, and when breakfast was called I met the great man. He told story after story with a stone-straight face and a subtle, sincere voice that had everybody in tears from laughter, including myself even though I could barely understand a word.

After meals we took turns washing dishes and pouring water onto each other's hands to wash up with soap. When we ran out of water I went to a cistern with Nael to get more. A small hole in the ground opened into a stone-lined chamber about twenty feet in diameter and twenty feet deep with three feet of water in the bottom. Nael drew water out with a bucket, and I held a funnel to fill the jugs. The water had a few spiders and chicken bones in it but was clear and cold and good enough for washing. Nael glanced up at the Zufin settlement.

"You see what we have to do for water?" he said. "The settlers never have to do this. They have access to all the best, purest water here."

I'd written a report about Israeli water use practices in the West Bank. Some of the largest settlements, including Ariel, were built over major aquifers, and the Wall's convoluted route isolated countless springs and wells, grabbing water along with land. Israelis used four times as much water per capita as Palestinians, and many Palestinians were forced to buy their own water back from the Israeli national water company, Mekorot, at inflated prices. Some families couldn't afford it, and people in Jayyous often had to wash their hands with buckets of water borrowed from neighbors. I'd seen Qais and Karim straining under the weight of two five-gallon buckets each taking water to one of Qais's sisters. Meanwhile settlers were topping off their swimming pools and watering their lawns a few miles away.

We talked and joked and had a good time while we harvested. Abu Dia even managed to make Umm Nael laugh a few times. But the laughter was interspersed with long moments of unnatural, empty silence. Umm Nael had cried after last year's harvest, knowing things would only get worse. This year she walked around as if someone had been killed in some kind of obscene way. Her whole, full life of raising a big family and all their olive trees had come to this sorry state, and for what? Despite the normalcy we pretended to, an abyss was yawning just ahead of us. This kind of life, already crippled beyond recognition, might be finished soon. Who decides, who controls, whether all of this will fall into oblivion?

MONDAY MORNING I packed a small bag for three days of camping with the mayor's family on their land. They were tired of dealing with the Wall every day, and so was I.

The days passed pleasantly, and time seemed to move along at just the right speed. Hours of clean work with our hands under the sun were interspersed with heavenly drinks of cold, clear water in the shade of an olive tree and picnics of pickles, yogurt, hummus, tuna, fried potatoes and eggplant, tinned mackerel, boiled eggs, fire-roasted tomato sauce, *halaweh*, and sweet black tea. Occasionally a cousin would bring a platter of *maqlouba* or a garlicky green stew called *molokhiya* from town and we'd eat like kings.

We harvested each day until we couldn't see anymore, then we'd take tea and watch the last lights of sunset fade and chat or just think our thoughts while the stars broke out of the crystal sky one by one. In those moments, leaning against an ever-growing pile of ripe olives, breathing in the deep, rich, subterranean scent of a hard day's work, I felt completely content and at peace. My nerves were mellowed and my spirit refreshed in ways words couldn't describe and money couldn't touch. On evenings like this, in a world like this, it seemed downright ungracious ever to despair. It was, after all, absurd to hate the slaughter and waste and hardship and destruction without acknowledging the flipside: that life was here, that the whole reason we hated waste and destruction was because we loved life and this world so much.

WHEN I CAME in from the groves on Wednesday evening, Qais invited me to stay at his house so I could join his family for the harvest the next day. I stayed in Marwa's room, and Qais joined us in his yellow-and-blue track suit. Marwa served as our chaperone, and we talked and laughed like it was a slumber party until Shadi poked his head in and told us it was time for bed.

I noticed for the first time that neither Qais nor Shadi had a bed. Both slept on foam mattresses on the floor of a bare room. Even the parlor, the showcase of any Palestinian home, had only an ancient couch and a few battered chairs that looked like they'd been salvaged from a hospital waiting room. Faded portraits of grandparents, a framed Quran verse with gold lettering against a black background, and the requisite rendering of the Dome of the Rock were the only decorations. It's strange now to realize how little I thought about the poverty this pointed to. In Jayyous, even if a house didn't have a stick of furniture except for a few plastic chairs, there wasn't a culture of poverty. Lack of access to gainful employment was a nuisance, not an identity, and for many it could be blamed directly on the occupation. With education such a high priority, a lot of sparkling conversations went on over plastic dinner tables.

After a predawn breakfast the next morning, we loaded up like possums, three men on the tractor and three women squeezed in the trailer with all the supplies. Qais drove us down to the Wall, and when it was our turn to go through the gate, Shadi hopped off and gave our documents to the soldiers. I laughed in my delirious tiredness that Israel should think it might take three soldiers and an armored Jeep to subdue Shadi. Qais waved to the soldiers as we passed them. I couldn't tell if it was a deliberate gesture of humanity or just the Arab hospitality tic.

We tractored to a plot of land under a hillside that had been blasted bare for the construction of the Wall. An enormous retainer wall and army access road had been built above Qais's family plot. Huge boulders heaved from deep in the earth by Israeli dynamite littered the land. We could climb on some of the boulders to get to higher branches; others just got in the way. All were incongruous symbols of something dreadful.

I asked Qais how many of his family's trees used to be here.

"Twenty," he said.

"How many are here now?"

He pointed to each one and counted off: "Seven."

He said it in an expansive way, a transparent attempt to hide his bitter anger. It was nearly impossible for Westerners to grasp what these trees meant to their owners. Each tree was like a member of the family, raised and cared for and climbed and combed over many lifetimes, an endlessly renewable source of dignified income and indispensable olives and oil. I'd heard families have bitter arguments over the fate of a single tree. Losing thirteen at once must have felt like a massacre.

Shortly after we sat down to breakfast, an armored Hummer roared by along the narrow dirt road next to us, kicking up dust. The soldiers laughed and waved at us through their bulletproof windows as if it were a joke or a joyride. We paused our meal to look up at them and make sure we weren't in danger. Then we looked at each other in disbelief. After everything they had done, they were now robbing us of our last defense—the ability to block it out so we could go about our day without being in a constant state of wounded rage and impossible cognitive dissonance. I could feel fury rising like bile in my esophagus.

Then I looked around at Qais's family, stuck in this situation that was nightmarish to the point of absurdity, and my anger, curiously, began to drain away. We knew who we were. There was no reason to let a couple of teenagers with military hardware, who probably didn't really understand what they were doing, ruin our morning. We shook our heads and continued eating.

We spent a day and a half in the valley with the seven trees, then we moved to the top of a nearby hill and joined several young cousins and their parents. The kids were adorable and funny and full of energy, and they played any game they could think of while we picked olives. Armored vehicles patrolled the access roads that ran along the Fence, and each time they came into view the kids would excitedly yell, "Hummar! Hummar!"

Qais was the pruning expert, and he climbed to the top of each tree to trim and shape the branches with a *moonshara* (hacksaw) to maximize next year's olive yield. He mentioned that he was study- ing French at university, and he kept asking me how to say things in French while we climbed around on the trees. His accent was as good as mine had been after two years of study. He'd probably speak better than I did in a matter of months. Nursing a bruised ego I muttered, "I'll have to learn Swahili or something to stay ahead of you."

I loved spending whole days with Qais and his family, so full of love and kindness and jokes. Tractoring back to town in the evenings, passing through Main Street and waving to everyone I knew, I felt like a kid in a parade back home.

During the long harvest days Qais and I got to know each other better and came to new understandings, moving toward something richer and more enduring than a fling, though God only knew where it could go. It didn't matter. When your train has no destination you're free to enjoy the view. Deep down in that place that secretly knows everything, I knew that this, too, would pass. But this was high tide. I savored it.

IT WAS CHILLY when we got back to Jayyous one evening, so we went inside and turned on the television instead of starting up a *nargila* cir- cle on the porch like usual. The whole time we'd been harvesting, the Israeli army had been killing people at an astonishing rate in Gaza. It was shaping up to be one of the largest military offensives of the second Intifada. It started after a crude homemade rocket launched by members of Hamas killed two Ethiopian-Israeli toddlers in a town near the Gaza Strip.

Israeli troops, tanks, jets, and helicopters were attacking homes, schools, and businesses and killing dozens of Gazans, many of them children, in gruesome ways. Gaza is one of the poorest and most crowded places on earth. Most of its inhabitants are refugees from the 1948 war—dispossessed once, and now being bombed as they sat help- less in their shabby camps. The news was showing videos that turned my stomach. Hospitals and morgues overflowing with the dead, wounded, and mourning. Mothers wailing. Fathers with thousand-mile stares, too shocked to cry. Children with eyes wide, forming their opinions about the nature of the world. All of it funded by my tax dollars.

Secretly and shamefacedly, I was so thankful to be in Jayyous picking olives among friends instead of back at the office being death's secretary and destruction's bookkeeper. Even without having to keep detailed track of everything, the images from Gaza were tearing me apart.

ANOTHER BOMBING

When we came in from the groves on Friday evening, one of Qais's hot-headed cousins, a pudgy, bearded young man, relayed the "good news" that thirty people had been killed in a bombing at a Hilton Hotel in Taba, an Egyptian resort town a few miles south of the Israeli border that's known to be frequented by Israelis. About half the victims were Israeli, most of the rest Egyptian.

Qais said softly, *"Allahu akbar."* He turned to me. "Are you happy?"

I felt cagey and uncomfortable. I hedged and said, "Not happy, not unhappy."

He said with disturbing relish, *"Ana ktir mabsoot."* (I am very happy.)

A dense, hard knot of sickness rose from my abdomen toward my heart. For a brief moment I heard a voice in my head say, *All Israelis pay taxes and join the military. And the Egyptians, if they were at a Hilton, were probably corrupt elites. Now they know what it feels like to be a Gazan.*

Then I caught myself, aghast. What was I saying? Was this what happened when you spent too much time in the Holy Land? Did the raw bite of pain give way to the pathetic, futile satisfaction of vengeance so quickly? If I could justify bombing a tourist hotel, anyone could justify anything. There'd be no bottom to it. There had to be rules, even in war, even when you were feeling the deepest, most impenetrable grief—especially when you were feeling that way. Killing random civilians in a hotel for something the Israeli government did was no more just—or effective—than punishing civilians in Gaza for something Hamas did. There's a reason collective punishment is a war crime.[17]

But I felt backed against a wall, and I wasn't even Palestinian. I could witness the Palestinian plight all day, but a foreign army would actually have to occupy my country, build a Wall through my land, destroy my father's livelihood, jeopardize my education, imprison my cousins, build a checkpoint between my pregnant sister and the hospital, bulldoze my neighbor's house, and kill thousands of my countrymen in order for me to be able to really stand in their shoes. If this was my reaction, I couldn't imagine what it was doing to the people around me, much less the people of Gaza. It made no sense for Israel to do what it did, year after year, and not expect that somebody, somewhere, was going to decide he had no better option than to bring a building down on top of himself. Security isn't a one-way street. If you treat someone's life like garbage, you can't seriously be surprised if it's dumped on your door one day.

I had always marveled at the way the Dalai Lama kept his cool even when things looked hopeless for his homeland. I resented it a little, too. It wouldn't be productive for him to rage and foam and smolder and give himself ulcers. But in some ways his peace of mind looked callous or even like a form of denial. Tibet still wasn't free.

---

17. Under the 1949 Geneva Conventions, to which Israel is a signatory, "No protected person may be punished for an offense he or she has not personally committed. Collective penalties and likewise all measures of intimidation or of terrorism are prohibited . . . Reprisals against protected persons and their property are prohibited." According to the Wikipedia entry for "Fourth Geneva Convention," "By collective punishment, the drafters of the Geneva Conventions had in mind the reprisal killings of World Wars I and II. In the First World War, Germans executed Belgian villagers in mass retribution for resistance activity. In World War II, Nazis carried out a form of collective punishment to suppress resistance. Entire villages or towns or districts were held responsible for any resistance activity that took place there. The conventions, to counter this, reiterated the principle of individual responsibility. The International Committee of the Red Cross (ICRC) Commentary to the conventions states that parties to a conflict often would resort to 'intimidatory measures to terrorize the population' in hopes of preventing hostile acts, but such practices 'strike at guilty and innocent alike. They are opposed to all principles based on humanity and justice.'"

There had to be a difference between feeling fine out of callousness or denial and finding ways not to let madness and hatred find a reflection inside of you and thus grow stronger. But what was it? I hoped I would figure it out soon, because the emotional state I was in now was clearly unsustainable.

DAYS OF PENITENCE

Watchtower: *It's a little girl. She's running defensively eastward.*

Operations room: *Are we talking about a girl under the age of ten?*

Watchtower: *A girl of about ten, she's behind the embankment, scared to death . . . I think one of the positions took her out.*

Captain R: *I and another soldier . . . are going in a little nearer to confirm the kill . . . Receive a situation report. We fired and killed her . . . I also confirmed the kill. Over.*

This invasion of Gaza, called Operation Days of Penitence after the Jewish High Holiday season during which it was carried out, started on September 30 and was still going on when I got back to the office on October 11. The incursion concentrated on a refugee camp called Jabalya, where ninety thousand refugees were crowded into three square kilometers. The stated goal was to destroy the infrastructure that supported the manufacture of crude, unguided Qassam rockets.

The rockets appeared to be the next generation of violent Palestinian resistance. Walls were no use against them, and even though they caused relatively few casualties,[18] they created very real and constant terror. Entire Israeli towns near the Gaza Strip ducked into bomb shelters whenever a Qassam launch was detected and bomb sirens went off. Given the near impossibility of stopping launch-and-flee assaults using conventional military power, Israel's aim in the operation was actually deterrence—to "exact a price," as Israeli Defense Minister Shaul Mofaz put it, for firing rockets.[19]

---

18. Qassam rockets have a kill rate of about 0.5 percent. In all of 2004, four Israelis were killed within Israel by Qassam rockets and two were killed in settlements in the Gaza Strip.

19. Jaime Holguin, "Fed-Up Israel Turns Up Gaza Heat," CBS/AP, October 1, 2004.

By the time the Israeli government pulled out of Gaza on October 15 (the first day of Ramadan), the army had killed 130 Gazans, most of them civilians, including thirty children. Hundreds more were wounded, many disabled for life. Bloodied body parts littered the streets of the Jabalya Refugee Camp, according to Israeli journalist Amira Hass.[20] Nearly a hundred homes were demolished, leaving 675 Palestinians homeless. Bulldozers, shells, and missiles damaged roads, wells, sewage and electrical lines, mosques, shops, and factories. Seven schools were damaged, including a kindergarten serving five hundred kids. Dozens of acres of orchards and farmland were flattened. Thirty greenhouses were destroyed.

The event that got the most attention was the killing of a thirteen-year-old girl named Iman al Hams on October 5. She was on her way to school in the southern Gaza Strip city of Rafah, nowhere near the Jabalya Refugee Camp, carrying a backpack and wearing her school uniform. Somehow she wandered into a "closed military zone." These zones are rarely marked and shift constantly; she probably had no idea she was in one. She was shot by an Israeli sniper from about seventy meters away. An Israeli commander identified only as Captain R approached her as she lay injured or dead in the street and shot her twice in the head at close range to "confirm the kill." He then put his weapon on automatic and emptied the rest of his clip into her body. A fellow soldier explained, "He was hot for a long time to take out terrorists and shot the girl to relieve pressure."[21]

Hundreds of Palestinian children had been killed during the second Intifada, and the Israeli army rarely launched investigations into such killings.[22] But Captain R's fellow soldiers complained publicly

---

20. Amira Hass, "Half an Hour Later, People were Still Collecting Body Parts," *Haaretz*, October 1, 2004.
21. "Israelis Probe Gaza Girl Shooting," BBC, October 11, 2004.
22. "Since the beginning of the [second] intifada, IDF [Israeli Defense Forces] soldiers have killed at least 1,656 [noncombatant] Palestinians [including 529 children] . . . Many of these deaths result from changes in the Rules of Engagement, which now allow soldiers to open fire on Palestinians in a variety of non-combat situations, even when the soldiers are not in danger . . . [Between 2000 and 2004] the IDF conducted

about his behavior and described it on Israeli television, and a transcript of the soldiers' conversation during the shooting was released. The Israeli public, which had always been told that theirs was "the most moral army in the world," was shocked, and the soldier was put on trial. But he was only charged with illegal use of weapons, obstruction of justice (for his initial false report), improper use of authority, and behavior unbecoming an officer.

Another girl, Ghadeer Mukheimar, was shot in the stomach with heavy ammunition as she sat at her desk in her elementary school classroom on October 12. Teachers at the school said Israeli soldiers fired toward the school from the Neve Dekalim settlement on a quiet day with no warning. Ghadeer arrived at the hospital in critical condition and died from her wounds the next morning.

The stories went on and on, shells and bullets and shrapnel meeting the fragile heads and hearts and limbs of children. But the Qassam threat wasn't neutralized, and it was easy to surmise that the operation had created more militants—more of the despair, shock, and numbing rage that turned young men into easy recruits—than it killed.

I turned my attention to the West Bank after I finally got caught up on Gaza. Nael had told me that shortly after I left, two Jayyous farmers were beaten by Israeli soldiers who'd been hiding among their trees. Not long afterward three teenagers were arrested. Many more foreigners, including Israelis, showed up to help with the harvest and deter the soldiers' violence, then the soldiers decided to ban all foreigners from crossing the gate.

But that was a picnic compared to what was happening elsewhere. On October 11, a twenty-six-year-old Palestinian farmer named Hani Shadeh was shot in the neck by an Israeli settler while he was picking olives on his land in the Nablus region. The settler was from Yitzhar,

---

only 89 military police investigations into deaths and injuries of Palestinians. Of these investigations, only 22 resulted in indictments. To date, one soldier has been convicted of causing the death of a Palestinian. Thus in the vast majority of cases, no one is ever held accountable." See: "Rules of Engagement and Lack of Accountability Result in Culture of Impunity for Palestinian Civilian Deaths," B'Tselem, November 24, 2004.

a settlement notorious for its violent ideologues. On September 27, an Israeli settler from Elon Moreh, also near Nablus, pulled a Palestinian father of eight out of his taxi and shot him dead because he'd refused to stop when the settler told him to. The settler was released on bail less than twenty-four hours after the murder.

On October 20, a settler drove into a village near Nablus, hit three Palestinian schoolgirls with his car, and fled. Two of the girls had broken bones and the other had broken teeth. On October 26, another settler from Yitzhar shot and killed an unarmed eighteen-year-old named Salman Safadi near Urif village in the Nablus region. Settlers in the Salfit region set a Palestinian olive grove on fire and threw rocks at the villagers when they tried to put out the flames. Other settlers were waging a campaign of intimidation against international and Israeli human rights activists to try to eliminate the presence of witnesses. Two U.S. citizens, members of the Christian Peacemaker Teams, were beaten with clubs and chains by masked Israeli settlers, resulting in a broken arm, a punctured lung, and other serious injuries. The activists had been trying to protect Palestinian children on their way to school from settlers south of Hebron.[23]

The Israeli army typically responded to these events by imposing extra checkpoints, curfews, and other restrictions on the Palestinians in these so-called "friction zones"—"for their own protection"—instead of on the settlers.

I found it impossible to think of all these victims as real. I couldn't fit my head around it, because it would be like fitting my head around Qais or Shadi or their father being hurt or killed, and that was too much. If only I had known all the Palestinian kids who'd been killed. If only I could feel for all of them and didn't have to wait until it was one of my own. I'd have died six hundred times already. And that number would be hopelessly out of date in a week. The list of eighteen-, nineteen-, twenty-, twenty-one-, twenty-two-, twenty-three-year-olds was even longer, an age when you're just coming to grips with life, exhilarated and liberated

---

23. Alison Weir, "Heroism in the Holy Land," *San Francisco Bay View*, October 6, 2004.

and terrified. Then your eyes close, all your lessons turn to ashes, your fate is a box, a memory, perhaps a poster on the wall.

I called Qais, hoping it would make me feel a little better. After a few weary civilities he began complaining about a pain in his chest.

"Have you seen a doctor?" I asked.

"No. These may be my last days. In a way, I hope so." I couldn't tell if he was joking or not. He sighed exhaustedly. "*Ya skuchaiu po-Allah.*" (I miss God.)

I closed my eyes. *We're all thinking it, Qais. We all miss God, or whatever you want to call the pure thing that runs through all this. And you're trapped here, imprisoned, in a way so obscene it's impossible to contemplate. And still you have to live it. You, a lucky kid who made it past his twentieth birthday.*

Qais asked why I was crying. He said he didn't want to hear me cry; he couldn't endure it. Sometimes I wasn't sure I could endure it, either. How was I supposed to think about a world where the life of a Palestinian was utterly disposable?

I wondered if I would break down if the strain became too much. But breaking down wouldn't help anything. I could leave, but leaving wouldn't help anything, either. I thought about suicide for the first time not as an abstraction but as a genuine option—a way to drop out of the whole diabolical game. But I dismissed it immediately. It would just be more of what I hated, which was early, pointless, preventable death. If all else failed and I gave up on the human condition entirely, I'd be better off wandering into southern Siberia and tending gardens for a living than killing myself. A single cup of tea in the morning light, a single act of resistance to injustice, would be better than oblivion.

I once asked a Lebanese friend at Stanford how people in his country dealt with tragedy after tragedy, year after year. He said one *hadith* (saying) of the Prophet said that if the day of judgment came and you had a baby palm tree in your hand, even if you saw imminent death approaching, you should still plant it. Every moment is an integral part of the totality of existence, and any act of faith and kindness is a victory in itself.

He offered the Palestinians as an example of a people who kept up hope despite decades of unremitting tragedies. They were still living, still getting married and having children and looking for a better tomorrow, if not for themselves, for their children; if not for their children, for their children's children. They had what they called *sumoud*—steadfastness. This was only the smallest taste of what that really meant. How could I, who was living under occupation *voluntarily*, possibly look any Palestinian in the face and do any less?

Such thoughts only kept it at bay, though, and only imperfectly. Someday I would have to face up to the lake of sorrow gathering behind my defense mechanisms. Somehow I'd have to learn to navigate the territory between crushing pain and numbing denial in a world where these things happened.

CHAPTER 7

Arafat's Funeral

One day while Majnun was sighing deeply for Laila,
his beloved, someone came and said to him: "Majnun,
leave off with your laments, for Laila is coming to see you.
Even now she is at your door." Majnun immediately raised
his head. "Tell her to go away, for Laila would prevent me
for a moment from thinking of my love for Laila."

—From *Kitaab al Aghani* (*The Book of Songs*),
an Arabic literary text from the ninth century

Ramadan was shockingly different in Ramallah than it had been in
Jayyous. I still appreciated the idea of it—a whole month of special
sweets, giant meals, strengthening family and community ties, and
taking time to remember why you're here on this earth. Hassan, the IT
guy at our office, explained that the most basic way we can empathize
with our less-fortunate fellows is through hunger. To be reminded of
the pain on earth, so much of it unnecessary, can be a very healing
exercise, and Ramadan is a wonderful time for charities.

But almost no one in my office was fasting, and most of my friends
in Ramallah were ex-pats or Palestinians with no family nearby, so
invitations to home-cooked Iftars were few and far between. If I was
invited to an Iftar but hadn't fasted, I felt like a cheat, but when I fasted

for only a day or two at a time my body had no time to adjust. I never could get into a good rhythm. But I loved the star- and crescent-shaped lights glowing in windows and public squares and the special greetings of the season.

On the first of November, I was finally able to move into the apartment provided by my employer. It had a huge living room with comfy blue couches, satellite TV, a sunroom, a bright, clean kitchen, and three bedrooms. The windows overlooked the Plaza Mall shopping center, which has a Western-style supermarket, hair salon, Italian restaurant, and dry cleaners on the lower level. Upstairs is a coffee house popular with teenagers, a fast-food joint called McChain Burger, a toy store, and an astronomically expensive United Colors of Benetton.

Palm trees lined the front of the mall, and a mosque with a tall white minaret blasted the call to prayer five times a day from behind it. Empty villas sat in the hills above, the abodes of diaspora Palestinians who had left due to the violence or been denied IDs or visas and thus had been bureaucratically expelled. I frequently heard gunfire from the settlements nearby, but it was usually far away and soon became part of the normal background noise.

Osama called a few nights later and invited me to a restaurant called Ziryab. We walked down Main Street and turned into a darkly ornate door a block east of my office. I must have passed it scores of times, but I'd never noticed it before. Inside was a stairway decorated with funky marble mosaic designs and posters that advertised concerts and film screenings. The stairway led to a coffee house with subtle sconce lighting, heavy wooden tables, cozy booths, and a blazing fireplace. The tables were set with olivewood ashtrays and candles covered in lines of Arabic poetry.

"The owner did these himself," Osama said, indicating the carved wooden art pieces on the wall. I nodded as I took in the stunning space. This was what I loved about the Middle East. You never knew what surprises were waiting behind humble, unmarked doors.

We joined three men at a table near a window that overlooked Ramallah's Main Street. Osama introduced one by saying, "This is

Majed. He's on his way to meet his wife in Sweden and finish his PhD in experimental theater."

Majed was a tall man with a thin face and curly hair who was slightly manic in a controlled way, as if he'd learned to keep a lid on his creative energies among pedestrians. He did several impressions for us, including one of Yasser Arafat that was so devastatingly spot-on we were all gasping with laughter.

It seemed a strangely irreverent thing to do given that only a few days earlier, Arafat had been flown to a hospital in Paris suffering from a mysterious illness.

REST IN PEACE, ABU AMMAR

Rumors about Arafat's health swirled and worsened. Ramallah was ensconced in a strange bubble of dread, resignation, and semi-denial while waiting for the president to die, masked under the usual flurry of shopping for the post-Ramadan holidays. Finally the news arrived early in the morning on November 11, 2004.

The French Honor Guard held a funeral at a military airport near Paris. President Jacques Chirac stood by Arafat's body as a show of respect. International coverage of the story was intense. CNN predicted chaos in the Palestinian streets, and we held our breath waiting for it.

The demonstrations in Ramallah were strangely halfhearted at first but gained steam over time. Red leftist flags flew alongside black Al Aqsa Martyrs Brigades flags, yellow Al Mubadara flags, and green palm fronds. Everyone wore *keffiyas*. Muzna looked glamorously mournful in Audrey Hepburn sunglasses with a black-and-white scarf draped around her shoulders. Posters of Arafat were held aloft, splashed across walls, and taped onto passing cars and taxis.

To everyone's relief it appeared to be a time for mourning, reflection, and respect, not violence or anger. Things were even more sedate than the disappointed journalists on CNN tried to convey. The power transition was carried out in accordance with Palestinian Basic Law and accepted even by Hamas. Arafat's soft-spoken aide, Mahmoud Abbas (also known as Abu Mazen), would replace him as chairman of the PLO, and elections would be held within sixty days to choose a new PA president, if Israel would allow them.

It was a heartening display of unity on a day in Palestine that was bigger than party politics. Even the most anti-Fatah people gave Arafat his nod that day. Viewed variously as a revolutionary hero, a terrorist, a sellout, or all three, his means were often questionable and his ends ever-shifting. Initially opposed to Israel's existence, he changed his position in 1988 when he accepted the "land for peace" formula of UN Security Council Resolution 242, recognized Israel, and renounced violent resistance—a historic compromise that no other Palestinian leader had the popular legitimacy to make.

The signing of the Oslo Accords in 1993 was the first time Israelis and Palestinians publicly recognized each other as partners for peace rather than enemies to be defeated by force of arms. The handshake between Yasser Arafat and Israeli Prime Minister Yitzhak Rabin on the White House lawn is one of the most famous photographs in Middle Eastern history. In 1994 Arafat was invited back to the territories to lead the Palestinian Authority. The PA had limited administrative and security duties in the West Bank and Gaza while Israel retained control of water, airspace, and borders. This arrangement was supposed to last for a five-year period during which Israel and the PA would engage in trust-building measures leading to the negotiation of a comprehensive peace treaty.

Arafat also accepted Israel's division of the West Bank into three areas: Area A (17 percent) fell under the security and civil control of the PA, although Israel reserved the right to enter at will. Area B (24 percent) fell under Israeli security control, with the PA responsible for civil affairs. Area C (59 percent) fell under total Israeli civil and military control. Area C includes virtually all Israeli settlements and settler roads, the huge buffer zones around them, all of East Jerusalem, the Jordan River valley, and the Dead Sea coast. Areas A and B are divided into twenty-five "islands" in a sea of Area C.

Area C was supposed to transition to Palestinian control in five years. Instead, the Israeli government restricted Palestinian access to it, made it nearly impossible for Palestinians to build on it, and continued to fill it with settlements. No matter how hard Arafat cracked down on his own people, the Israeli government was never satisfied. Yet cracking down harder when no fair peace deal was on the horizon made him look like a quisling. In all, 380 Palestinians and 260 Israelis were killed during the "Oslo peace years" of 1993–2000, and the settler population surged from 250,000 to more than 400,000.

For their part, the Israeli public was only dimly aware of settlement expansion and the crushing hardships of occupation. But they were acutely aware of the fourteen suicide bombings carried out by Hamas and Islamic Jihad during the Oslo years, and they felt jilted by the Oslo process as well.

Arafat's star began to wane as the Palestinian people began to resent the PA's corruption, cronyism, and mismanagement. Arafat made sure Fatah dominated all branches of government, the best private sector and export jobs, and the top security positions. He ignored reformist laws passed by the Palestinian Legislative Council,[1] and his security forces intimidated, imprisoned, and sometimes tortured or killed rivals. The PLO and the PA became Byzantine tangles of business interests, semi-independent militias, and corrupt bureaucrats posing as revolutionaries. And whatever the truth about the Camp David peace summit of July 2000,[2] Arafat had failed to present his side to

---

1. The PLC, the legislative branch of the Palestinian Authority, is a unicameral body with 132 members elected from 16 electoral districts in the West Bank and Gaza.
2. President Bill Clinton, in his last months in office, met with Israeli Prime Minister Ehud Barak and Yasser Arafat at Camp David, Maryland, for a last-ditch effort to negotiate a two-state solution. The talks failed spectacularly. From the Israeli perspective, Barak made a "generous offer"—including more than 90 percent of the West Bank and parts of East Jerusalem—and Arafat walked away. In the view of the Palestinian delegation, Palestinians had already conceded 78 percent of their homeland by recognizing Israel in 1988. Barak's "offer" was to annex additional areas of the West Bank (including most of East Jerusalem), deny Palestinians genuine sovereignty, and ignore international law and the question of refugees. For a more nuanced explanation of these events, see: Hussein Agha and Robert Malley, "Camp David: The Tragedy of Errors," *The New York Review of Books*, August 9, 2001.

the world effectively, and it had been a massive public relations coup for Israel. The only thing that saved him from complete pillory was the fact that Israel put him under house arrest in his ruined Muqataa, which turned him into a kind of martyr.

But he was the father and hero of a movement that turned a bunch of dispossessed and broken refugees into a political force to be reckoned with, against enormous odds. He was a man who survived a plane crash in the Libyan desert, slipped through the fingers of the Israeli army in Beirut, dodged several assassination attempts, led the first fledgling Palestinian government, and was imprisoned in a war ruin for three years until he was flown to Paris, grinning all the way, where he died at age seventy-five, a global icon.

Either way, many Palestinians were quietly relieved to be given a fresh start with a new president. Arafat's death signaled the gradual passage of the Fatah Old Guard who had held power since the 1960s, known as "the Tunisians" because of their long exile in the seaside villas of Tunis and their reputation for being corrupt and out of touch.

Arafat's likely successor, Mahmoud Abbas, was another Old Guard member, but he wore a business suit and tie, not a uniform and *keffiya*. He looked like an ordinary democratic leader and was known for his opposition to suicide bombings. If he came to power in peaceful elections, it would be difficult for the Israeli government to label him a "terrorist," "irrelevant," and "no partner for peace" as they had done with Arafat and refuse to deal with him.

The odds weren't good, but you never knew. Maybe, just maybe, things could finally take a turn for the better.

THE DAY AFTER Arafat died, his body was flown to Cairo for a formal funeral attended by heads of states from all over the world. I watched it on CNN and then rushed to the Muqataa to attend Arafat's Palestinian funeral in person.

Palestinian bulldozers had finally cleared the Muqataa's enormous grounds of rubble, and it was overflowing with press and mourners. Estimates of the crowd's size ranged from 100,000 to 700,000. It might have been over a million if Israel hadn't closed most of the roads. I made my way to the middle of the crowd, covering my ears when I got too close to men firing bursts of gunfire into the air and batting away the hands of teenagers who used the cover of the crowd to make a grab for my ass.

Soon a hush fell over the crowd. The helicopter carrying Arafat's body had left Cairo. It was on its way. Everyone watched the skies. When at last I caught my first glimpse of the helicopters, the first sounds of the rotors, my breath caught in my throat. It was a moment of pure history, and each person absorbed it in his or her own way.

The choppers landed in a clearing in the crowd. Within minutes the figurehead of the Palestinian movement for the past four decades was planted in the ground. He was replaced by a yawning vacuum. And the most tenuous scent of a new hope.

Holiday in Jayyous

"Why are you still fasting? It's the Eid, isn't it?" I asked Rania.

"Oh, yes," she said. We were in her kitchen in Jayyous stuffing date paste into balls of semolina dough, packing them into decorative wooden molds, and whacking them against the table to dislodge the little cakes, which would be baked until browned and dusted with powdered sugar. "But women are not supposed to fast during the menses. So we fast an extra week after."

"Oh." I laughed. "I wish someone had told me that."

Once the Eid cakes were finished and I had sampled my fill, I headed to Qais's place. I mentioned to Qais that I'd been hanging out with Communists lately and said jokingly, "Maybe now that Arafat is gone, Palestine will become a Communist state."

He shook his head. "Anyone who thinks Palestine will be Communist doesn't understand Palestine or Islam."

I was taken aback. "What do you mean?"

"The Quran is comprehensive and includes politics and governance."

Now I was stunned. It was as if I were looking at a stranger. When had he become an Islamist? He hadn't seemed particularly religious the year before, when he'd just come back from Russia. What had changed? Had it happened all at once or gradually? Had the stress of occupation finally gotten to him or was it something else? And how had I missed it?

"You can see man's law has been a disaster," he went on. "But God's law can bring peace and plenty."

"God's law isn't always so great, either," I mumbled. "Look at the Taliban."

He shook his head. "The Taliban do not understand Islam. No one can force you to wear a veil or follow Islam. But anyone who truly understands Islam will follow it naturally." To my dismay he went on and on about miracles and punishments, angels and demons, rules and rewards. He even said religious people tended to die younger because God missed them—an alarmingly defeatist statement that gave me an inward chill.

My own spirituality had been in flux ever since I realized that the scientists, the cult of the observable, were missing the whole point, which was: What is the whole point? From my position in purgatory, how could I blame Qais for choosing a story that gave him comfort, meaning, and community in times as hard as these? I had to admit, I was jealous he had a place to go where he could prostrate himself before the mystery of the universe among friends.

But even if there was another life, there was never another *this* life. All I could think while Qais was coloring in his worldview for me was, *If not for all these religious restrictions, we could have been together all this time. It may be the only Paradise and we're wasting it with words.*

He ended his little sermon as more people joined us. We went back to chatting as if nothing had happened, but something had shifted between us.

OMAR'S STORY

I was harvesting with Qais's family the next day when my good friend Ali found me, a dapper high school counselor with a mellow baritone voice and an impeccably groomed goatee.

"*Ya Bam*," he said with a grave, apologetic look. "I would not ask you for this, but I think there is no other way. There is a farmer's son named Omar. When Arafat died, the *shebab*[3] were burning tires at the south gate of the Wall. Omar's father was on the land, and Omar went to the gate to wait for him. When the soldiers came, the *shebab* started throwing stones at them. I don't know if Omar was throwing stones or just waiting. Anyway, the soldiers came through the gate with their guns, and Omar ran away with the others. A soldier shot him twice in the back."

"My God."

"Yes, and then they took him away to a hospital in Israel. We called and found out which hospital. It's in Kfar Saba. He is OK, he is alive, but he has had many surgeries. When we call the hospital, they are very rude and won't tell us anything. His parents are going crazy. They want to visit him, but the hospital says they cannot get a permit to visit him unless they come to the hospital and take a paper that tells about his condition. So you see . . ."

"Yeah, there's only one catch," I said disgustedly. "Well, look, I can go to the hospital and get the paper."

He sighed. "Really, Bamila, I know this is a holiday for you, and we wouldn't ask . . ."

"I know."

I called Dan to see if he could pick me up in Jayyous and take me to Kfar Saba. He apologized and said he'd recently sold his car, and he didn't have time to borrow one at the moment.

So I got up early the next morning and made my way south to Ramallah, then to the Qalandia checkpoint, crossed on foot, took a minibus to East Jerusalem, caught a cab to the Jerusalem Central Bus Station, and caught another bus back up north to Kfar Saba. It was a journey of more than a hundred miles and six hours that would have taken ten minutes if Dan had been able to pick me up on the settler road.

Finding the hospital took a bit of hunting, but once I found it the

3. *Shebab* is Arabic for "youth" or "young men."

task didn't seem so daunting anymore. All I had to do was ask for a paper, say hey to the injured kid, and I'd be on my way back to Jayyous in no time. It might even be one of those bridging-the-divide moments with the Israeli doctors. Who could fail to sympathize with a young man who'd been shot in the back, or a young American woman trying to help him? It was easy to be rude over the phone. I was confident that, in person, they would see us as human beings and treat us as such. By the time I walked through the front doors of the hospital I was feeling almost cheerful. I found a receptionist and told her, "I have a friend from the West Bank who's been injured and is being treated here. I need to get a paper that explains about his condition so his parents can come and visit."

She looked uncomfortable, as if she feared I might be mildly crazy or criminal. "You'll have to talk to someone in administration," she said. "I don't handle these things." She directed me to a small back office, where I found a man in his forties with thick grey hair. I asked if he spoke English.

"Of course!" he said, widening his eyes as if the likes of me asking if he spoke English were the most preposterous indignity he'd suffered that day. I told him why I was there. He waved his hand dismissively. "We don't give papers about West Bank people here. We're not allowed. It's like a secret that he's here."

I checked his voice for irony or humor and found none. "I'm sorry, what do you mean you don't give papers about people being here? That's why they sent me. I just need a paper that says he's here so I can give it to the District Coordination Office so we can get a permit for his parents to visit."

"We don't give out information like that," he said without meeting my eyes. "You have to call Dalia in Beit El. She's in charge of these things, not me." Beit El is a settlement north of Ramallah whose name means "House of God" in Hebrew. Palestinians often have to go there to deal with administrative matters related to the occupation.

"If we could have done this from Beit El," I said, "I'm sure it would have been done already. They sent me here, physically, to get a paper. All I need is a paper that says—"

He smiled mock patiently, as if I were simple or slow, and interrupted me. "Listen very carefully. You aren't the first person who has come here looking for information about these people, and you won't be the last. We don't give out papers. That's it. Don't ask anymore."

I had a feeling he was lying through his teeth. But what could I do? "Can I visit him?" I asked weakly.

"What do I care?"

I left his office with my face flushed and my fists clenched. The way he said "these people" had sent hot chills down my spine. If I had eaten anything that day, I feel fairly confident I would have thrown it up. At least I could visit the injured boy, so maybe the day wasn't a total wash. I walked up to his floor. The nurses pointed me toward the basement, where he was having a CT scan done. I went back downstairs and asked the receptionist at CT if she knew where I could find the boy I was looking for.

She looked at me blankly. "Maybe that's him?" I looked back and saw a good-looking blue-eyed young man with pale skin and curly brown hair in a gurney in the middle of the waiting room. He had an IV drip in his arm and looked alert but tired. His eyes seemed naturally sharp but dulled now, resigned to a casual bit of violence that would drastically affect the rest of his life—something simultaneously offhand and unthinkable.

"Omar?" I asked. He nodded, his expression wavering between wariness and polite confusion.

Suddenly I felt shy. He wasn't expecting anyone, least of all a foreign woman he didn't know. I told him in halting Arabic that I was a friend of Ali's in Jayyous. He nodded. "*Keef halak?*" I asked.

He gave the traditional pleasantly noncommittal answer: "*Hamdulillah*" (Thanks to God).

My eyes widened in disbelief. "*W'Allah?*" How could he even say it? He looked down at himself: "As you see."

I reported on this kind of thing daily at my job. This was actually mild compared to the things that made the news. Omar had survived, had no brain damage, was not in critical condition, and had not lost several limbs and/or family members. He was just in a hospital having surgeries and CT scans done far away from his family, not knowing how bad his injury was. This was nothing.

And yet it was overwhelming. So where did that leave all the other things I reported on, all the bloody and senseless things I didn't have to see for myself?

I swallowed hard and asked who else he knew in Jayyous. I asked how old he was, and he said twenty. I wanted to ask more but I didn't know the Arabic for words like "prognosis" or "paralysis."

A doctor soon emerged and walked toward Omar's gurney. I introduced myself and asked if he could explain Omar's condition so I could tell his family.

He looked at his watch. "I need to eat soon." I smiled. "Yeah, me too." It was late afternoon and I hadn't eaten all day. I was trying to highlight our shared humanity and gently suggest that this injured, helpless, isolated boy's terrible predicament was slightly more important than lunch. He didn't smile back. "Wait fifteen minutes," he said and wheeled Omar into the CT scan room.

Fifteen minutes later two orderlies wheeled him back out. The doctor had escaped out another door.

My ears burning from the latest rebuff, I followed Omar and the orderlies up to his room, where I found a pretty young nurse named Sofya from Netanya. I asked her about his condition. She said brightly, "Well, his kidney is damaged and his spine is broken, and he can move one leg a little, but the other not at all."

I steeled myself. "Will he walk again?"

She shrugged nonchalantly. "Mmm, I don't think so, probably not."

The room turned grey and looked sharper and farther away as tears stung my eyes. For nothing he was in this state, no reason at all. Not just injured but paralyzed, probably for life. And nobody cared. It was like a bad parody of man's inhumanity to man.

I tried to keep my voice steady as I told the nurse what I was here for. She looked like she had no idea what I was talking about. I asked if I could use the phone to call Ali in Jayyous.

When I heard Ali's baritone voice, clear and reasonable and familiar and friendly in this sea of obtuse hostility, thick hot tears fell. I pulled myself together and told him what I had learned. Then I gave the phone to Sofya so he could tell her exactly what we needed. She said she would try her best, but she didn't sound very hopeful. She tried calling Dalia in Beit El, but there was no answer.

Sofya shrugged. "Maybe you can come back tomorrow?"

It wasn't clear how anything would be different tomorrow, and my desire to get back to Jayyous as soon as possible, among friends and olives and kindness, was so visceral it was painful. So I went on the trail of the paper again. After another hour of hunting and asking and negotiating, Sofya finally conceded that the paper could be issued here after all. "But the doctor who does these things is very busy today. She is receiving many children, and she is the only one who can receive them."

"How long does it take to make the paper?"

"I don't know, about fifteen minutes."

"She can't spare fifteen minutes?"

I'd learned an important lesson in Russia. If something important is at stake and hostile bureaucracy is standing in your way, you have to make it harder for them to ignore you than to fulfill your simple request. "Look, can I just talk to her real quick?"

Sofya narrowed her eyes and pursed her lips. Then she rolled her eyes and sighed. "Come with me."

I followed her into a darkened office. The doctor was a tasteful-looking Russian blonde woman who sneered slightly when she saw me. She wasn't receiving any children. I tried to explain what I needed. Before I could finish my sentence she was tearing paper off a pad and writing in Hebrew. She affixed an official label and stamped an official stamp and handed it to me.

"Thank you so much. Is this is all I need?"

"Yes."

A kind orderly helped me fax the paper to Dalia in Beit El, then Sofya gave me the phone to try to call Dalia again and see if she got the fax. Dalia finally answered. She grudgingly admitted that she got the fax and everything was in order.

"So that's it?" I asked. "Is that what you need to give his parents a permit?"

She paused, then said challengingly, "We don't know how long he will be there."

I couldn't believe it. She was acting like this was some kind of game and she was still trying to win. "His spine is broken," I said evenly. "He is not going anywhere."

Another pause, then testily, "I can give you three days. OK?"

Back in Omar's room, Sofya gave me the phone again. I dialed Omar's parents in Jayyous. Omar was so weak he could barely hold the phone. I'd been on the other end of the phone many times in a family's home as they spoke with a relative in an Israeli jail or faraway hospital. People always tried to act cheerful so they wouldn't upset each other. The mother didn't want her son to think about how she'd been sick with crying. The son didn't want his mother to know he'd been lonely, injured, ill, humiliated, terrified, starving.

After Omar hung up, he touched my arm and pulled up his shirt. The surgery scar was immense, from his heart down past his waistband. He put his shirt back down and pointed to a spot on one of his swollen legs. I touched it. He shook his head, and tears welled slightly in his otherwise impassive young face. He couldn't feel it.

Soon it was time for me to go. Dan had agreed to pick me up and take me back to Jayyous in a borrowed van. I shook Omar's hand and held it for a while as I met his pale blue eyes with mine.

I left the hospital in a daze. After walking a few steps in the fresh air, I ducked behind a column and sank to the ground and wept.

When Dan arrived I had no idea how to tell him about my day. I mostly stayed quiet and felt terrible that I couldn't bring myself to act happy to see him or express how grateful I was that he was taking me back to Jayyous. All I wanted, desperately, was to get back to the olive groves and to my friends who understood how I felt without words.

Dan and I had kept in touch over the phone, but I hadn't seen him in months. We were both so busy with work and life. When I did talk with him, we were usually both depressed about something horrible that had just happened. I hated for him to always see me like this. I hated to bring this gloom into his life when I had no idea how to fix it. Even though Dan was sitting right next to me, I missed him.

As we entered the West Bank on a settler road, I caught sight of the twenty-five-foot concrete Wall surrounding Qalqilia. Forty thousand people in a cage at the dawn of the twenty-first century.

"Look at that!" I exploded stupidly, rising out of my seat and banging my head on the roof of the van.

"I know," Dan said flatly. "I can't believe it. It's like some movie about South Africa or something. And it's happening right here."

My Boss Decides to Run for President

Dr. Barghouthi called an emergency meeting a few days after I got back from Jayyous. I was annoyed because I already had my evening perfectly planned. I was going to a restaurant called Beit Sini (China House) to get spicy Kung Pao chicken, then I was going to go home, curl up around some hot cocoa, and watch a mindless Angelina Jolie action movie on MBC2 in my pajamas. For two restful, thoughtless, soft, warm hours, I could forget about everything else.

Except now I had to sit through this stupid meeting that probably had nothing to do with me.

We gathered around the big wooden table in the conference room. As soon as we were seated and quiet, Dr. Barghouthi dropped the bombshell.

"So, I have decided to run for president against Mahmoud Abbas."

That perked me up, but I still didn't see what it had to do with me. I was sure he could run for president even if I was at home eating Chinese take-out.

As I surreptitiously glanced at my cell phone (it was already after six, and the movie started at seven), I heard him say he'd need someone to volunteer to be his foreign press coordinator. Whoever that unlucky person was would have to stay in the office tonight for five or six hours and compile, organize, and prioritize the contact information for all the foreign correspondents in Israel and Palestine. He or she would then represent Dr. Barghouthi to the world's press throughout the campaign in addition to his or her usual responsibilities.

"The election will be in early January," he said, "so we have less than two months to consult with our constituencies, prepare offices, organize supporters, design and distribute campaign materials, and many other things. Time is of the essence."

Suddenly I had a sinking feeling. No one was looking at me, but everyone knew the other foreigners in the office would be jetting off to England or Spain or Australia for the Christmas holidays. I'd be the only native English speaker left.

Slowly through my hazy, unhappy sense of duty, something began to filter through my thick head: My *boss* was running for *president*. And I was being offered a front-row seat. Was I simple?

I took a deep breath and braced myself. "I can do it."

CHAPTER 8

Running for President in a Nation Without a Country

When you are taking part in events like these you are, I suppose,
in a small way, making history, and you ought by rights to feel
like a historical character. But you never do, because at such times
the physical details always outweigh everything else.

—George Orwell, *Homage to Catalonia*

I stayed at the office until the wee hours compiling the emails, faxes, and phone numbers of every major foreign news correspondent in the region. A few days later I wrote my first press release, faxed and emailed it to all my contacts, and followed up with calls: Dr. Barghouthi would announce his candidacy for president of the Palestinian Authority at the Ambassador Hotel in East Jerusalem on November 29, 2004.

The setting was significant because he was planning to enter East Jerusalem, his birthplace, without an Israeli permit. This bit of civil disobedience would put Israel over a barrel. If they arrested him, it would shine light on Israel's illegal annexation of East Jerusalem and score points with the Palestinian public. If they didn't, it would be seen as a small victory against Israel's unfair and illegal policies.

I arrived at the venue early and watched the camera crews set up in the plush conference room. When a critical mass of reporters arrived, I handed out the materials we'd written. By the time Dr. Barghouthi approached the podium, it was standing room only.

I held my breath all through the conference. At least a dozen cameras were pointed at Dr. Barghouthi as he spoke confidently and eloquently. He said he was speaking for the "silent majority" of Palestinians who criticized Fatah's corruption and autocracy but also rejected Hamas's fundamentalism and violence. "This is a majority whose voice is being drowned out by the noise of guns and tank shells, a majority that can have a voice only if they are allowed to cast a vote."

Real democracy was crucial, he said, because negotiations were meaningless if the leadership didn't fully represent the people. One of the first things he would do as president would be to hold elections for the Palestinian Legislative Council, which hadn't held elections in nearly a decade. He also called for the modernization and democratization of Palestinian institutions, and above all an end to corruption and nepotism in the Palestinian Authority.

He sought the creation of a viable, contiguous, independent Palestinian state on the West Bank and Gaza with the Green Line as its border, East Jerusalem as its capital, and a fair resolution to the 1948 refugees' legal claims for repatriation or restitution. These parameters are based on UN General Assembly Resolution 194, which resolves "that the refugees wishing to return to their homes and live at peace with their neighbours should be permitted to do so at the earliest practicable date, and that compensation should be paid for the property of those choosing not to return," and UN Security Council Resolution 242, which calls for Israel to withdraw from territories it occupied in 1967 in return for peace.

In 2002, the Arab League unanimously adopted the Arab Peace Initiative, which promises peace, recognition, and normalization if Israel conforms to these parameters. Poll after poll suggested Palestinians would accept this, but so far the Israeli government had ignored the offer. Dr. Barghouthi said he would call for an international forum like the Madrid Peace Conference of 1991[1] to press for these parameters on the world stage. He said negotiations should be internationally brokered because leaving the Palestinians alone with the vastly more powerful Israelis would be like leaving a lion and lamb to negotiate about what to have for lunch. If the Israeli government refused, he would call for nonviolent resistance, including pressing for international boycotts and sanctions against the Israeli government.

In short, Dr. Barghouthi wanted to take the Intifada off autopilot and move it in a reasoned, deliberate direction that was neither reflexively violent nor in thrall to American and Israeli interests. He and other reformers had been marginalized by the Oslo process, which entrenched Arafat and his corrupt inner cadre. With these elections, Palestinians finally had a chance to elect leaders who were responsive to their legitimate rights and aspirations.

At the end of the conference, Dr. Barghouthi fielded difficult questions with humor and eloquence in Arabic, English, and Russian. Cameras followed him out of the hotel to his waiting car, where he answered a few last questions, smiled and waved, and drove back to Ramallah without incident.

I left the hotel with my head in the clouds. He'd pulled it off—he'd held his press conference without getting an Israeli permit or being

---

1. The Madrid Peace Conference was held in the aftermath of the 1991 Gulf War. The governments of the United States and the U.S.S.R. invited Israel, Syria, Lebanon, Jordan, and the Palestinians to attend. It was the first time these countries met face-to-face on the international stage, and the aim was to begin a comprehensive peace process based on the principle of "land for peace"; Israel would cease to occupy southern Lebanon, the Syrian Golan Heights, the West Bank, and Gaza in exchange for peace with its neighbors. Although none of these objectives was realized, the conference nearly doubled the number of countries willing to recognize and have diplomatic relations with Israel, including China, India, Oman, Qatar, Tunisia, Morocco, and Mauritania. The long-running Arab boycott of Israel also began to decline as economic and diplomatic relations improved. Dr. Haidar Abdel-Shafi, the widely respected and beloved Gaza physician who cofounded Al Mubadara, was head of the Palestinian delegation to the Madrid Conference, and Dr. Barghouthi also participated. It was one of the most promising attempts at genuine peace in the history of the Israeli-Palestinian conflict. But it was overshadowed by the Oslo Accords, which were secretly negotiated between the Israeli government and the PLO behind the backs of the Madrid delegates and the emerging on-the-ground leadership in the West Bank.

arrested. And now the campaign had officially begun. He was only running for the privilege of administering a territory under a foreign army's rule. But at least, and at last, the Palestinians had a choice. It wouldn't simply be a coronation of the next in line of the Fatah Old Guard.

I felt like I'd been present for a birth—the birth of democracy in Palestine.

I didn't know if Dr. Barghouthi had a chance of winning, and I didn't know if he would make a good president if he won. His agenda didn't differ from Abbas's platform in its broad outlines. Abbas also rejected violence, promised to fight corruption, called for negotiations, and supported a Palestinian state on the West Bank and Gaza. They were both politicians, and they spoke like politicians, in inspiring but vague generalities. The question was, who could deliver?

As I was walking toward the Old City to catch a service taxi back to Ramallah, I caught sight of the golden Dome of the Rock. On impulse I decided to visit it for the first time.

The walls of the Jerusalem Old City were built by the Ottoman sultan Suleiman the Magnificent in 1538. They enclose the densest square kilometer of holy sites in the world. The Old City is divided into Muslim, Jewish, Christian, and Armenian Quarters, each buzzing with homes, cobblestone lanes, tourists, religious pilgrims, and colorful shops selling everything from figs and fresh slaughtered goats to ornate hookahs and T-shirts saying, I GOT STONED IN ISRAEL.

I entered the Damascus Gate and walked through the Muslim Quarter toward the Haram al Sharif (Noble Sanctuary). The Haram is a thirty-five-acre plaza that takes up one-sixth of the Old City and is home to the Dome of the Rock, the most iconic structure in Jerusalem, and the Al Aqsa Mosque. The Dome was built in 691, making it the oldest extant Islamic building in the world. It is believed to have been built over the place from which Mohammed made his night journey into the heavens with the Archangel Gabriel to receive the word of God. Only Mecca and Medina are holier to Muslims than Jerusalem is.

Jewish tradition holds that the Haram, known to Jews as the

Temple Mount, is the former site of the Second Temple, which was destroyed by the Romans in 70 AD. The Western Wall, one of the retaining walls for the Haram, is believed to be the last remnant of the Second Temple. A massive open-air prayer plaza was built below the Haram next to the wall. It is the holiest Jewish site in the world and the focal point of prayers for religious Jews.

Israeli soldiers were guarding the entrance to the Haram. They questioned me briefly before allowing me to pass into the bright, spacious plaza. People from all strata of Palestinian life were ambling around or congregating and chatting. A group of kids was playing soccer under a copse of pine trees near a stone gate. The Dome of the Rock itself, intricate, delicate, and immense, was resplendent against an azure sky. A likeness of it can be found in virtually every home in the West Bank, but no likeness can do it justice. It is truly one of the marvels of the world.

It's also where the second Intifada started. After the bitter failure of the Oslo years and the impasse at Camp David, Ariel Sharon, leader of the right-wing Likud opposition party, had marched on the Temple Mount with hundreds of police in riot gear. Sharon claimed he was merely exercising his right to access a Jewish holy site. But it was clearly a political ploy meant to strengthen his position among Likud hard-liners. And to say he was a controversial figure engaging in a provocative act would be wild understatement.

Shortly after the West Bank was occupied in 1967, Jews had been banned from the Temple Mount by order of the chief rabbinate of Israel on the grounds that they might tread on the holy of holies while ritually unclean. This dovetailed with Israeli Defense Minister Moshe Dayan's fear that Jewish control of the Haram might provoke a war with the entire Muslim world. Islamic authorities were allowed to maintain control of the top of the complex while Israel controlled access to it.

This arrangement is relatively peaceful but highly unstable. Muslims fear efforts to erode their hold on the Haram, and half a dozen attempts have been made by fundamentalist Jews and Christians to destroy or desecrate the Islamic sites to try and make way for a Third Temple. The Haram is also the anchor of identification with Jerusalem and a potent symbol of nationhood. Neither Israel nor the Palestinians seem willing or politically able to give it up. It is the single most hotly disputed piece of real estate in the world.

Sharon, a rotund former general with thick jowls and white hair, is viewed as a tough-minded war hero in Israel. Palestinians consider him a war criminal due to, among other things, his role in a massacre of unarmed Palestinians in the Sabra and Chatila refugee camps in Lebanon in 1982. An Israeli commission found him to bear "personal responsibility" for the carnage. He was also one of the champions of the settlement enterprise. He used his various cabinet posts between 1977 and 1992—agriculture, defense, and housing—to dole out government grants, low-cost loans, and tax breaks to settlers. In 1998, he famously told the settlement movement, "Everybody has to move, run and grab as many hilltops as they can to enlarge the settlements, because everything we take now will stay ours. Everything we don't grab will go to them."

The subtext of Sharon's march on the Temple Mount was clear: If he became prime minister, he would never bargain it away to the Palestinians. As far as he was concerned, the Mount, as well as the rest of East Jerusalem, belonged to Israel forever.

The response was entirely predictable. Palestinians from all walks of life engaged in massive protests. In the two weeks that followed, Israeli forces killed sixty-eight Palestinians, including fifteen children, and injured a thousand more. Twelve Palestinian-Israelis were also killed. One of them was a well-known seventeen-year-old peace activist named Aseel Asleh, killed by a shot to the neck at point-blank range.

In those same two weeks, Palestinians killed three Israeli soldiers and two civilians.

Thus the second Intifada was born.

A few months after his stunt on the Temple Mount, amid spiraling violence, a frightened Israeli population elected Ariel Sharon prime minister of Israel.

The first suicide bombing of the second Intifada took place on March 4, 2001—six months after the Intifada began. By that time more than three hundred Palestinians had been killed, including ninety-one children (half of whom were killed by gunfire to the head).[2] In the same period, fourteen Israelis were killed in Israel and forty-nine were killed in the West Bank and Gaza, one a child.[3]

Despite its contentious history, on this day the Haram was a rare haven of space and peace in this emotionally charged, crowded city. And the campaign kicked off today might be a tiny step toward making Jerusalem a peaceful, shared capital one day after all. At the very least it might reveal important clues as to how real change could happen—how peace might be made peacefully.

BEATEN IN THE STREET

Walking out of the HDIP offices was soon like walking into a Mustafa Barghouthi theme park. Every square inch of surface was fair game for posters, and Dr. Barghouthi's were by far the most professional looking. Abbas's were quite cheesy, with Photoshopped images of himself looking off into the future with a faint smile on his face and Arafat in the background, as if passing the torch. It was funny to walk down the street and see one shop plastered from baseboards to rafters with

---

2. Source: B'Tselem. According to Amnesty International, "The overwhelming majority of Palestinian children have been killed in the Occupied Territories when members of the Israeli Defense Forces (IDF) responded to demonstrations and stone-throwing incidents with excessive and disproportionate use of force, and as a result of the IDF's reckless shooting, shelling and aerial bombardments of residential areas. Palestinian children have also been killed as bystanders during Israel's extrajudicial execution of targeted activists, or were killed when their homes were demolished. Others died because they were denied access to medical care by the IDF. At least three Palestinian children have been killed by armed Israeli settlers in the Occupied Territories . . . Most of these children were killed when there was no exchange of fire and in circumstances in which the lives of the soldiers were not at risk . . . No judicial investigation into any of the cases of killings of Palestinian children by the IDF in the Occupied Territories is known to have been carried out." See: "Killing the Future: Children in the Line of Fire," Amnesty International, September 29, 2002.

3. Source: Israeli Ministry of Foreign Affairs.

Dr. Mustafa's face and the next one smothered by Abu Mazen mug shots. For Dr. Barghouthi it must have been like the scene in *Being John Malkovich* when Malkovich goes inside his own head.

Marwan Barghouthi, the popular leader of Fatah's Young Guard,[4] briefly threw his hat into the ring. Polls showed that if he did run he stood an excellent chance of winning even though he was serving a life sentence in an Israeli jail. No one knew if this would pressure Israel to release him or if the Palestinian Authority would have to be run from an Israeli jail. But the question remained moot. Marwan withdrew several days later under pressure (some say threats) from Fatah Old Guard leaders.

Three independent candidates, a Communist, and a candidate from the Democratic Front for the Liberation of Palestine (DFLP) were also running, but none was expected to win more than 3 percent of the vote. Hamas was boycotting the campaign because they didn't recognize the creation of the Palestinian Authority under the Oslo Accords. Once Marwan dropped out, Dr. Barghouthi was the only serious opposition candidate left.

ARIEL SHARON HAD announced it was "important that it should be clear to the entire world that Israel has made possible free, fair, and effective elections."

But more than a week into the campaign, he still hadn't made arrangements to allow free movement for any presidential candidate except Abbas. The other candidates hadn't even been given permission to travel to Gaza, where one-third of Palestinian voters resided. Dr. Barghouthi had to risk arrest if he wanted to campaign freely in

---

4. The "Young Guard" are the Fatah members who came to prominence as on-the-ground leaders during the first Intifada (as opposed to the "Old Guard," mostly corrupt septuagenarians who spent most of their lives in exile). When the Old Guard came back to Palestine in 1994, they largely displaced and ignored the Young Guard, but the Young Guard remain popular among the people. Most Palestinians believe Marwan Barghouthi's trial on terrorism charges was a sham and consider him to be a political prisoner. (Marwan and Dr. Mustafa are only distantly related. "Barghouthi" is a common Palestinian surname.)

East Jerusalem, where more than 200,000 Palestinians lived. He was denied entry to Nablus, detained at a checkpoint for two hours in the Salfit region, and surrounded by Israeli soldiers in Hebron and denied access to its Old City. (This resulted in one of our best posters, with Dr. Barghouthi surrounded by aggressive-looking Israeli soldiers and calmly pushing one of their gun barrels away from his chest.)

Dr. Barghouthi held another press conference on December 8 to protest this de facto favoring of Abbas by Israel, which he feared might undermine the legitimacy of the elections. He demanded that Israel cease all arrests and assassinations for the duration of the campaign, allow free movement for all presidential candidates until election day, and allow free movement for all Palestinians on election day. If these demands were not met within thirty-six hours, Dr. Barghouthi said he would lead major peaceful demonstrations in protest.

The weather had turned cold, and we were all exhausted from campaign work. I was constantly reading fifteen things, writing fifteen things, answering emails, and taking calls in addition to keeping up with the usual death and destruction. It was all I could do to stumble home at night and watch CNN or a movie for an hour or two before collapsing into bed.

I had just finished cooking dinner on the night of December 8 and was settling in to watch *Frasier* on MBC4[5] when my phone rang. It was one of the HDIP administrators, an officious woman with short brown hair. I rolled my eyes and thought, *What now?*

"Yes, hi, Pamela. I am sorry, but you need to come to the office right away. Dr. Mustafa has been beaten by Israeli soldiers."

"What? Is he all right?"

"Yes, he is in the hospital, but we think he is all right. We need you to write a press release."

When I got to the office, Muzna told me that Dr. Barghouthi and his entourage had been stopped at a checkpoint on their way back

---

5. MBC4 is another branch of the Middle East Broadcasting Center. It plays American shows like *Friends*, *Dr. Phil*, and *The Biggest Loser* in English with Arabic subtitles. *The Oprah Winfrey Show* has become a huge hit in Saudi Arabia as a role model for women.

from a meeting in Jenin. They'd been pulled out of their car at gunpoint by Israeli soldiers, beaten to the ground, and forced to stay there for an hour and fifteen minutes in the freezing cold. They were beaten if they tried to move or talk to each other. One of the guys, Adnan, was an administrator with a shaved head and a goatee who could be witheringly sarcastic. He was dating the British woman, Emily, in our office. She was beside herself because he'd been choked by the soldiers. Another sweet but tough-looking man named Luai had been hit in the head with the butt of a gun. Dr. Barghouthi had been hit on his back and thigh. It was chilling to imagine the fear and fury of the scene.

Our press release said, "If Israeli soldiers felt they could get away with doing this to Dr. Barghouthi, a person sure to get publicity, imagine what they do to Palestinians with no protection or attention." We sent it to all our contacts and headed to the hospital.

Several journalists were already there. Dr. Barghouthi's X-rays showed that, luckily, nothing was broken. He told the cameras that this kind of harassment and intimidation was exactly what he had been protesting earlier in the day. Democracy could never be meaningfully established, he insisted, while voters and candidates alike were trapped inside virtual prisons defined by Walls and checkpoints.

THE ISRAELI ARMY had done something so outrageous this time, I was sure the press would have to write about it and finally expose this type of routine abuse. But when I opened *The New York Times* the next day, to my horror, I found the story relegated to an afterthought in an unrelated article about an eight-year-old girl who'd been killed by Israeli gunfire in her home in Gaza.

> Elsewhere . . . Mustafa Barghouti said he and his associates had been struck by Israeli soldiers at an Israeli checkpoint in the northern West Bank. Dr. Barghouti said he intervened when one of his associates was being hit, and was himself hit by the soldiers. He said the five were forced to sit on the ground for more than an hour.

An Israeli military official disputed the account, saying that soldiers had requested to see identification, which is standard at checkpoints, and that Dr. Barghouti and the others had refused. After 20 minutes, the men presented the identification and were allowed to pass. The official denied the men had been hit.[6]

I was flabbergasted. Not only was it buried. It was left completely up to interpretation. I called Greg Myre, the journalist who'd written the piece, and asked if he had gotten our press release, and if so why he hadn't written more substantively about the incident.

"I just don't have time to go into the kind of detail you cited," was all he would say.

I wanted to retort, "If an Israeli presidential candidate had been beaten up by Palestinians, I am sure you would have found the time." But I knew it wouldn't do any good. I hung up in disgust thinking, *You're a journalist, for Christ's sake. Aren't you supposed to report the truth? If I say the sky is blue and someone else says it's red, do you print both claims with equal weight? Is that what "fair and balanced" means these days?*

In any case the beatings didn't intimidate Dr. Barghouthi or his staff. If anything it tripled everyone's resolve.

TWO DAYS LATER I joined Dr. Barghouthi on a campaign visit to the Qalqilia district. My friend Ali, it turned out, was a campaign coordinator for Dr. Barghouthi in the region. He was waiting for us at the entrance to Jayyous, looking even more dapper than usual in his best suit and tie. He led us to the Town Hall, where an audience was waiting.

Dr. Barghouthi gave his usual speech denouncing corruption and emphasizing that if the Israelis wouldn't negotiate fairly, the way to peace and justice was through nonviolent resistance. He said the real heroes of Palestine were the farmers and teachers and doctors who

---

6. Greg Myre, "Palestinian Family Says Girl, 8, Was Killed by Israeli Bullet," *The New York Times*, December 10, 2004.

had the fortitude to stay on their land even when the pressure to leave was overwhelming. Living with humor and grace under these circumstances was a major act of resistance in itself.[7]

A farmer in a blue work shirt and *keffiya* stood up and said, "I have over a hundred dunams[8] isolated by the Wall. The PA promised help, but they have done nothing. I need support or I will have to leave my land."

Dr. Barghouthi said, "More than half a billion dollars comes into Ramallah yearly, but much of it misused or embezzled by the PA. With proper leadership, transparent and fair, nobody needs to go hungry in the short term while we struggle for our rights in the long term."

Another man asked, "Aren't you afraid of trying to clean house in the Palestinian Authority?"

Dr. Barghouthi replied, "My second day in office, you can watch. The Allenby Bridge will be very busy."

He was implying that corrupt officials would be fleeing the country. The only person in the audience not visibly delighted was the PA representative from Qalqilia—who was sitting in the front row! I hoped Dr. Barghouthi knew what he was doing. I couldn't help but think, *You and what army?*

I was standing next to Ali in the back while Dr. Barghouthi spoke. I whispered to Ali, "Your job as a high school counselor is PA-funded, right? Are you worried you might lose your job since you're volunteering for Dr. Mustafa?"

He sighed. "The Authority is very stupid, and I may lose my job. But I will support who I want to support. If I lose my job, I lose it."

"Do you think Dr. Mustafa can win?"

"I'm not sure. Some people see him as soft and European, even if his thinking is very good. It takes more than good thinking to be a leader here."

This was frustrating to hear, especially coming from Ali. But I knew what he meant. Dr. Barghouthi was a rare free agent in a region where nearly everyone was a proxy or a client. Fatah was beholden to the

---

7. Hence the popular Palestinian phrase, "Existence is resistance!"
8. Twenty-five acres.

United States and Israel for arms, money, and recognition while Hamas was supported by Iran and Syria. Dr. Barghouthi's strength—his independence—was also his greatest weakness. No superpower or regional power supported him, and he didn't have much money or any guns. It would require an enormous leap of faith to vote for someone who supported nonviolent resistance and essentially had nothing on his side other than international law. Still, more and more people were realizing it was foolish to play into the hands of Israeli hard-liners. The violence was noise that was drowning out the real issue: the occupation and colonization of Palestinian land. Someone had to be the first to put down weapons. It seemed incumbent upon Israel, the vastly more powerful party, to do so. But Palestinians couldn't sit around forever waiting for Israel to do the right thing.

Dr. Barghouthi was taking an enormous risk just by running for president. If he won, it could shake up the entire region. He'd be the first Palestinian in a top leadership position who'd be difficult to marginalize given his very public calls for and history of nonviolent resistance and the fact that, unlike Abbas, he spoke impeccable English and could communicate directly with Western audiences. Even if he only split the vote, it would have major consequences for Fatah, which was quite content with its near total domination of the Palestinian Authority. The Israeli government clearly wanted Fatah to remain in power, too, because it was a known quantity. For Israel, as for Fatah, the status quo was the preferred state of affairs.

Dr. Barghouthi was trying to say through his campaign that it wasn't up to Israel or Fatah. It was up to the Palestinian people, for whom the status quo was a decades-long disaster.

I whispered to Ali that I sometimes feared for Dr. Barghouthi's life. He grimly agreed. I recalled a quote by Gandhi: "First they ignore you, then they ridicule you, then they fight you, then you win." I hoped the fight would stay somewhat civilized.

WE DROVE TO the campaign office in Qalqilia next and met with a down-home group of doctors, lawyers, teachers, and volunteers who formed the core of the campaign in that region. Spirits were high and people were smart and funny and kind. I couldn't help but contrast this group with the crowd at the Grand Park with their grim faces and overpriced cell phones. *How different things would be*, I thought wistfully, *if these people were in charge and representing Palestine to the world!*

It was long after dark by the time we headed home. I sat in the back of the presidential (*insha'Allah*) Isuzu next to Dr. Barghouthi. He opened a black plastic bag and pulled out a piece of pita bread lightly stuffed with hummus and *baba ghannouj*. He tore it down the middle and offered half to me. It was the only food either of us had eaten all day. For a moment I wondered if I should take it. It wasn't entirely outside the realm of possibility that someone might try to poison him. But my hunger quickly overcame my paranoia.

Dr. Barghouthi had been taking calls all day as we traveled between villages, speaking with the press, volunteers, and campaign aides in Arabic, English, and Russian. He was still at it all the way home. After he hung up with one caller he said, "That was Mr. Abbas."

"Really? What did he want?"

"He was asking if I was OK after being beaten on Wednesday."

"What'd you tell him?"

"I'm a little sore, and a little stiff. But overall I am fine."

It was on the tip of my tongue to ask if he feared a more serious attempt on his life or health. But I couldn't bring myself to say it. Instead I asked, "Are you worried about being arrested and prevented from running?"

"That won't prevent me from running," he said with a trace of amusement in his voice, as if I'd missed something obvious. "I'll run from jail."

DIRE STRAITS IN BETHLEHEM

The highlight of my Christmas came early, on December 21, with a Bach festival at the Ramallah Cultural Palace. Palestinian and international musicians played and sang transcendently in Baroque

German. The last two songs were conducted by a woman so old and frail it took ages for her to make her way to the podium. She was obviously well known and well respected, and when she cracked a joke in Arabic on the way up, everyone laughed. She presided over a traditional Palestinian song, and the feeling of joy and pride in the audience was palpable. The European singers must have felt it. The standing ovation at the end went on and on and evolved into synchronized clapping like I'd heard at the Bolshoi Theater in Moscow. I wished it could go on all night.

The employees in my office had a choice between taking Christian or Muslim holidays, and of course I chose the Muslim ones. No way was I going to be stuck in an office all alone while my friends in Jayyous were stuffing themselves with *maqlouba*, *qatayef*, coffee, and good cheer.

Luckily Christmas fell on a weekend in 2004, and I made my way south to Bethlehem after work on Thursday, December 23. Noura, the friend of a brother of a friend of a friend of Yasmine's, had agreed to host me over the Christmas weekend in her home in Beit Jala, a wealthy Christian suburb of Bethlehem. She was on the short side, smart, bubbly, and comfortable, and she welcomed me with bread, butter, and apricot jam.

"The jam is from our land just west of here," she told me proudly.

I asked her how many Christians lived in the West Bank and Gaza. I guessed about 15 percent. She shook her head. "Before, yes, but now it's maybe 3 percent. Many Christians left after the Nakba, mostly to America. Others left after '67. Now with the second Intifada, even more are leaving, especially in Bethlehem and Ramallah."

"Are there tensions between Muslims and Christians?"

She smiled. "We are all Palestinians here. The Muslims have bad elements, like any society. But it's nothing compared to the occupation. For example, most of my family's land is in Area C, and now it's on the other side of the Wall. We have apple and pear and apricot trees, and we always had picnics there when I was growing up. Now we can't access it at all. This apricot jam"—she picked up the nearly empty jar—"may be the last." She set it down hard. "I work at the Beit

Jala municipality, and some families have come to us ten times for new water tanks after Israeli soldiers shoot holes in the ones on their roofs. And almost every house in my neighborhood has been damaged by shelling from Gilo."[9]

She stopped short, as if surprised by her own words. "You know, these things happen," she said wonderingly, "and you can't believe it. You can't imagine it. You think it can't possibly happen here. And then it does, and you are surprised. But slowly you get used to it. And then something else happens, something worse, and you are shocked again. And then you get used to it again."

She shook her head. "It keeps going on like this."

The next morning was Christmas Eve, and I caught a taxi to the center of Bethlehem. The Old City is gorgeous, made of light-colored stone with metalwork painted a cheerful shade of teal. Manger Square, the huge central plaza, is surrounded by the Church of the Nativity, the Mosque of Omar, and the Palestinian Peace Center. Girl and Boy Scout troops, bagpipers, and drummers marched down Star Street and through Manger Square, and a few teenagers dressed up like Santa Claus handed out candy and balloons to kids.

But overall it would barely have passed for Christmas Eve in Stigler, Oklahoma, much less in the birthplace of Jesus Christ. The sky was grey and spitting rain, and most of the gift shops and businesses were shuttered even on this biggest weekend of the Bethlehem year. The only tourists were a busload of Nigerian pilgrims, an intrepid Japanese contingent, and Israel's Filipino and Thai domestic workers negotiating purchases of olivewood Nativity scenes with Palestinian hawkers in Hebrew.

Back at Noura's house that night, we were joined by her brother

---

9. Gilo is an Israeli settlement south of Jerusalem. Much of the land on which Gilo is built was confiscated from the Palestinian villages of Beit Jala, Beit Safafa, and Sharafat. Approximately forty thousand Israeli settlers live there. During the first two years of the second Intifada, there were more than four hundred shooting incidents by Palestinian gunmen who infiltrated Beit Jala and targeted Gilo, causing no deaths but some damage and injuries and a great deal of fear. The Israeli army responded with devastating force against Beit Jala.

and a friend of his. Her brother was a tall musician who played the bagpipes and the oud (lute) and wore a black leather jacket. His friend had a John Cusack vibe and was always worrying a toothpick around in his mouth. They invited me out for a drive.

We listened to Dire Straits and Nirvana as we drove around the steep, narrow back roads of Bethlehem on that dark, rainy Christmas Eve. With the music and the laid-back aimlessness, I felt like I was back home dragging Main with high school boys. The only thing missing was a Sonic cup full of vodka and cherry limeade.

The Cusack character reminded me of Qais, and I realized with a pang that Qais hadn't returned my calls in more than a week. It wasn't his fault that we were both insanely busy and he was under so much pressure from school, his culture, his parents, and the occupier. It wasn't his fault that the last time he tried to visit me he was abducted and interrogated for thirty-two hours. But I was getting tired. He had another vacation coming up, and he mentioned that he might try to visit me. I wouldn't bring it up again. But if he didn't make the effort on his own, I'd probably let our relationship, such as it was, fade. It was a heavy, depressing thought. I decided to put it out of my mind until the elections were over.

Finally we drove to the Church of the Nativity to check out the scene outside the Midnight Mass. Mahmoud Abbas, Dr. Barghouthi, and Michel Sabbah[10] were making their way through the crowd, which caused a moderate amount of excitement. A few choirs sang in the drizzle on Manger Square. But the weather was as cold and damp as the spirits, and the sparse crowd quickly dispersed. The only comfort was the *sahlab* sold by street vendors, a thick, white pudding drink with coconut and cinnamon sprinkled on top, creamy and sweet and warming.

I THANKED NOURA for her hospitality the next morning and caught a cab back to the Church of the Nativity for the big day. The door to

---

10. Michel Sabbah is the first Palestinian to serve as the Latin patriarch and Catholic archbishop of Jerusalem.

get inside the church is curiously small and unadorned, a square portal about four and a half feet tall in an otherwise plain stone wall on one end of Manger Square. The first church on this spot was dedicated in 339 AD by Helena, mother of the Roman emperor Constantine. Most of what remains dates from renovations by the Crusaders. Inside the church was cavernous, with dark Corinthian columns, silver filigree chandeliers hanging from the ceiling, and robed men wandering past dark icons.

I made my way to the cavelike chamber beneath the church where the place of Jesus's birth is marked by a silver star. The tiny room was crowded with pilgrims, tourists, and irate Spanish monks yelling, "Don't push! Two at a time! Wrong door! Stop hogging Jesus!"

They didn't actually say "Stop hogging Jesus," but I found it difficult to feel properly numinous. I went back upstairs and found a passage that led to St. Catherine's Church, a newer and more modern wing with blinding white walls and columns, golden accents, and tall stained-glass windows. A Jesus doll had been placed on an olivewood manger near the front of the church. People lined up to kiss him, run their hands over him, pray, or pose with their arm around him while their partners snapped photos.

Small services were held in different languages throughout the church. The Catholics and Greek Orthodox had the biggest services, and the Assyrians, Armenians, and other denominations were tucked away in smaller chambers. I didn't see any Protestants. All the rituals were alien to me, and I missed the comfort and familiarity of my family's Methodist Church in Stigler. It suddenly seemed bizarre to me that I had sung about Bethlehem all my life and never once thought to wonder what was going on there now.

MASS DESTRUCTION

Monday morning it was back to the pressure cooker of the campaign. After Dr. Barghouthi's team was finally granted permission to enter the Gaza Strip, Dr. Barghouthi was delayed for an hour and a half at the Erez crossing. His team, including his campaign manager Dr. Khaled Saifi, were forbidden from entering with him despite the fact that they had permits.

On Christmas Eve, twenty volunteers for Dr. Barghouthi's campaign in Hebron were detained by Israeli soldiers for two and a half hours in the rain. Their IDs were taken, and they were verbally abused and humiliated. On Christmas night in a village called Yatta near Hebron, two volunteers for Dr. Barghouthi's campaign were assaulted by Israeli soldiers and detained for two hours. The next day, the director of an advertising firm in East Jerusalem, who was putting up billboards for Dr. Barghouthi, was told to remove them and was taken in for questioning by the Shin Bet.[11]

While the world was focused on the elections and I was scrambling to keep up with my campaign duties and full-time job, the Lidar Company,[12] a real estate venture linked with Israeli billionaire Lev Leviev,[13] was hard at work in the West Bank. It's a lucrative business to build settlements and satisfy the ever-growing demand for attractive, inexpensive housing within driving distance of major Israeli cities. For the price of a two-bedroom apartment in Tel Aviv, Israeli Jews can get a multi-bedroom house in a settlement like Zufin with clean air, wide open spaces, and settler roads linked seamlessly with Israeli highways.[14]

In early December the company quietly bulldozed 650 olive trees on Jayyous land isolated by the Wall, where a new settlement

---

11. Conal Urquhart, "Israel Accused of Obstructing Palestinian Election in East Jerusalem," *The Guardian,* December 28, 2004.
12. Also known as the Leader Company, Ltd.
13. Lev Leviev made his fortune in the diamond trade with Apartheid-era South Africa and has business and real estate interests all over the world. A close associate of Ariel Sharon, he has been implicated in human rights abuses in Angola and is active in the business of settlement expansion throughout the West Bank. In March of 2009, the British government reversed a decision to rent space for a U.K. embassy in Tel Aviv from Leviev's Africa-Israel Company due to his involvement in illegal settlement expansion in the West Bank.
14. Settlement housing is subsidized through housing grants from the Israeli government, which receives money directly from the U.S. government without the oversight of USAID. Israel is the only recipient of U.S. foreign aid to enjoy such an arrangement.

called Nofei Zufin was planned. The trees belonged to a farmer named Tawfiq Salim, a relative of the mayor Abu Nael. The company claimed they bought the land and had a permit to uproot the trees. Mr. Salim strongly denied selling the land and said the company was using an inaccurate map. The Israeli authorities ordered Mr. Salim to pay for a new survey and prove in court that the land was his. He was assured that the bulldozing would not continue while legal proceedings were ongoing.

That promise was broken. All 650 trees, some of them six hundred years old, were uprooted and destroyed or taken and sold in Israel and the settlements.

NEW YEAR'S EVE fell on a Saturday night, and I joined several friends and officemates for a party at a hotel in Jericho. On the way back to Ramallah, I got a call informing me that one of our campaign volunteers, a high school student named Riziq Ziad Musleh, had been shot while putting up posters for Dr. Barghouthi's campaign near the city of Rafah in the southern Gaza Strip. There were no clashes. There was no warning. The bullet, which came from the nearby Rafiah Yam settlement, lodged in his heart. He died in the hospital that night. Our campaign filed a complaint with the European Union Election Observation Mission, for what it was worth. Nothing seemed to have any impact.

There was some good news to report, though. More than a hundred Israeli peace activists had traveled to Jayyous on New Year's Eve to help the farmers plant a hundred olive saplings on the land where the 650 trees had recently been uprooted.[15] The activists tried to march toward Jayyous but were stopped by Israeli soldiers. Most Jayyousis were unable to get past the Fence and join them because they didn't have permits. One of the Israeli participants, Uri Avnery, was a Jewish

---

15. The Israeli activists were members of groups such as Gush Shalom (Peace Bloc), Taayush (Arab Jewish Partnership), the Israeli Committee Against House Demolitions, Machsom Watch (*machsom* is Hebrew for "checkpoint"), and Anarchists Against the Wall.

former member of the Knesset and a veteran of the 1948 war who had since become an ardent peace activist.

Mr. Avnery said to the assembled crowd: "Two years ago, when the Fence was built here, we had a hard time convincing people in Israel that the purpose of the Fence was not security or prevention of suicide bombings, but was erected for political and settlement purposes. First they separated the people of Jayyous from their land, preventing them from working on it, now . . . Now everything is clearly visible: They are passing the land to settler possession."

Abu Azzam, the jolly Jayyous farmer who'd been active for so many years in nonviolent resistance, was later quoted in *Haaretz* saying, "The Israelis . . . walked several kilometers on foot because the army did not permit them to bring their vehicles to the fields. Even the elderly among them went on foot . . . Several hundred villagers from Jayyous watched us from behind the fence. They were extremely moved. It was a very good feeling to see the Israelis planting the trees with us."[16]

Israeli settlers uprooted the new trees a few days later.

SHIFTING AND SWIFTING

At last January 7 arrived, the final day of campaigning. I was so proud of everything we had accomplished—I was giddy and so exhausted I was almost incoherent. But we had a full day scheduled, including another press conference in East Jerusalem and a meeting with Jimmy Carter, who was in town to monitor the elections, before making one last round of campaign stops.

When Dr. Barghouthi emerged from his meeting with the former president, he announced to the gathered press corps, "Right, we are going to the mosque for Friday prayers." He had a permit to be in East Jerusalem until 2:00 PM, but he knew the Israeli authorities probably wouldn't allow him to visit the Dome of the Rock. Sure enough, an

---

16. Meron Rapoport, "The Fruits of his Efforts Lie on the Wrong Side of the Separation Fence," Haaretz, September 5, 2009.

Israeli police checkpoint was waiting for him outside the gate leading to the Haram al Sharif. Dr. Barghouthi told the police he was a presidential candidate and showed them his permit. They said the permit was only valid to meet with Jimmy Carter, nothing else. When Dr. Barghouthi refused to turn back, he was escorted into an unmarked white pickup truck and hauled away.

After two hours we got word he'd been expelled from East Jerusalem. We had just enough time to pick him up and make it to a rally in Abu Dis, a suburb of East Jerusalem badly affected by the Wall. Then we headed to Beit Ummar and Surif, two villages southwest of Bethlehem. No other candidate had made stops here at all, and they seemed grateful simply to have been thought of. As we were leaving, a group of Fatah supporters gathered and chanted slogans in support of Abbas, but they were quickly drowned out by the chanting of Dr. Barghouthi's supporters.

Back in Ramallah, Dr. Barghouthi finished the day with two TV interviews, one with CNN and another with the BBC. The lights and cameras were set up on a rooftop inside the Muqataa, and he was lit up against an inky black sky. The CNN journalist made no mention of his being beaten, of a high school student having been killed on New Year's Eve in Gaza, of the bulldozed trees in Jayyous or the increase in checkpoints in the run-up to elections.

In any case, Dr. Barghouthi had just spent more than a hundred hours a week on the road visiting villages, getting arrested and beaten, reviewing press releases, administering thousands of volunteers, repeating himself endlessly in stump speeches while always sounding fresh and inspired, answering difficult questions at press conferences, and struggling against the combined forces of Israel and Fatah. Anyone who knew what he'd been through knew he must have been close to collapse.

He answered her questions patiently and cogently, but it was occasionally a bit beyond him to maintain a train of thought. He was trying to make the point that his campaign had put pressure on Abbas toward truer democratic reform, and that Abbas had changed his position on several key issues as a result. What he said was something like, "Due to our pressure, Abbas keeps shifting a . . . and swifting his positions on at least three issues . . ."

I must have been a bit delirious, too, because all night I was cracking myself up imagining Abbas "shifting and swifting" all over the place. It was unreal how real all of this was. The world was such a funny, local little place. It really was what we grunts made of it.

Still, the odds were long against Dr. Barghouthi's campaign. For one thing, the PA was by far the largest employer in the Palestinian territories. Many were afraid that if Abbas lost, aid might dry up and their jobs might evaporate. Plus, Abbas's team shamelessly used PA resources in violation of Palestinian law. Ninety-four percent of Palestinian state television coverage was allocated to Abbas. By election day, hundreds of thousands of people still had no idea who Dr. Barghouthi was. A British paper quoted one East Jerusalem merchant saying, "There should be more happening. How can we have proper elections if nobody knows who the candidates are?"[17]

Worse, many people had long ago lost interest because they believed the international, Israeli, and Arab[18] media's mantra that Abbas's win was a foregone conclusion. Dr. Barghouthi was referred to, if at all, as "a long shot candidate" and "no serious challenge." He had to get himself arrested to grab any headlines, and he still didn't get the kind of press you'd expect for something as exotic and exciting as the first serious democratic opposition candidate in Palestinian history.

Aside from all that, when I asked people why they'd vote for Abbas, many said something along the lines of, "The world wants Abbas. Israel says they'll negotiate with him, and America and Britain say they'll support him. It probably won't come to anything, but maybe at least there will be a ceasefire. Probably there will be a few years of 'relative calm' while the settlements keep expanding and the Wall

---

17. Conal Urquhart, "Israel Accused of Obstructing Palestinian Election in East Jerusalem," *The Guardian,* December 28, 2004.
18. For obvious reasons, the autocratic governments in the region didn't want their people getting too many big ideas about representative democracy.

keeps being built, we'll be made even poorer and more desperate, negotiations will continue to go nowhere, and there will be a third Intifada. I hope not. But we'll give Abbas a chance. If nothing good happens, we'll vote for someone else next time."

ELECTION DAY

I hadn't felt this way in years. Like Christmas morning when I was a kid. I couldn't eat, sleep, think. It was Election Day, January 9, 2005. During the short but grueling campaign, I hadn't had the energy to focus on anything but getting through each day. Now I finally had a chance to savor how historic this was.

The results trickled in throughout the day as we waited anxiously in the campaign office eating pizza and watching the phones and computers. There were irregularities, as expected. All campaigning was supposed to stop forty-eight hours prior to the election, but Abbas supporters carrying campaign materials were present at some polling stations. East Jerusalem was especially problematic. Many people reported intimidation and obstruction by Israeli security forces.[19] Others complained of confusion over registration lists. In the end only 4 percent of eligible voters were able to vote in East Jerusalem. The rest had to brave the checkpoints to vote in suburbs deeper in the West Bank, and there were many reports of voters having trouble passing checkpoints.

Then just before the polls were supposed to close, the Central Elections Commission (CEC), which had otherwise been widely praised for its professionalism and transparency, controversially extended voting for two hours and changed the voting rules to allow unregistered voters to cast ballots using only their ID cards. One official said the changes came

---

19. A few months earlier, when Palestinians were registering to vote, Israeli special forces had raided and shut down several East Jerusalem registration centers because, according to Gil Kleiman, a spokesman for the Israeli police, they were considered a challenge to Israeli sovereignty over East Jerusalem. See: Conal Urquhart, "Israel Accused of Obstructing Palestinian Election in East Jerusalem," *The Guardian*, December 28, 2004.

due to heavy pressure from Fatah, who feared low turnout might weaken Abbas's mandate. It raised fears of multiple voting to pad Abbas's lead. Several members of the CEC later resigned in protest.

Otherwise things went about as well as could be expected. Stations opened on time and voting was conducted in an orderly and peaceful manner, with fair representation of women, refugees, the young, and the elderly of the West Bank and Gaza. At the end of the day Abbas's lead was strong enough—62.5 percent to Dr. Barghouthi's 19.5 percent—that most people believed the results represented the will of the people. International observers, including Jimmy Carter, certified the elections "free and fair." It was declared a victory for democracy in the Middle East.

Twenty percent was certainly an impressive figure given the enormity of what Dr. Barghouthi was up against. For an ex-Communist with a Christian wife, a man who both preached and practiced Gandhi-style nonviolent resistance, to garner so much support in such a jaded, besieged, overwhelmingly Muslim population was at least as surprising as if Ralph Nader or Ron Paul won 20 percent of the popular vote in America. It was a huge protest vote—a harbinger of things to come. Yet it was virtually unreported in the international and Israeli media.

As proud as we volunteers were, we couldn't help but feel a little morose. We wished we could have found out what might have happened in a fair fight. But it was heartening to know that both Israel and Fatah had had to work hard and sometimes embarrass themselves—reveal themselves—in order to defeat him. Meanwhile, Al Mubadara had been built into a vibrant opposition party that could run for seats in the Legislative Council and hold Fatah more accountable to the people.

Even with Abbas at the helm, the Palestinian situation had a chance of improving. With Arafat gone, the PA might finally move toward much-needed reforms. And there was talk of a ceasefire and resuming negotiations with Israel. Furthermore, Ariel Sharon was planning on removing all Israeli settlements from the Gaza Strip in the fall of 2005, part of a proposal known as the Disengagement Plan. Many Palestinians were cynical about his reasons, and some refused to believe it would happen at all. But if it did it would be an unprecedented move—perhaps an important step on the road to removing settlements from the West Bank as well. Maybe the old general was beginning to realize his country would never have peace and security unless the Palestinians had it too.

The tiniest crack of hope had been opened. It was a cautious, cynical, desperately fragile hope, but it was hope nonetheless, and it had been so long since anyone had had even pthat.

If only we could keep it open. If only we could build on it.

CHAPTER 9

Holy Land Spring

*Maybe it just sags
like a heavy load.*

Or does it explode?

—Langston Hughes, "Harlem"

One January evening around midnight, Tino and Maeve and I caught a cab home after a party at Sangria's. Tino was a tall blond photographer from Germany who'd recently begun volunteering with the *Palestine Monitor*. He and his Canadian girlfriend Maeve, who worked with Medical Relief, had moved into my apartment in late December. Just after our cab passed the Muqataa, we braked to an easy halt behind a vehicle stopped in the middle of the road.

In a matter of seconds our eyes adjusted to a surreal and sinister reality.

The vehicle in front of us was an Israeli army Jeep. To its right a soldier stood between the Jeep and a tall building. He was pointing his gun wildly in all directions, manic and terrified, as if he saw invisible enemies surrounding him. Another soldier rose silently out of the top of the Jeep and trained his gun on our windshield. It had a much larger bore than an M-16. I was always hearing about kids in Gaza being shot with heavy ammunition. *This*, I thought fleetingly, *is probably what they were talking about.*

To my surprise, my fear was overshadowed by extreme indignation. It was viscerally outrageous to think my life was hanging by the finger twitch of a frightened nineteen-year-old on my way home from a party in a place where innocent people were regularly killed with no repercussions. My mind recoiled from the asinine possibility that my life could end here, for nothing, with a bullet paid for by my own tax dollars.

But these thoughts and feelings were very quiet and in the background. At the forefront was a calm, preternatural awareness of a simple and incontrovertible fact: I didn't control anything but my own behavior. My eyes darted and my mind flew. If I ducked or reached for my documents, the soldier might consider it a provocation and shoot. Even if I managed to crouch to safety, the others would be exposed. The door wasn't locked and my seatbelt wasn't buckled, so opening the door and rolling out was an option if shooting did break out. But of course that would be a last resort.

Then I had a thought that froze my blood. Tino was a fearless photographer. The night of Abbas's electoral victory, he'd snapped dozens of photos of Fatah supporters as they celebrated in the streets. One of them was standing on the hood of a yellow taxi plastered with Abbas posters as it inched its way down a crowded Main Street. He was holding an assault rifle aloft in a vaguely victorious manner, but the look on his face was of embarrassment and mild irritation. I wasn't sure why. Maybe he didn't really like Abbas but his paycheck demanded he pretend like he did. Perhaps he felt like an actor in an increasingly absurdist drama and was tired of playing but felt helpless to stop. Or maybe it was because Tino was in his face with a camera.

An image flashed through my mind of Tino leaning out of our cab's window to snap a photo of the Jeep with the soldier on top, thinking this was a similar situation, and getting a bullet to the forehead for his trouble.

"Tino, don't move," I barked. "Don't reach for anything and don't touch the window."

Tino and Maeve silently obeyed. The rest was out of our hands. If a Palestinian in the building to the right got the fool idea in his head to try defend his capital-in-exile from yet another military invasion, or if our driver decided to bail on us…

The fabric of time had a strange texture in those rarefied moments when we didn't know whether some of us might soon have holes punched in us. It was impossible to describe or even remember exactly once the danger had passed. We could only look at people who'd had similar experiences with new understanding.

After an indeterminate amount of time, a third soldier emerged from the building and got into the Jeep. The twitchy soldier lowered his weapon and followed. The soldier on top of the Jeep raised his gun and sank into the vehicle. The Jeep drove away.

No one said anything. Our driver calmly put his car into gear and continued on to the address I had given him a few minutes earlier.

When we arrived at my flat, I didn't know what to say to the driver. We had just survived a brush with death. His panic or ours could have gotten us killed. But we made it through together. It seemed absurd simply to give him his ten shekels and say goodnight.

After paying and getting out, I looked back and said with a sideways smile, "*Hamdulillah ala salaama.*" The phrase, which means 'Thank God for safety,' is commonly said after someone has recovered from an illness or returned from a long or perilous journey.

He laughed. "*Habibti.*"

Tino and Maeve and I walked wordlessly up to our apartment and never mentioned the galling incident again.

Winter Living

Other than the odd brush with death I was thoroughly enjoying life in Ramallah, and now that the campaign was over I finally had time to relax and enjoy it. My favorite spot was Pronto, an Italian restaurant overlooking Ramallah's City Hall Park. Yasmine introduced me to John, a half-Palestinian from Horse Cave, Kentucky. He was a counselor at the Friend's School, the most prestigious high school in the Palestinian territories, founded in 1869 by Quakers, and his father was from one of the founding Christian clans of Ramallah. John was rapidly learning Arabic, and I never tired of hearing him speak it with his thick Southern drawl. We met at Pronto every week and talked endlessly about religion, politics, and our love lives over cherry cheese-cakes and cappuccinos as we watched the sky fade over the park's leafy trees and broken fountains.

Every month I picked up a glossy magazine called *This Week in Palestine*. Each issue focuses on a different topic such as Palestinian tourism, health care, farmers, the elderly, the disabled, technology and investment, architectural treasures, and festivals. It also runs restaurant reviews, profiles of local artists, listings of concerts, plays, and films, and recipes for herbal remedies from local plants. I saw one of the winter's performances, *Al Hajez* (The Checkpoint), at the Qasaba Theater. Young dancers wordlessly acted out their first time seeing the Wall, a bride who couldn't get past the Wall to attend her wedding, a boy unable to make it to his birthday party, and a woman forced to give birth at a checkpoint. For the finale, all the dancers came out at once waving their *hawiyas* (IDs), dancing in increasing agitation, waiting and waiting for the soldiers to take the pause button off their lives. What made it all the more powerful was that many of the performers would have to go through actual checkpoints to get home that night.

Meanwhile, things were beginning to move politically in the wake of Abbas's election. Israel and the international community had been saying peace talks could resume if the Palestinians fulfilled three preconditions. The first was a peaceful transition of power following Arafat's death, which had already been accomplished. The second was elections at all levels, from village councils to the Palestinian Legislative Council (PLC). Local and regional elections were scheduled in a phased manner throughout the year, and Abbas promised PLC elections would follow soon after.

The first round of local elections was held in twenty-six districts in the West Bank and ten in Gaza. They were already revealing a major shift in Palestinian politics. Islamic candidates, mostly from Hamas, won one-third of local council races overall. In Gaza they won control of seven out of ten.

Hamas had an armed wing called the Izzedine al Qassam Brigades, but "approximately 90 percent of its work is in social, welfare, cultural, and educational activities" such as schools, orphanages, health clinics, and sports leagues, according to Israeli scholar Reuven Paz.[1] Like Americans, Palestinians put a high priority on domestic considerations. For many, a vote for Hamas meant voting for the less corrupt party, the "values" party, the party that provided certain public services, or simply the only viable alternative to Fatah.

In a village north of Ramallah called Bani Zeid, Islamic candidates won five seats on the thirteen-member council. Fatah members also claimed five seats, which meant Fatah and Hamas had tied—a shock, since the village was considered a bastion of the Left and Fatah.

Hamas members teased Fatah members, saying, "You can learn about being in the opposition, it won't hurt you."

Fatah members retorted, "And it won't hurt Hamas to learn about the responsibility of governing."[2]

Fatah insisted on electing a Fatah member as mayor, but the Islamic members, along with a Communist and a Socialist who were fed up with Fatah's corruption, overruled them. They pulled together the majority needed to elect their own chosen candidate.

Her name was Fathiya Barghouthi—the first female mayor elected in the West Bank. Women overall claimed 52 of 306 open seats in the West Bank—nearly three times the minimum required by Palestinian law. It was exciting to see things shaken up after so many decades of ossification under Fatah.

---

1. "Backgrounder: Hamas," Council on Foreign Relations, August 27, 2009.
2. Amira Hass, "PA Town Gets Female Mayor," *Haaretz*, January 23, 2005.

Eid al Adha

I invited Tino and Maeve to join me in Jayyous for the Eid al Adha (Festival of the Sacrifice), a Muslim holiday commemorating God's mercy in staying the hand of Abraham and allowing him to sacrifice a ram instead of his son. It's the preferred time for a pilgrimage to Mecca, and it's a tradition on this Eid to butcher a sheep or goat and distribute one-third of the meat to your family, one-third to friends and neighbors, and one-third to the poor.

Ali invited us to his parents' house for the first day of the feast. His father was a tall, thin man who talked slowly, as if weighing every word, and had the air of a holy man. He would later be elected mayor of Jayyous on a Hamas ticket. One of Ali's brothers led a nervous-looking goat into the front yard. To be *halaal*,[3] it had to be killed by cutting its jugular vein and allowing all the blood to drain out. The rain puddles in Jayyous ran red that day. (I couldn't shake the thought that the streets of Gaza must have looked similar after Operation Days of Penitence.) The goat was skinned and butchered in the yard, and we had fresh fried goat liver and onions for lunch.

We walked to the olive press in the afternoon to show Tino and Maeve the olives going in all washed and ripe and the warm oil coming out a spigot on the other side, the color of molten gold. Abu Nael was there, and he presented me with an RC Cola bottle full of fresh oil from his land. I used it for months, full of gratitude and memories of the good times we had gathering it.

In the evening I left the foreigners in the care of Ali and made my way to Qais's house. He met me at the gate outside his family's yard. After some halfhearted pleasantries, I took a deep breath and looked up at him. "I don't think we can be together anymore."

He sighed sadly. "Yes, I know." He said it as if it wasn't news to him—as if he'd given up weeks ago as well. I looked down. I couldn't think of anything else to say. I nodded, turned, and slowly walked away.

---

3. *Halaal* means permissible by the laws of Islam, similar to the Hebrew word *kosher*. It is the opposite of *haraam*.

I made my way to the house where Tino, Maeve, and I had been invited to stay the night. Our hosts were relatives of Ali's, a couple named Ghaleb and Ghadeer and their famously adorable son Osama. Ghaleb was a tall, energetic, affable man and Ghadeer was short, pretty, and lively. Osama, a dark-haired toddler with a sweet round face, was the serene center of gravity of the family. Their home was painted in cheerful pastels, and their parlor was set up Bedouin-style with cushions along the walls. I wanted nothing more than to sink into one of those cushions and fall into obliterating sleep. But all of us would be sleeping in this room, so I was obliged to sit and chat with feigned cheerfulness until everyone was ready to go to bed.

When it was nearly midnight and I was nearing the end of my rope, Maeve left without explanation. I assumed she was brushing her teeth. When she returned, to my horror, she was carrying a cake with a candle in it. I'd completely forgotten. Now that it was past midnight, it was January 21, 2005. My twenty-fifth birthday. I summoned all my strength to fake a smile as they sang me a Happy Birthday song and cut the cake.

Then the dancing started. Ghaleb blasted Arabic pop music, and everyone pulled me up to shimmy and laugh and spin for what seemed like hours.

When at last the lights were out and I was surrounded by sleeping revelers, I could properly mourn my loss. Lying on my back under a thick fuzzy blanket, I thought back over our entire intense, chaste relationship, from our first happy meeting on Amjad's porch to this final empty night. Tears streamed from the corners of my eyes and into my ears. It was a soothing feeling, like drowning in warm water.

THE NEXT MORNING I tried to take Tino and Maeve out to the land, but soldiers wouldn't let us pass through the Fence. So we went on a walk around Jayyous instead, visiting everyone I knew. We were invited to Rania's house for dinner, and she told us about college life and showed us some of her coursework in psychological counseling. I had visited her at her college once. It was clear she was thriving and well-respected by her peers and professors.

After dinner I visited Jayyous's Internet café to see if I had any birthday wishes in my in-box. As soon as I entered the café, I stopped cold. I had forgotten that the tall, quiet, friendly young man who ran the café was the son of Tawfiq Salim, the man who'd just lost 650 olive trees.

"I'm so sorry," I faltered after we exchanged quiet greetings. "I heard about . . ."

He nodded and looked down. The expression on his face was a bleak and ravaged landscape. There was no way to express what the loss meant to his family. Not just their pride and livelihood but centuries of love and memories on a living landscape as familiar to its owners as their own skin.

"I'm so sorry," I said again and fled without checking my email.

THERE WAS RARELY a holiday when I didn't come back to my desk in Ramallah and find at least two or three fresh child killings. This time three Palestinian boys age thirteen, fourteen, and fifteen had been shot dead by Israeli soldiers. On January 26, a three-year-old girl eating breakfast in Deir al Balah in the central Gaza Strip was shot in the head by an Israeli soldier and instantly killed. A dozen more were killed or mutilated when an Israeli antipersonnel shell sent a cloud of metal darts into a group of a children, aged eleven to seventeen, in a strawberry field in northern Gaza. The Israeli army claimed they had fired at militants who were launching rockets.[4] These fatalities brought the number of Palestinian children killed in the second Intifada to 650.

And on and on, same old story—more people arrested while visiting their families, more eviction notices, more destruction orders with little hope of appeal.

To keep from sinking totally into despair, I threw myself a birthday party in Ramallah at the end of January. Tino and Maeve were there, and John the half-Palestinian from Kentucky, and Osama the Commie and his friend Bashir, a cameraman, and Ali from Jayyous. My upstairs neighbors, Hussein and Fares, joined us as well. Fares was

---

4. Gideon Levy, "The IDF is Investigating," *Haaretz*, January 14, 2005. See also: "Israeli Shell Kills Seven in Gaza," BBC, January 4, 2005.

short and soft-spoken with large, expressive black eyes. He worked in finance and danced with a *dabka* troupe. Hussein was tall and pale skinned, a refugee from 1948 whose family lived in a tiny village west of Ramallah. The village was now being surrounded by the Wall, which meant he might soon be a double refugee. He was a deeply mellow guy who volunteered with Medical Relief in addition to his full-time job, and his eyes crinkled up like George Clooney's when he laughed. Sometimes we hung out over dinner and watched *The Daily Show with Jon Stewart* when we could find a rerun of it on CNN International.

When I tried to introduce my friends to each other, they started to laugh. Nearly all of them already knew each other. Bashir and Osama were comrades in the People's Party, and Hussein and Bashir had met at countless disasters, one carrying a stretcher and the other filming.

"This is the first time we ever met at a happy occasion," Hussein said with his George Clooney smile.

Hussein baked spiced chicken with onions for dinner, and I made borscht, mashed potatoes with sautéed garlic and *labaneh*,[5] and salad with fresh goat cheese, avocado, tomatoes, lemon juice, and Jayyous olive oil. John entertained us with stories about his students. Two of them had proposed that a delegation from their school be sent to Amman, Jordan, for a Model United Nations conference. John was sent as their chaperone. The students set up economic, social, and security councils and an International Court of Justice, and each kid adopted a country to represent. They made speeches and debated resolutions on issues like child labor, POW rights, arms trade, the oil crisis, international banking regulations, espionage, the AIDS epidemic, and the Israeli Wall.

John said it reminded him of church camp, which as any good Southerner knows is never as much about religion as it is about meeting attractive members of the opposite sex. One of his seniors shared a table with a beautiful girl from Kuwait. They fell for each other, spoke to their families, and applied for the same college in England—despite the fact that the young man already had a girl-friend back home in Ramallah.

---

5. Strained yogurt, similar to cream cheese but softer and tangier.

"But what can I say?" John said. "I remember doing the same stuff at church camp!"

We talked and laughed our way through three bottles of red wine from Bethlehem. In that house, on that night, despair was nowhere to be found.

CEASEFIRE

The third precondition for resuming peace talks was a ceasefire that incorporated all Palestinian armed factions. Everyone was exhausted by the violence anyway,[6] and Sharon needed calm so he could implement the Gaza Disengagement at the end of the summer.

So on February 8, 2005, Abbas met with Sharon in a resort town at the southern tip of Egypt's Sinai Peninsula called Sharm el-Sheikh to work out a ceasefire deal. Israel pledged to halt military operations against Palestinians if Palestinians ended violence against Israelis. Israel also agreed to release 900 Palestinian prisoners, cease carrying out targeted assassinations, and withdraw its forces from five West Bank cities.

It was hard to imagine that the Palestinian security forces, still gutted from the attacks of 2002, could ensure Israel's security by force of arms where Israel's mighty army had failed. If virtually any militant faction chose not to respect the ceasefire, there would simply be no ceasefire. Hamas didn't endorse the ceasefire because they didn't approve of the terms. They demanded the release of all 8,000 prisoners, not just 900. And they said it wouldn't be a true ceasefire unless settlement expansion ceased. Otherwise it would be like Israel saying, "Hold your fire until I agree to negotiate how much of this pizza each of us will get. Meanwhile, I'll keep eating the pizza."

Still, Hamas seemed likely to uphold the calm since public

---

6. In 2004 alone, 823 Palestinians were killed (including 181 children) and more than 1,500 Palestinian homes were demolished, while Israel lost 68 civilians (including 8 children) and 40 soldiers. Source: B'Tselem.

opinion was in favor of it and Hamas was trying to join the political fold. The second Intifada was essentially over.[7]

But Uzi Benziman warned in *Haaretz*: "The ceasefire hangs by a thread . . . Israel will make a mistake if it makes do with the minimum. It must seek a permanent solution and not take comfort in a period of calm for a few months or, at most, an interim agreement for a few years . . . Now is the time to break free of the delusions about the Greater Land of Israel and to accept the fulfillment of the Zionist vision inside the borders delineated by the Green Line. It would be terrible if Israeli society only reaches this sober conclusion after another round of bloodshed."[8]

SUICIDE BOMBER'S FAMILY SHUNNED

The day after the ceasefire was announced, Israeli soldiers raided the Gaza Strip and arrested six Palestinians. Hours later, gunfire from a settlement killed nineteen-year-old Ibrahim Abu Jazar of Rafah while he was standing near his home. Hamas fired forty-six rockets in retaliation, damaging one settlement house. Hamas announced that it would respect periods of quiet, but it would not stand idly by while innocent Palestinians were killed. The PA considered the rocket fire a direct challenge to Fatah.

A week later Alaa Dar Khalil, fifteen, of Beitunia near Ramallah was shot in the neck and killed by Israeli soldiers while he and a friend were walking near the Wall. His friend, Osama Hamdan, fourteen, was seriously wounded. Hours later a pregnant Palestinian woman was denied passage through the Qalandia checkpoint and forced to give birth in a car.

A week later, a suicide bomber blew himself up outside the Stage nightclub on the Tel Aviv promenade, killing five Israelis and

---

7. During the second Intifada (September 2000 until the end of January 2005), a total of 3,253 Palestinians were killed, most of them civilians, including 643 kids. A total of 958 Israelis were killed, 654 of them civilians, including 123 kids. Source: B'Tselem.
8. Uzi Benziman, "Not the Time for Chest Beating," *Haaretz*, January 26, 2005.

wounding fifty. Islamic Jihad claimed responsibility. They said it was retaliation for Israel's violations of the ceasefire.

According to *Haaretz*, support for the bombing was at 29 percent, compared to 77 percent for the previous bombing. Several men from the Al Aqsa Martyrs Brigades gathered in Al Manara to denounce the bombing.

The bomber was from a village near Tulkarem called Deir al Ghusun, where Israel's Wall isolates 825 acres of farmland from its owners. The dead man's family set up chairs for the funeral and made the customary bitter coffee to serve to guests. But no one came. The town boycotted the funeral.

Conal Urquhart of *The Guardian* spoke with the bomber's family. "He wanted to be a teacher, to get married and get a home," said his brother Ibrahim, who'd been imprisoned by Israel for eighteen months without trial in 1989. "He seemed optimistic in spite of everything. It never occurred to any of us that he would blow himself up . . . I don't know who [recruited him] but we want them to stop this and reach out their hands for peace. That is the only way the situation will improve."[9]

It seemed clear by now that the vast majority of Palestinians would not support suicide bombings if a fair peace deal were on the horizon. It was heartening to see that this was the case in a period when things were merely getting worse less rapidly.

A few days later I talked to Qais for the first time since we'd broken up. We exchanged pleasantries like old times, wondering about each other. He related the devastating news that his mother had had a stroke and lost movement in one arm. "Life never goes the way you think it will," he said wearily. He was worried and confused but gracious and cool as always. He told me about a party he was going to for a friend who'd won a trip to Mecca. It was difficult to keep the tears out of my voice when I told him to have fun. He told me in Russian not to be shy, to call if I ever needed anything. We said good-bye in all languages.

---

9. Conal Urquhart, "Tel Aviv Bomber's Family Shunned," *The Guardian*, March 1, 2005.

NABLUS IN APRIL

The Jewish holiday of Purim came in late March complete with parties and good humor, a comprehensive West Bank closure, and costumed settlers rampaging through Palestinian villages on what *Haaretz* described as "pogroms." Settlers in the Hebron area poisoned Palestinian fields by spreading barley seeds boiled in rat poison over a large area in an attempt to kill grazing animals and starve out the local shepherds.[10]

Meanwhile, the editor of a new *Encyclopedia of the Israeli-Palestinian Conflict* asked me to write an essay about holy sites, and Nablus had two juicy ones: Joseph's Tomb and Jacob's Well. On April Fools' morning, I caught a service taxi to the Huwara checkpoint. The drive up was gorgeous in the Holy Land spring. The olives trees had been washed clean of dust by the winter rains, and the fields were carpeted with succulent grasses and young crops in every shade of vivid green.

Nablus was surrounded by a dozen checkpoints, and Huwara, six kilometers south of the city, was the busiest. The chaotic jumble of concrete barriers, narrow gates, and barbed wire was nestled in a broad green valley. Every day thousands of people were searched and questioned and (if they were lucky) herded single file through revolving metal doors, often with loaded M16s pointed casually at the crowd. I walked toward the checkpoint nervously. I didn't even make it past a pre-checkpoint roadblock before a soldier called me out. He asked where I was from, and I said America. "You can't pass," he said dismissively.

"Why not?"

"No Americans allowed." I tried to argue, but it was no use. I asked if there was someone else I could talk to, like the District Coordination Officer.

"Yeah, the DCO will be here in . . . thirty minutes."

I'd begun to think of the DCO as a semi-mythical beast invoked when soldiers didn't want to deal with whatever was in front of them.

---

10. Anna Baltzer, "The Twisted Easter Egg Hunt," *Anna's Eyewitness Reports from Palestine*, March 27, 2005.

People routinely waited hours for the DCO to show up, sometimes days. Thirty minutes? He probably made that up. An hour later he'd ask me to wait another half hour. An hour after that, *Sorry, the DCO left for the day. Come back tomorrow.*

I had no heart to wait around and see if the typical scenario would play itself out. I called Chris, a red-headed Brit who'd volunteered with the *Palestine Monitor* and was now living in Nablus. Unruffled, he suggested I meet him and a friend, Nick, in a village near Huwara. "There's a path to walk over the mountains into Nablus from there." He handed the phone to Nick. I asked if it was safe to bypass the checkpoint.

Nick said in a thick Manchester accent, "I mean, bypassing checkpoints is never 100 percent safe. There's a small chance a soldier or settler might take a shot at us if he thinks we're Palestinians."

"What do you mean, 'a small chance'?"

It's difficult to explain why I even entertained the notion of risking my life just to visit some holy sites and eat some *kunafa*. But by then it seemed perfectly natural to me that people—mothers and students and professional people with things to do—routinely risked their lives to sneak around checkpoints just to get on with life.

A cab dropped me off on a high hill on the outskirts of a village near a dirt path that led into the mountains. The view was stunning, a crazy quilt of cultivated land spreading out in silky greens on the steep, convoluted landscape. It looked like Tuscany but more lush and vibrant. Switzerland maybe, minus the snowy white peaks towering above. I sat in the grass between two houses to enjoy the vista and wait for the boys.

A family soon spotted me from across the road and motioned me over. I joined them on their porch and talked with about six adults and fifteen kids, complimenting the nice house and the beautiful land and the cute babies. Two Israeli settlements were visible on hilltops on either side of the village. I asked the father about them.

His jolly face darkened as he told me their names: Bracha and Yitzhar. My eyes widened. Some of the worst settler attacks came from Yitzhar: beating up farmers and old people, hit-and-run attacks on children, destroying trees and greenhouses, and occasional cold-blooded murder. It was, in the words of American journalist Jeffrey Goldberg, "one of the flagship settlements of the zealots."[11]

We changed the subject and entertained each other until a platter of *maqlouba* the size of a small tractor tire was plopped down in front of us. Rice spilled down the sides of it like an avalanche. We ate it along with salad, soup, and yogurt until we couldn't eat another bite, leaving massive leftovers.

The level of hospitality here never ceased to amaze me. When people asked me to describe Palestine, sometimes I said, "If you ask for directions, you get invited to dinner." This time I hadn't even asked for directions.

Chris and Nick arrived just as we were washing up. I thanked the family for the lovely meal and company, and we set off into the hills.

Nick was a tall Brit with a confident, friendly bearing, intelligent eyes, and a penchant for sarcasm. He was wearing flip-flops, a T-shirt, and cargo shorts that had seen better days, and his fine red-brown hair stood up as if he'd forgotten about it for several months. We introduced ourselves only briefly before starting up the steep mountain path. They were out of breath from the hike, and I was so full of *maqlouba* I was visibly waddling.

As we topped the first ridge, an astounding view opened up in front of us: a village built on a rising cultivated hill that fell away steeply on one side—a scene as grand and lush as a medieval Scottish castle but more inviting and alive. Beyond the bluff more hills and valleys stretched into the distant golden haze.

For a land as small as the West Bank, there's an incredible number of unexpected treasures packed away in its numberless nooks and crevices. With so few proper maps or travelers, you don't have to go far off the beaten path to feel like you're exploring a ten-thousand-year-old undiscovered country. We sat next to a white stone wall under a fig tree

---

11. Jeffrey Goldberg, "Among the Settlers: Will They Destroy Israel?" *The New Yorker*, May 31, 2004.

to take a breather. A feeling of profound peace settled over us as we munched on fresh-picked figs and soaked in the beauty around us.

The next phase of our trek would be the most dangerous, passing through Area C land near the settlement of Bracha. We veered off the trail to avoid a checkpoint occasionally manned by soldiers, walking quickly and saying nothing.

As frightened as I was, I also felt jubilant. It was novel and exciting to feel like fugitives from laws we didn't recognize as legitimate, like the von Trapp family fleeing into Switzerland. But it was horrifying to think how many Palestinians had to act like fugitives, criminals, strangers in their own land on a daily basis.

At last we topped the final ridge and the white stone city of Nablus came into sight. Nick took a deep breath. "God, I love this view."

From up here it looked like a picture of well-ordered serenity—white homes in a long valley bounded by smooth hillsides leading up to tree-crowned heights—except for the massive blight of an Israeli military base built on top of the hill across from us, towering above the city like an overlord.

The guys were starving, and we scrambled down the steep hillside to a café in a fancy hotel called the Yasmina. Nick and I introduced ourselves more properly over sodas and hummus on the café's glass-walled catwalk. Nick was a law student at a top university in England. He'd come to the West Bank to study at Bir Zeit University for a summer and decided to stay on in Nablus and study Arabic on his own. They told stories of late-night shoot-ups in the Old City, neighborhood kids who always wanted the *ajanib* (foreigners) to entertain them, and the militants who would probably shoot out their kneecaps if they did inappropriate things with Palestinian women.

Nablus was a profoundly harder town than Ramallah, more conservative and much more dangerous. The Old City, where Nick lived now, was invaded almost nightly. The refugee camps were known to turn into killing fields at a moment's notice. Even on peaceful spring days, the specter of death and violence almost tangibly haunted the minds and hallways of the town. Unspeakable things had happened and kept happening here. Posters of the dead didn't have time to fade before more were pasted over them.

A colorful stained-glass inset of a small-town mosque decorated one of the hotel's picture windows. The mosque's clear aquamarine dome had been shot cleanly through by a single bullet, a small but powerful monument to the everyday hatred and violence that plagued this city. Yet it was strangely evocative of hope, of rising above meanness and ugliness. It was damaged, but it was still there and beautiful, seeming to smile beatifically and ironically, the cracks in its limpid glass catching the sunlight prettily.

According to scriptures, Joseph was the favorite son of Jacob, patriarch of the twelve tribes of Israel, and a grandson of Abraham. Joseph's brothers were so jealous they sold him into slavery in Egypt and told their father he'd been devoured by wild animals.

Joseph went on to save Egypt from an epic famine through his interpretation of the Pharaoh's dreams. His family was forced to move from Canaan to Egypt to escape the same famine and, as his earlier dreams had prophesied, they now had to bow before him.

Joseph died a wealthy man in Egypt, and the book of Joshua relates that Joseph's bones were brought by the Israelites out of Egypt and buried in Nablus (known as Shechem in Biblical time) on land Jacob had bought long ago for a hundred pieces of silver. Archaeological evidence is patchy at best, and the structure now known as "Joseph's Tomb"—a squat, white-domed Ottoman-era shrine located near the Balata refugee camp in Nablus—is just as likely the final resting place of a Muslim *sheikh* named Yusif. Either way, right-wing Israeli settlers claimed it in the 1980s and founded a *yeshiva* (Jewish religious school) at the site. Israeli soldiers followed and turned it into a fortified military base.

Shortly after the second Intifada began, clashes broke out around the tomb. Six Palestinians and one Israeli were killed. After the Israelis retreated under fire, a Palestinian mob ransacked and destroyed the army outpost and the tomb. (An Israeli mob torched a mosque in the city of Tiberias the next day in revenge.)

I stayed in a hostel near the Nablus Old City, and the next morning Chris and I set out to visit Joseph's Tomb. We knew vaguely where it was, and when we thought we were close we asked two teenagers for directions.

Tucked away in a back alley of a poor residential area, it was a burned, blown-up, neglected ruin. The grounds were overgrown, the top of the dome had been blown off, the walls were black with soot, and the tomb itself had been reduced to rubble. Even the stone stairs leading up to it had been smashed. The destruction had apparently been orgiastic, which seemed a pity. It would have been a nice place for pilgrimage and reflection no matter who was buried there. But the ugly reality of occupation had obliterated any holiness or serenity it might have possessed.

We made our way to the nearby Church of Jacob's Well and pushed a buzzer in a massive metal gate at the entrance to the grounds. The gate swung slowly inward to reveal a solemn-looking Palestinian man in his forties. He nodded in greeting and walked to the front of the church to open the doors for us.

The church wouldn't have been out of place in Paris or Florence except that it was so new. Two graceful white bell towers flanked the entryway. The ceiling rose majestically to a larger-than-life portrait of Christ. Paintings and stained-glass windows lined the walls leading to a beautiful altar. The floor was of dirt and gravel, and there were no pews. I thought the intention was to be closer to the earth or to humble yourself before God, but it turned out they'd just run out of funds. The Greek Orthodox priest was in Europe soliciting for floor cash.

The real treasure was below the altar. According to the Gospel of John, Jesus met a Samaritan woman at this well and asked her for a drink. When she hesitated, wondering whether a Samaritan should help a Jew, Jesus revealed he was the Messiah, saying, "Everyone who drinks this water will be thirsty again, but whoever drinks the water I give him will never thirst. Indeed, the water I give him will become in him a spring of water welling up to eternal life."

A bucket of the holy water had been drawn from the well, and the groundskeeper allowed us each a cool swallow. He told us there were not many visitors lately due to "the situation," but next week an Italian group was coming, and usually a few people trickled in every couple of weeks.

I couldn't help but contrast Joseph's Tomb with the Church of Jacob's Well. Both were European non-Muslim presences in an overwhelmingly Palestinian Muslim town. But the settlers had come as conquerors and oppressors while the Greek Orthodox church behaved like respectful neighbors.

I noticed a small commemorative plaque on one wall dedicated to a priest who'd been killed in 1979. A triptych showed a bearded, bespectacled Greek being bludgeoned and bloodied by a robed madman at the foot of the holy well.

"This happened here?" I asked, aghast.

"Yes, he was killed right here. And here it shows the settler who did it."

"A settler did this?"

"Yes. A rabbi." The rabbi and his followers had come to the monastery in November of 1979 and demanded that the icons and crosses be taken down. They claimed the site belonged to the Jews because their patriarch Jacob had built the well. The priest refused and explained that it had been a sacred Christian site for centuries. A week later the rabbi and his men came back, tortured and killed the priest, and desecrated the church. No one was arrested for the crimes.

I kept thinking I couldn't be shocked anymore. This place never ceased to impress.

PASSOVER

I was in a strangely good mood the next week at work. It wasn't until April 9, when three children were killed in Gaza, that I figured out why. Until that day there hadn't been any violent deaths for three entire weeks. It was like three weeks without some putrid smell I'd gotten so used to I didn't even notice it anymore until it was gone. Not having to report on killings every day did wonders for my state of mind.

In all of March, April, and May, no Israeli civilians and only one soldier were killed, and eighteen Palestinians were killed, including six children—a staggeringly small number compared to any other three-month period since the second Intifada began.

The three Palestinian boys killed in Gaza were fifteen years old. Palestinian witnesses said they were playing soccer and running after the ball when they were shot. Israeli soldiers said they were running for the border with the intent to smuggle weapons, and that they ignored warning shots. The soldiers claimed they aimed for the legs, but each of the boys was killed by a single shot to the head or back. Either way, there was a wall at the border and the boys had been unarmed. For many reasons, the Israeli story made no sense.[12]

Still, the violence was slowing down and the mood in the West Bank lightened considerably.

IN THE THIRD week of April I was invited to attend my first Passover seder in Herzliya Pituach, a wealthy Israeli neighborhood north of Tel Aviv, by an Israeli friend named Etan. He was a fellow Stanford physics major who'd racked up awards in math and science, then made a surprising and cool switch to art and film studies. His mother was a charming woman with short brown hair and glasses. His white-haired uncle, an Israeli war veteran, joined us along with a few others, including a cousin with long blonde hair and a kind, open face. They were taken aback when Etan told them I lived in Ramallah. Most Israelis imagine Ramallah to be a cross between the Wild West and the seventh circle of hell.[13] But they seemed open minded about my opinion that Ramallah was a charming and livable city full of gracious, educated people with many great restaurants, coffee houses, and a strong sense of culture.

---

12. Chris McGreal, "Snipers with Children in their Sights," *The Guardian*, June 28, 2005.
13. Near the beginning of the second Intifada, two Israeli soldiers took a wrong turn and ended up in Ramallah. The soldiers were lynched by a mob enraged by the million-plus bullets that had been fired at Palestinians during the first few days of the Intifada. See: Reuven Pedatzur, "More than a Million Bullets," *Haaretz*, June 29, 2004. When most Israelis think of Ramallah, the only image that comes to mind is a triumphantly screaming man with the blood of an Israeli soldier on his hands.

The phone soon rang. It was a grandaunt who couldn't make it in for the holidays, calling from L.A. While Etan was talking with her, his mother turned to me and whispered, "She's a Holocaust survivor. She saw all of the worst things. She was in Dachau."

I nodded, my mouth dry, thinking about the sweet old lady on the other end of the phone and what she must have seen as a kid in a place whose name I shudder to write. My skin began to crawl. I'd seen several Holocaust movies and documentaries, but being this close to an actual person involved in the Holocaust made it less abstract in a shockingly sudden way.

I lost my appetite until chatting with people distracted my mind and the delicious smells from the kitchen brought my stomach around.

The food was homemade and lovely—matzo and parsley to symbolize the hasty retreat from Egypt eating unleavened bread and bitter herbs, my first gefilte fish, charoset (fruit wine compote), guacamole with egg and onion, delicious tamarind chicken, and baked bananas with almond slivers and chocolate mousse for dessert. We did readings and sang songs before and after the meal. I followed along with the Haggadah (telling), a fulfillment of the scriptural commandment to "tell your son" about the Jewish liberation from slavery in Egypt.

After the readings we played Whist and talked a little softball politics. None of us was in any mood to argue. After my rainy and underwhelming Christmas in Bethlehem, it was lovely to have an extra warm, cheerful family holiday thrown in for the year.

When I got back to Ramallah, a massive parade was making its way down Main Street. Marching bands, festive flags, and Girl and Boy Scouts troops made their way past several rows of spectators. At first I couldn't tell what it was for. Hamas? Fatah? Communists?

Then I noticed a group of marchers in flowing black robes carrying an ornate cross on a wooden pole, and I realized it must be the Greek Orthodox Easter. Little kids were wearing new white clothes, some were dressed like angels, and they all looked like, well, kids at Easter. I walked home feeling, for lack of a better word, blessed.

BAB AL SHAMS

Not long after Passover, a movie called *Bab al Shams* (Gate of the Sun) screened at the Qasaba Theater, a two-part epic about the Nakba and its aftermath. The first part told the story of a village called Ein al Zeitoun (Olive Spring) in the northern Galilee. The main character, a young woman named Nahila, liked to sneak over to the fence surrounding the new Jewish settlement next to her village and watch the girls in their athletic shorts play sports and study in open-air schools. It inspired her to learn to read and write.

I felt a devastating sense of loss as I watched this. Many believe Palestinians are descendents of the original Canaanites and Israelites, the first Jews and Christians, keepers of the ancient culture of the Holy Land. European Jews are often on the vanguard of Western civilization. The Arabic and Hebrew languages are similar, Jewish and Muslim dietary laws are virtually identical, and both peoples were furious at European betrayals. They had so much in common and so much to teach each other, if only their relationship could have been based on partnership rather than conquest.

When the fighting began, the residents of Ein al Zeitoun were driven out of their homes by Zionist forces. Each time the growing tide of villagers began to settle down in a new area to rest and recoup, they were attacked and driven further north. At one point, when people from dozens of towns were crowding around a strange village square fighting over scraps, Nahila just stopped and laughed at how pathetic they had become. It was like some absurdist nightmare, impossible to take seriously. And yet it was happening.

Most of the Palestinians of the Galilee were driven inexorably north toward Lebanon, Syria, and Jordan. After the war, Israeli forces razed more than four hundred Palestinian villages to the ground. Any "infiltrators" trying to get home were shot or rounded up and expelled repeatedly. Sixty years later, millions of refugees and their descendents are still not allowed even to visit their homeland.

I tried to imagine Jayyous being emptied, its inhabitants forced to stumble toward ever more concentrated camps of displaced persons until they were banished from Palestine altogether. I tried to imagine the whole jolly village, so familiar, full of so many centuries of memories, reduced to rubble. I tried to multiply it by four hundred. It didn't compute.

This was what the Nakba meant to the Palestinians—a great drowning, a great subjugation that millions were forced to watch helplessly as uncountable names and memories and stillborn futures were eradicated from the face of this earth.

The second half of the film was even more devastating than the first. It was the late 1960s. Nahila's descendents were living in an ugly concrete refugee camp in Lebanon. After decades of being dispossessed and beaten down and ignored by both Israel and their Arab hosts, Palestinians began taking matters into their own hands. The battle cry of the 1960s was *Revolution*, embracing the whole world with a feeling that the whole world was fighting with you, so young and perfect, the heart of a bull, you'd do anything for Liberation, for self-determination, for a chance to define your own destiny. As I watched the film, the same pathetic fire burned in my chest.

But any time the Palestinians gained real momentum, they were crushed by the Israelis, the Jordanians, the Lebanese, all of whom had their own reasons to feel threatened by the resurgence of stateless people who were heroes in the eyes of a morose and defeated Arab world ruled mostly by dictators beholden to the West.

Some Palestinian factions began engaging in high-profile terror attacks and hijackings. Lebanon became entangled in a brutal civil war. Syria and Israel stepped in. Everything became bloody, smoke-charred chaos. The rhetoric of Liberation got lost in petty skirmishes, retaliations, power grabs. Mothers, fathers, sisters, friends, and ideals were crushed and left for dead, dreams and egos shut up in cinder-block cells, desecrated, bombed, slaughtered. Before you know it you're middle-aged (if you're lucky) and no better off than you were before. Your kids just want name-brand jeans and an engineering degree from Michigan, because everything else seems like a dead end.

Dreams of home retreat further and further, and the thieves of your innocence are still there dancing on your ancestors' bones, forcing more than half a nation to live naked, without roots, with resolution so tantalizingly close—just a few miles, really!—and so utterly impossible. You fester in your concrete shantytown with open sewers running down narrow alleyways and dream of the wide spaces, carved stone homes, and lemon-scented air of your stolen coastal home while you watch your fathers and grandfathers die in exile, and you can't stand it, but you have no choice.

CHAPTER 10

Okies in the Promised Land

Let the beauty we love be what we do. There are
hundreds of ways to kneel and kiss the ground.

—**Rumi**

I'd written dozens of letters to my parents by now, but it was no substi-
tute for experiencing Palestine for themselves. I wanted them to visit so
that for the rest of our lives, they would never have to wonder whether
I had exaggerated either the beauty or the horror. My mom had never
left the States before, and she and my stepdad, Bill, had been talking
about visiting me for months. But I knew they'd put it off indefinitely
unless drastic measures were taken. Finally I said to Mom, "If you love
me, you'll come see what my life is like over here."

They arrived at Ben Gurion Airport on Friday, June 3.

We caught a cab to their hotel on the Mount of Olives, which
had an unparalleled view of the Jerusalem Old City and the Dome
of the Rock. After freshening up and having a bite to eat, we headed
down to the Old City and walked along the Via Dolorosa, the path
Jesus walked while carrying the cross. It took us through the Muslim
and Christian Quarters with their bustling mix of shops catering to

tourists and residents alike. Mom quietly soaked everything in. As we left through the Damascus Gate she said, "It all looks like an old Cecil B. DeMille movie set."

We walked up Nablus Road past the Garden Tomb to the Jerusalem Hotel, where I'd made dinner reservations at the Kan Zaman Restaurant to give my parents their first taste of Arabic food, music, and ambience. We ordered *mezze*, traditional appetizers served on small plates, everything from smoky *baba ghannouj* and fresh *tabouleh* to spicy chicken wings and fried cauliflower. They loved it. For the rest of the trip we rarely ordered anything else.

An oud player and drummer played and sang, and scented *nargila* smoke hung sweetly on the air. A woman spontaneously stood up and started dancing, and the rest of the patrons encouraged her by clapping and dancing and singing in their seats. Mom and Bill smiled and clapped along, totally at ease. We couldn't have had a better first day.

THE NEXT MORNING we caught a bus to the Qalandia checkpoint. Somehow I forgot to prepare my parents for the impact of seeing a checkpoint for the first time. As we walked through the dirty, fenced-in path that ran parallel to the outgoing terminal where men, women, and children were being corralled like sheep and treated like criminals on their own land in the shadow of a sniper tower, tears were streaming down my mother's face. Part of me wanted to comfort her. But another, hardened part thought, *Welcome to the real world, Mom.*

The sad truth was, by now going through a checkpoint seemed as ordinary to me as standing in line at a grocery store. I felt angry when I was harassed or turned back, of course. But it had simply become a part of the landscape of life. People, like frogs in slowly boiling water, can apparently get used to anything, a fact as amazing as it is terrifying. It's one of the reasons I enjoy tour guiding people in the West Bank—to remind myself what normal emotional reactions to this place are supposed to be like.

"Good Lord," Mom said. "How can this be happening over here and no one in America even knows or cares?"

I repeated something Yusif had said to me a long time ago: "That's a very good question, Mom."

When we reached Ramallah, I showed them my office and the Al Karameh Café across the street where I got a five-shekel cappuccino after lunch every day, as much for the barista's shy smile as for the best coffee in town. We followed Main Street toward Al Manara, where I showed them the stone lions, each representing one of the founding families of Ramallah. I told them *Ramallah* means "Height of God" due to its scenic beauty and fresh sea breezes. It had been a mostly Christian town until it was inundated with refugees in 1948. Since then many Christians fled to America or Europe to wait out the conflicts. But the mayor's office was still reserved by law for a Christian.[1]

I led them to Pronto, where the owner Bassem heartily greeted his regulars. We ordered cappuccinos on the veranda overlooking City Hall Park. When I introduced my parents to the waiter, his face lit up.

"Ah, welcome!" he said, and refused to charge us for the coffees.

I looked at my parents and laughed. "You see what I have to deal with here?"

We caught another cab to my clean, spacious apartment. I showed them the huge Bravo Supermarket next door, where I could get anything from Nutella and peanut butter to deli sliced smoked turkey and hummus. For dinner we drove to Al Fellaha (The Farmer Woman), a restaurant in the countryside surrounded by olive groves. It specialized in homemade *musakhan*, a dish of tender roasted chicken, onions, sumac, allspice, and saffron baked on top of crispy, chewy wheat bread and sprinkled with toasted almonds and pine nuts. The food was delectable, the atmosphere tranquil, and the restaurant owners a charming family. I told every funny story I could think of, and my parents asked lots of questions. When I was trying to explain about the ideological settlers, Bill remarked, "So they're kind of like NRA Baptists?" Mom and I cracked up. The meal at Al Fellaha was one of our favorite memories of the trip.

---

1. In December 2005 Ramallah would elect its first female mayor, Janet Mikhail, a Roman Catholic.

THE NEXT DAY we headed to Jericho and caught a cab to the Dead Sea, the lowest and saltiest point on earth. Just as the dark blue water was coming into view through the desert haze, a soldier stopped us at a flying checkpoint. He squinted at our documents.

"Sorry, the road is closed," he said.

I leaned out the window. "What do you mean, closed?"

"I mean go back, the road is closed."

"Why?"

"No Palestinian cars allowed."

Most of the Jordan Valley and Dead Sea rift are off-limits to Palestinian traffic. But I hadn't thought to check our driver's license plates. Even if he had Palestinian plates, I assumed he would know a way to bypass the checkpoints. Now I didn't know if the driver had taken our money, knowing we'd get turned back, or if this soldier was just on a power trip.

Either way, seeing a soldier arbitrarily deny my mother a glimpse of one of the wonders of the world on her once-in-a-lifetime vacation awakened a primal rage I didn't realize I was capable of. For the first time I experienced the literal truth of "seeing red." I started yelling at the soldier, much to his amusement and my mother's horror. She pulled me back into my seat and the driver backed up and turned around. I can't imagine what I would have felt, or what I might have been capable of, if the soldier had been denying my mother life-saving medical treatment instead of just messing up her vacation plans.

The silver lining was that we'd have more time to explore Bethlehem. We found a service taxi to take us through Wadi Nar to bypass Jerusalem and its roads that are off-limits to Palestinian cars. I took my parents through the Church of the Nativity, the Shepherds' Fields, and the Milk Grotto, where Mary allegedly spilled milk while nursing Jesus.

Finally we sat down for baklava and coffees at a café near Manger Square. Soon the call to prayer sounded from the Mosque of Omar. The mosque had been built on the site where an early Muslim caliph had prayed after issuing a law that guaranteed respect and protection for Christian shrines and clergy in the city.

Mom leaned toward me and asked, "What's he saying?"

It was just the ordinary call to prayer, but I pretended to listen intently as if attempting a difficult translation. "He's saying . . . 'Kill the infidels, kill the infidels.'"

My stepdad nodded thoughtfully, as if this were an interesting bit of cultural trivia. Mom froze in terror, her coffee halfway to her lips.

I couldn't keep a straight face for long. "I'm kidding, Mom. Don't worry. He's just saying it's time to pray."

We made our way to the main checkpoint between Bethlehem and Jerusalem, located in a northern Bethlehem neighborhood. The Wall passed a few feet from the houses in this area, which had been reduced to a near ghost town. Most of the restaurants and businesses were shut down, and several commandeered apartment buildings were draped in camouflage netting. Striking graffiti images were painted on the Wall, including a sign that said WELCOME TO THE GHETTO. Like the Qalandia checkpoint, this one was miles from the Green Line.

I passed first through the metal detector in the massive checkpoint terminal. When my parents followed, I heard a female Israeli guard say to Mom, "Are you a tourist?"

"Yes," my mother said.

"We love tourists," the guard said earnestly.

Mom nodded miserably as she watched Palestinians just a few yards from us getting searched, questioned, and harassed by other soldiers. Walking away from the terminal to try to find a taxi into Jerusalem, with the giant concrete Wall hiding from sight the friendly, strangled, ghettoized birthplace of Jesus Christ, my mother cried for the second time.

THE NEXT DAY, hoping for a more relaxed and touristy atmosphere, we headed back to the Jerusalem Old City to visit the Haram al Sharif and witness the unforgettable sight of the Dome of the Rock shining against the azure sky. The Old City was more crowded than usual as we made our way to the Western Wall prayer plaza. When we reached the entrance of the ramp to the Haram, an Israeli soldier stood in our way.

"It is closed," he informed us.

I looked at him in astonishment. "Why?"

"It's Jerusalem Day."

"What does that mean?"

He pointed vaguely toward the crowd and shrugged. "It is closed. Sorry."

Slowly we figured out what was going on. It was Yom Yerushalayim, an Israeli celebration of the 1967 "liberation and reunification" of Jerusalem. Thousands of American Jews had descended on the city and were parading around as if they owned the place while Palestinians were kept out of sight and under control by hundreds of Israeli police, soldiers, checkpoints, and closures. Visiting the Dome of the Rock was entirely out of the question.

As we were walking back through the Muslim Quarter, a young shopkeeper asked us what we were looking for. "We wanted to see the Dome of the Rock," I said glumly, "but it's closed for Jerusalem Day."

"Go up on the roof of the Armenian Hospice," he said. "It has the second-best view of the Dome of the Rock." He gave us directions, and we were welcomed into the hospice and onto the roof, where the view of the golden Dome was indeed almost as resplendent as that from the Haram itself.

The Church of the Holy Sepulcher was our last must-see site in the Old City. The labyrinthine structure was built on Golgotha, the Hill of Calvary where Jesus was believed to have been crucified and buried. Several Christian sects compete for administration and maintenance of the church and its grounds. Their infighting prompted Salah al Din (Saladin) in 1178 to appoint a Muslim family, the Nusseibehs, to be custodians of the keys to the church and mediate disputes.

Mom insisted on hiring a guide to take us through the church. No sooner had she spoken than a kindly man offered us a tour. To our delighted astonishment he turned out to be Wajeeh Nusseibeh, the keeper of the keys himself. Off we went into the most crazy amalgam of churches, with a different sect controlling every corner and level, chamber and chapel. Each room was more intriguing than the last.

One entire hallway of rock walls was covered with crosses carved by Crusaders during their occupation of the city.

At the end Mr. Nusseibeh opened an old wooden safe and showed us pictures of himself in the official book of the church with various global VIPs, including popes, presidents, and movie stars. Then we took our own picture with him. The whole tour cost only $20. Mom said it was the best $20 she ever spent.

After rounding out the day with lunch at the Jerusalem Cinematheque and an afternoon at the Israel Museum, we caught a cab back to our hotel. Things were going fine until we hit the first Jerusalem Day roadblock. The driver turned around and tried to find another route, only to be blocked again. When we hit the third roadblock guarded by tense, sweaty, machine gun–wielding soldiers, the driver started cursing and careening around every back alley in Jerusalem trying to find a way through, demanding more money, and nearly hitting cars and cats and people as he sped along. Mom began clutching her shirt and singing "How Great Thou Art" under her breath.

As we finally neared our hotel, the driver said in alarm, "This is an Arab neighborhood!"

"Yes," I said. "It's the Mount of Olives in Palestinian East Jerusalem."

"You're not scared?" He seemed genuinely flabbergasted.

Mom muttered, "Not half as scared as we are of your driving."

THE REST OF our trip would be in Israeli cities, hopefully with no more guns, checkpoints, or insane Jerusalem cabdrivers. Our first destination was the Sea of Galilee. We rented a car to visit the Biblical sites scattered among the green hills surrounding the lake, including the Mount of Beatitudes where Jesus delivered his Sermon on the Mount; Tabgha, with its Church of the Multiplication of the Loaves and Fishes; and Capernaum, where Jesus began his public ministry after leaving Nazareth. The apostles Peter, Andrew, James, and John had lived in Capernaum, and Mom's favorite site was the ruin of St. Peter's mother-in-law's house. A guide told us she had been rich and lived by the beach, and the boys used to hang out there on weekends. Mom said she had a mental picture of Jesus and the twelve shooting pool in her basement.

We moved on to Nazareth to see the Church of the Annunciation, built on the spot where the angel Gabriel told Mary she was pregnant with the Messiah. The courtyard was lined with beautiful mosaics from dozens of countries showing Mary and baby Jesus, each with its own twist. The Japanese Jesus looked Japanese and the Thai Madonna was wearing a traditional Thai headdress and sarong.

On the way out of town we saw a sign for Nazareth Illit (Upper Nazareth). I pointed it out to Mom and said, "It means—"

"Even I know what that means," she said.

It was an extension of Nazareth built on land expropriated from Palestinian-Israelis. "Its 50,000 inhabitants live in a dynamic urban space that keeps expanding and developing. The 70,000 Palestinians of old Nazareth live in a city half the size that is not allowed to expand by a single square meter; indeed, one of its western hilltops was recently requisitioned for Upper Nazareth."[2] It appeared that Israel's discriminatory land policies weren't confined to the West Bank and Gaza.

Our last major stop was Acre,[3] a mainly Palestinian-Israeli seaside city north of Haifa. We toured its incredibly picturesque Old City, including the Knights' Halls, the prisoner's hall, the Citadel, the Great Hall, the Crusader's tunnel, and the Turkish bath used by Zionist militants to spring their comrades out of British prison in 1947.

In the late afternoon we walked to the pier to see if we could take a boat ride to see Acre from the sea. A tour boat was just leaving, and we asked if we could board. They looked at us strangely but took our shekels and let us on.

Soon Arabic music came on over the loudspeakers and at least thirty kids got up and started dancing and singing along with two teenagers dressed up like cartoon characters.

Now we knew why they had looked at us strangely. We had crashed some kid's birthday party. We couldn't pay attention to the

---

2. Ilan Pappe, "In Upper Nazareth," *London Review of Books*, September 10, 2009.
3. *Akka* in Arabic, *Akko* in Hebrew.

views of Acre for watching all the cute, funny kids. Two of them grabbed plastic swords out of a shopping bag and started brandishing them at each other. Their mom yelled at them in Arabic and pointed to the swords then pointed to her eye.

Mom laughed. "You don't need to translate that. She's saying what I always say: 'You'll put someone's eye out with that thing!'"

Rum Night

As much fun as we'd had, I was dog-tired by the time my parents left. I was looking forward to a relaxing weekend at home, cooking and watching movies, before heading back to work. Until I looked at my planner and realized, to my horror, that it was time to renew my Israeli tourist visa again.

Israel rarely granted work visas to people in the Palestinian territories unless they worked with major international organizations. The rest of us were forced to live on tourist visas, which meant we had to leave the country every three months and hope they'd let us back in and give us another visa. Even putting aside the expense and hassle, there was nothing I hated worse than going through Israeli borders. They had the power to give you a one- or two-week visa instead of the standard three-month tourist visa or turn you back entirely. Your life always hung by this thread. Palestinians who'd lived or studied abroad for several years were sometimes unable to renew their Israel-issued Palestinian IDs. If so, they, too, were forced to live on tourist visas. Such instability was enough to keep many of the best and brightest from building a life and career in the West Bank.

At the border I never mentioned my real job. One journalist told *Haaretz* that "the treatment given to all of the foreign correspondents upon arrival in Israel is hostile . . . worse than what they now receive in Egypt or than what was once the case at the border crossings to East Germany and Russia."[4] If I wanted to work as a journalist in the West

4. Anat Balint, "Let the Journalists Suffer," *Haaretz*, July 21, 2003.

Bank without appalling treatment at the border and a constant threat of deportation, I had to either overstay my visa or act like a tourist.

At a crossing back in December, they caught me in a weak moment and grilled me until my tourist story fell apart. They pulled me into a back room and did a full body search, then they went through every compartment of every bag I had, shaking my clothes, opening every little compact and bottle, going through the secret inner lining of my purse, and reading every page of my day planner. Nearly all the names in my cell phone were Arabic, and it was sickening to watch them click through my friends' phone numbers and read all my text messages, including many sweet notes from Qais. I wanted to scream.

They held me for a total of fifteen hours and threatened to deport me if I didn't give them information about everyone I knew in the West Bank. I refused. For all I knew, my friends might be harassed at their next checkpoint, arrested, beaten, or (God forbid) targeted based on the fact that I'd given the authorities their names. Going back to Palestine wasn't worth that.

Finally they gave up and told me to wait. I spent hours on a cold metal bench staring at a clock, hungry and thirsty, my stomach twisting into hard little knots as I thought about all I had to lose. My job. My friends. My plans. The new apartment I'd just started fixing up.

In the end, through whatever vector summation calculus they use to determine our fate, they let me through. But it was a nerve-shattering, ulcer-inducing game every time.

This time they only held me for a couple of hours on my way out of Israel, and I made my way to Wadi Rum, the desert valley in southern Jordan where *Lawrence of Arabia* was filmed. The setting was spectacular, with golden valleys surrounded by ancient stone mountains sculpted into grotesquely beautiful shapes by a billion years of seas and winds. Some of them looked like slightly melted gothic cathedrals, with flying buttresses and everything.

A Bedouin guide took me and some other foreigners on a Jeep tour to see natural bridges, ancient rock carvings, and watering holes where Bedouin men served tea and sold five-minute camel rides to shirtless Hungarian tourists. At night our guide set up camp next to a sheer rock cliff and rustled up some roasted chicken, tomatoes, and onions. We shared sweet tea and crisp, tart apples for dessert while our guide played his lute by the fire.

The scene before us was otherworldly beautiful. A full moon lit up the sand and mountains to the west while we were still in the moonshade of the wall. The moon-shadow advanced on us until midnight, when the moon cleared the cliff above us. I wandered away to find a nice dune to sit on and take it all in.

The moon had a bright ring around it twenty moon-diameters across, which made it look like the dome of a great cathedral. The jagged stone mountains were like pillars conjured by God. The surrounding sea of silken sand softly refracted the moonlight's radiance. The stars, subtly colored, brilliant, three-dimensional, embedded in the silvery ink of unlikely existence, were unbearably beautiful. The breeze, neither warm nor cool, seemed to blow through me.

Suddenly I felt as insubstantial as air, as if I had become a part of the scene around me. There was no difference between me and the air molecules at the tops of the mountains. There was no meaningful distance between me and the stars. It was a feeling of relief so profound I was overwhelmed, and yet it was the most natural . . .

Alas. My reverie was punctured by my Bedouin guide ambling up the side of my dune to investigate whether the romance of the setting might incline me toward romance with him. I couldn't bear to desecrate this night with anything as banal as his foolish hopes or my irritation. Claiming exhaustion, I walked back to camp and lay by the fire, sighing as my head descended slowly out of orbit and back toward the shared reality of the every day.

CIVIL SOCIETY'S UNIFIED CALL

I returned to Palestine spiritually refreshed and thrilled to be back with a brand-new visa and no distractions in sight. Just three solid months of normal work and normal weekends.

My first task was to write about the long-delayed release of 400 Palestinian prisoners. Israel had promised to release 900, but only 500 had been released in February, most of whom had already served at least two-thirds of their sentences. The other 400 were finally released on June 3. Palestinians were disappointed because most of them were held only on minor charges, and many were within a few months of being freed anyway.[5] Worse, even after the release, there would still be 8,000 Palestinians in Israeli jails—the same number as had been in prison prior to the first release—due to new Israeli arrests. Al Mubadara issued a press release entitled, "800 Arrests since Sharm el-Sheikh make a Mockery of Ceasefire Agreements."

Palestinian Minister for Prisoners Sufian Abu Zaydeh said, "This one-sided step does not meet the minimum of our demands. Our priority is to release young prisoners, the women, the elderly, the sick, and political leaders like Marwan Barghouti."[6]

Next I summarized a report called "Promoting Impunity" by Human Rights Watch (HRW). It described the Israeli army's failure to investigate the vast majority of the killings of Palestinian civilians between September 2000 and November 2004. Out of 1,600 Palestinians killed outside of combat situations, army investigations resulted in only six convictions, the longest of which was twenty months for "grave intentional harm." The soldier who served the sentence had shot a Palestinian man dead while he was adjusting his TV antenna.

HRW found that Palestinian civilian deaths were treated as "lowest priority" cases. They relied on soldiers' own accounts to determine whether the circumstances surrounding a killing merited serious investigation, in which case the army relied on "operational debriefings" in which Israeli soldiers "investigated" other soldiers, often from the same unit or command, without seeking evidence or testimony from victims or eyewitnesses.

---

5. Ken Ellingwood, "Israel Frees Nearly 400 Palestinians," *Los Angeles Times*, June 3, 2005.
6. Steven Erlanger, "Israeli Cabinet Backs Release of 400 Palestinian Prisoners," *The New York Times*, May 30, 2005.

Sarah Leah Whitson, the executive director of the Middle East division of HRW, characterized such investigations as "basically a sham" that "fails to meet even basic standards of impartiality and independence . . . The government's failure to investigate the deaths of innocent civilians has created an atmosphere that encourages soldiers to think they can literally get away with murder."[7]

Meanwhile we were approaching the one-year anniversary of the International Court of Justice ruling that the route of Israel's Wall was illegal. And still there had been no action by the international community to enforce the ruling. Palestinians were beginning to realize they would have to take matters into their own hands.

On July 9, 2005, Palestinian civil society, represented by more than 170 political parties, NGOs, civil rights groups, and unions of Palestinian women, farmers, teachers, lawyers, doctors, dentists, and professors, made a historic call:

> In light of Israel's persistent violations of international law, and . . . given that all forms of international intervention and peace-making have until now failed to convince or force Israel to comply with humanitarian law, to respect fundamental human rights and to end its occupation and oppression of the people of Palestine, and in view of the fact that people of conscience in the international community have historically shouldered the moral responsibility to fight injustice, as exemplified in the struggle to abolish apartheid in South Africa through diverse forms of boycott, divestment and sanctions . . .
>
> We, representatives of Palestinian civil society, call upon international civil society organizations and people of conscience all over the world to impose broad boycotts

---

7. "Promoting Impunity: The Israeli Military's Failure to Investigate Wrongdoing," Human Rights Watch, June 21, 2005.

and implement divestment initiatives against Israel similar to those applied to South Africa in the apartheid era. We appeal to you to pressure your respective states to impose embargoes and sanctions against Israel. We also invite conscientious Israelis to support this Call, for the sake of justice and genuine peace.

The Boycott, Divestment, and Sanctions (BDS) movement should continue, they said, until Israel ends its occupation and colonization of Palestinian lands, dismantles the Wall, recognizes the rights of Palestinian-Israelis to full equality under the law, and respects the rights of Palestinian refugees.

At last Palestinian civil society was giving people all over the world a way to resist the occupation nonviolently and with clear principles. If the governments of the world refused to stop the billions of tax dollars and political impunity flowing to Israel despite its record of human rights violations, people of good conscience could at least stop supporting businesses that profited from the occupation.

At the time it was a cry in the wilderness. Almost no one took heed, and very little would happen until nearly four years later.

TEL AVIV WITH NICK

After work one Sunday, I spent three hours relaxing in the Turkish bath near the Plaza Mall in Al Bireh. When I emerged from the warm mist, I saw that Nick had called. I called him back; he was in Ramallah and invited me to join him at Sangria's.

We sat in the clean air of the beer garden and talked all evening. He told me about his life back in London, and I told stories from my redneck past. He said his favorite Arabic word was *bjannin*, which shares the roots of the words *garden, heaven,* and *insane.* It implies something so good it makes you crazy.

Talk turned eventually to our mutual friend Chris, the red-headed Brit who'd volunteered with the *Palestine Monitor* and then moved to

Nablus. He was a walking contradiction—rather small for his age of nineteen but tough in that British soccer hooligan way, sweet and sensitive with a mouth like a sailor, brave enough to come to Palestine but terrified of everything once he got here. He made friends easily and had a knack for telling hilarious stories. Nick and I would always have a fondness for him, not least because he had introduced us to each other. But he couldn't pronounce anything in Arabic. He must have ordered seven thousand Taybeh beers, and he never said it right once. *Hamdulillah* was entirely beyond him. It usually came out something like, "Hum diddly widdly . . . Allah?"

I told Nick, "Once he said, 'I used to think it was pronounced Ramaaallah, but now I know it's Ramullllah.' I didn't have the heart to tell him both pronunciations were completely wrong. And he had us convinced for three weeks that he was on his way to Najaf, the holy city in Iraq. We finally figured out he was going to Al Najah University in Nablus."

Nick laughed.

"But the best Chris story," I went on, "happened when I wasn't there."

A Dutch anthropologist friend named Saskia had traveled with Chris to Dahab when he first arrived. I'd suggested it as a way to give him time to relax and get used to the Middle East. But instead of relaxing, he spent most of the trip dreading the Israeli border he'd have to cross to get back in.

When they reached the border crossing near the southern Israeli city of Eilat, Saskia made the mistake of letting Chris go first. When the female border guard asked for his passport, he blurted, "I'm with her, that's Saskia from Holland, sh . . . she is just a tourist, we're both tourists, we . . . I don't have much money on me, but Saskia does, so there's no problem, we won't try to . . . And I was also traveling with Pamela from America, but she's in Jordan right now, and . . . and . . . I'm not going to Nablus!"

Nick laughed uproariously. Somehow Saskia managed to talk her way out of that. But it took her a while to forgive Chris for putting her anthropological research in jeopardy.

Nick shook his head. "Ah Chris, your stories of bewildered agitation in the Holy Land will live forever. Man, I haven't laughed this long or genuinely in ages."

I felt the same. It had been months since I'd so thoroughly enjoyed someone's company.

Nick was traveling to Tel Aviv the next weekend for a retreat from the pressure cooker of Nablus, and before the night was over he invited me to join him.

After we crossed the Green Line, I found a restroom and changed into skimpy shorts and a tank top, just because I could. When I emerged, Nick was silent for a moment.

"You know," he finally said, "I think you may have the best legs in Ramallah."

I laughed. "How would you know? You never see anyone's legs in Ramallah. Henry Kissinger's bare legs would look good in Ramallah."

I felt so free after so many months of wearing pants in the hot Mediterranean summer I was practically prancing like a colt. We made our way to a restaurant by the beach and had heaping guacamole cheeseburgers for lunch and chocolate fudge soufflé sundaes for dessert. Then we changed into bathing suits and hit the water, playing in the waves and running under the sun, dispelling months of pent-up nervous energy. Once we were thoroughly exhausted, we found some rocks by the sea to sit on.

"I still can't get over this place," Nick said. "A few dozen miles from here, people in Nablus are living like they are. And here we are in our bathing suits on a golden beach. How can you wrap your head around it?"

"I don't know. But you know what's also weird? We've only been in Tel Aviv a few hours and I already feel nostalgic for the West Bank. You know what I'm talking about?"

He nodded slowly. "Yeah. I know. There's something about it . . ."

"Like, I was showing a Jewish friend around Ramallah the other day, this woman I know from Stanford named Lizzi. When we walked by Pronto, with all the Palestinians and foreigners sitting around smoking cigarettes and drinking wine and talking politics, she said, 'They look like the French resistance or something.'"

Nick agreed. There was an air of 1920s Paris or Casablanca about the place—a city cut off from the world except for a small group of dissolute, disillusioned expatriates who weren't sure whether to fight injustice or get drunk and forget about it. The atmosphere of mute shock expressed only in sidelong glances, of being on the right side of history against long odds, of knowing something few people knew, and of genuine connection and collective struggle was something tenuous and rare. Every foreigner who spent time in Palestine felt it. No matter where we were from or where we went afterward, the parts of Palestine where we lived, worked, and studied always felt like a home to us.

The price was manifestly not worth it. Losing a day at a checkpoint or worrying that a friend was being beaten (or worse) wasn't nearly as romantic as it sounded, and nothing was worth watching kids suffer and die. It was draining, it was cynical-making, it aged you prematurely and punctured your dreams. Everyone had to figure out how to deal with it in his or her own way—through denial, acceptance, action, or something else. But the fleeting, crackling magic of those endless, short years of war was a silver lining worth cherishing to the very hilt of possibility.

For dinner we walked south to Jaffa, a proud port city that had once been a glory of the Arab Mediterranean. Its Old City, formerly a teeming center of culture and commerce, was cleansed of Palestinians after 1948, polished up, and made into a picturesque tourist trap full of small art galleries, shops, and apartments. One expropriated home, all arches and verandas and cut stone worn smooth by years, had been turned into a charming café called Aladin—an Arabic restaurant with an Arabic name in an Arabic building selling Arabic food with Israeli waiters making Israeli profits at Israeli prices.

The view from the balcony was resplendent. A minaret topped by a sculpted metal crescent was framed against the sea spreading north to the bright Art Deco skyline of Tel Aviv and west to the setting sun.

A pleasant sea breeze was blowing. We ordered nineteen-shekel hummus (would have cost three in Nablus) and outrageously overpriced lemonade with mint.

Nick knew several people in Nablus who were refugees from Jaffa. They still had the keys to their homes and memories of their orange groves and orchards, just forty-odd miles away. The building we were sitting in might have belonged to the grandparents of one of his friends. Nick stretched theatrically as he looked over the gorgeous view and its aching history.

"Crime does pay," he said with a tragic sigh. "It surely does."

". . . he said, as someone exploded behind him," I added parenthetically.

Nick choked slightly on his lemonade. "Yeah . . ." He sighed grimly and shook his head. "No wonder they get such a kick out of that."

CHAPTER 11

The Gaza Disengagement

*Few of us can surrender our belief that society must somehow
make sense. The thought that The State has lost its mind and
is punishing so many innocent people is intolerable. And so the
evidence has to be internally denied.*

—Arthur Miller

A *Haaretz* editorial lamented: "This summer, Israel is going to do the
most ruthless thing it has ever done to its citizens . . . It is going to send
its soldiers into the homes of citizens to pull them out. And to destroy
all that they built, all they planted, all they believed."[1]

The author was talking about the removal of settlers from the
Gaza Strip during the upcoming Disengagement. Of course it was
awful for anyone to be evicted from his or her home. But as Gideon
Levy pointed out, "The specter of being evicted from his home is
what let him buy it cheaply in the first place, like all stolen property.

---

1. Ari Shavit, "Listen to the Calls of Distress," *Haaretz*, January 27, 2005. For a sobering
   rebuttal to similar dramatics, see: Gideon Levy, "From Khan Yunis, You Can't See the
   Settlers," *Haaretz*, January 9, 2005.

Thus he should have known that his home is liable to be temporary, yet he sees his eviction as an 'expulsion,' 'deprivation' and 'an infringement of civil rights.'"[2]

Settlers and their supporters had been holding massive demonstrations against the Disengagement for over a year. An *Associated Press* article quoted one man saying, "I have come to demonstrate against the disengagement of Jews from the land of Israel. If Sharon wants to disengage, he should do it to the Arabs, because they don't belong in the Land of Israel."[3]

The Gaza Strip, cradled in the southeast corner of the Mediterranean Sea, has changed hands many times over the millennia. "A city so rich in trees it looks like a cloth of brocade spread out upon the land," wrote the fourteenth-century Syrian scholar Al Dimashqi when he visited Gaza. Located at the crossroads of Europe, Asia, and Africa, its fertile land and value as a trade route were prized by successive invaders.

Until recently the Gaza Strip had been a rich agricultural area, producing fruits, vegetables, and cut flowers for lucrative export to European markets. But the Oslo Accords and their permit system had slowly squeezed Gaza's economy. After the second Intifada started, Gaza was enclosed by an Israeli wall, factories closed, and Palestinians had a harder time working in Israel. Unemployment and poverty among Gaza's 1.5 million residents skyrocketed.

As Nehemia Strasler said in *Haaretz*: "Not only did we not invest [in Gaza], not only did we not build or develop, but we exploited them as a cheap labor force, we sold them our 'Grade B' and 'freshness date expired,' and we did not enable them to build up an industry that might have competed with its Israeli counterpart, heaven forbid. In Gush Katif [the Gaza settlements], 7,500 people gained control over 20 percent of the land in Gaza, and over more than 20 percent of the water. If that is not cruel colonialism, then what is?"[4]

---

2. Gideon Levy, "Settlers, Tell Us, What do You Think will Happen?" *Haaretz*, January 3, 2010.
3. Jaime Holguin, "Israelis Protest with Human Chain," CBS, July 26, 2004.
4. Nehemia Strasler, "You Have to Read Sharon's Speech," *Haaretz*, August 18, 2005.

Sharon's Disengagement Plan included the removal of all Israeli settlers from the Gaza Strip, which was hard to argue with. But other aspects of the Plan were worrisome. For one thing, Israel would continue to "supervise the outer envelope on land, will have exclusive control of the Gaza airspace, and will continue its military activity along the Gaza Strip's coastline." In other words, Israel would still control all of Gaza's land, air, and sea borders. Under international law, it would therefore remain occupied territory.

Furthermore, "As a rule, Israel will enable the continued supply of electricity, water, gas and fuel to the Palestinians, under the existing arrangements and full compensation." Israel also "reserves the basic right to self-defense, which includes taking preventive measures as well as the use of force against threats originating in the Gaza Strip." Many feared the end result would be to turn Gaza into an open-air prison that would be subject to Israeli bombings, invasions, and siege any time it misbehaved.

Zooming out a bit, one could see why this kind of plan might make sense to Ariel Sharon. The population of Israel is around 7.7 million, including 5.8 million Jews and 1.6 million Palestinian-Israelis. The population of the West Bank and Gaza is approaching 4 million. Thus the number of Palestinians and Jews between the Jordan and the Mediterranean is almost equal. And the Palestinian population is growing much faster. Once Palestinians outnumber Jews, Israel's status as a "Jewish democracy" will be seriously imperiled. Israel will be forced to choose between two options.

The first is the two-state solution: a viable, sovereign Palestinian state in the West Bank and Gaza alongside Israel. The second is the one-state solution: turning the Holy Land into a single state in which power will be shared between Jews and Palestinians.

The one-state solution is out of the question as far as the Israeli government is concerned because it would mean the end of Israel as a Jewish-majority state. So far they've also rejected a two-state solution based on international law as proposed by the Arab Peace Initiative. And Palestinians reject anything less.

The only other option is to take measures to extend the occupation indefinitely.

Sharon's advisor Dov Weisglass made this explicit: "The disengagement plan . . . supplies the amount of formaldehyde that's necessary so that there will not be a political process with the Palestinians . . . The disengagement plan makes it possible for Israel to park conveniently in an interim situation that distances us as far as possible from political pressure. It legitimizes our contention that there is no negotiating with the Palestinians."[5]

Sharon himself openly stated, "The Americans have often asked us to sketch out the boundaries of the large settlement blocs in Judea and Samaria [the West Bank], and we have refrained from doing so in the hope that by the time the discussion on the settlement blocs comes, these blocs will contain a very large number of settlements and residents."[6]

Indeed, although nearly 8,000 settlers would be evacuated during the Disengagement, the settler population in the West Bank in 2005 was projected to grow by more than 12,500.

East Jerusalem Outrage

Tino and Maeve left at the end of the summer, and a Canadian journalist named Jon moved into my apartment. He was working on a story about a Palestinian village called Jebel Mukaber, south and east of Jerusalem but still within the expanded borders Israel drew when it illegally annexed East Jerusalem in 1980.[7] A huge new settlement called Nof Zion (View of Zion) was being built on its land.

5. Ari Shavit, "Weisglass: Disengagement is formaldehyde for peace process," *Haaretz Magazine*, October 8, 2004.
6. Shahar Ilan, "Sharon against the haters from Tel Aviv," *Haaretz*, August 25, 2005.
7. UN Security Council Resolutions 476 and 478 reaffirmed that "the acquisition of territory by force is inadmissible" and said Israel's attempts to alter the status of Jerusalem constituted "a flagrant violation of the Fourth Geneva Convention." All countries, including the United States, maintain their embassies in Tel Aviv rather than in Jerusalem because they don't recognize Israel's annexation of East Jerusalem.

The village is in a strategic and picturesque area with views of the Jerusalem Old City, the Mount of Olives, Mount Zion, and even the Dead Sea after a short hike uphill. The future site of the settlement was staked out across a hillside next to the village. A huge billboard depicted the four hundred luxury condos, shopping mall, country club, hotel, synagogue, and private kindergarten that would soon be built.

According to Israel's *Yediot Ahronot*, thirty yet-to-be-built apartments had already been sold to wealthy Jews from New York. The settlement was advertised as being built on "about thirty acres" of "private, Jewish-owned land." But half the land had been confiscated from its Palestinian owners by the Jerusalem Municipality under the auspices of public services. Villagers who owned the land were mounting a legal challenge, but it was doubtful it would come to anything. The Israeli courts almost always ruled in favor of settlements in such cases.

When Israel annexed East Jerusalem, it drew a boundary that went far beyond the city to include several villages and a refugee camp, the open spaces surrounding them, and even parts of southern Ramallah. The Israeli government declared most of the confiscated land "green areas," which meant it was illegal to build there, making it difficult or impossible for Palestinians to build new homes or improve existing ones, dig wells, or even plant trees. Many growing families build anyway and live under the constant threat of demolition.[8] Meanwhile, gleaming new Jewish-only villas are frequently built on "green areas" that are suddenly rezoned for settlement construction.[9] The importance Israel puts on maintaining control of East Jerusalem can be measured by the fact that nearly half of all settlers—almost 200,000—live in East Jerusalem.

Before 1967, East Jerusalem was the center of Palestinian culture and politics. Since the Israeli government occupied the city, it's

---

8. Around 60,000 Palestinian residents of East Jerusalem are living under threat of having their homes demolished. See: Akiva Eldar, "UN: Israel Must Freeze East Jerusalem Home Demolitions," *Haaretz*, May 1, 2009.
9. Most Israelis don't see the settlements in East Jerusalem as settlements. They call them "Jerusalem neighborhoods." In terms of international law, however, there is no difference between settlements in East Jerusalem and those in the rest of the West Bank and Gaza.

been using the settlements—and now the Wall, which snakes around to take maximum land with minimum Palestinians on it—to break East Jerusalem away from the rest of the West Bank and to fragment Palestinian communities within East Jerusalem.

Uri Bank, a leader of Israel's pro-settlement Moledet (Homeland) party, was very clear about this: "We break up Arab continuity and their claim to East Jerusalem by putting in isolated islands of Jewish presence in areas of Arab population. Then we definitely try to put these together to form our own continuity. It's just like Legos—you put the pieces out there and connect the dots. That is Zionism. That is the way the State of Israel was built."[10]

At the end of 2005, the Israeli High Court would find out the Israeli army had lied to it on several occasions when they claimed the route of the Wall was based solely on security considerations. In many areas, including Jayyous, the court found that the Wall route had in fact been based on future development plans of settlements.[11]

A *Haaretz* editorial summarized the situation: "While all the attention is focused on the highly publicized evacuation of the settlers from [Gaza], the real battle for Israel's borders is taking place in the West Bank. It could be years before the eastern border with the Palestinians is finally settled, but meanwhile, the bulldozers and builders are at work—as has been the custom of Israeli greed for the last 38 years of occupation—in an attempt to 'create facts on the ground' against all logic and against the long-term interests of the State of Israel."[12]

While Gaza grabbed all the headlines, the battle for East Jerusalem and the rest of the West Bank raged on.

---

10. Ben Lynfield, "Settlers Vie for East Jerusalem," *The Christian Science Monitor*, December 12, 2003. For a map of the Wall's path in East Jerusalem, see the map on p. 299. See also: Barak Ravid, "E.U. Envoys: Israel Trying to Sever East Jerusalem from West Bank," *Haaretz*, December 2, 2009.

11. A report was published jointly in December of 2005 by two Israeli organizations, B'Tselem and Bimkom (Planners for Planning Rights), entitled "Under the Guise of Security: Routing the Separation Barrier to Enable Israeli Settlement Expansion in the West Bank," which laid out the case in detail. See also: Meron Rapoport, "Lies of the Land," *Haaretz*, June 25, 2006.

12. "The Battle for the 'Fingernails,'" *Haaretz*, April 20, 2005.

HIP-HOP AND A GRENADE

The weekend of August 11 kicked off with a hip-hop concert, the last stop on a tour called Son of a Refugee.

The headliner was a trio of Palestinian-Israelis called DAM from Al Lyd (or Lod), a hardscrabble town southeast of Tel Aviv. Palestinian-Israelis face discrimination in many guises, official and unofficial. Police violence is much worse, and their towns languish with far fewer government resources than Jewish areas enjoy. Many Bedouin towns aren't recognized at all, which means they lack even basic infrastructure like electricity, water, and public schools. Some have been razed to make way for Jewish development.

DAM took the usual hip-hop lyrics about discrimination and living in ghettos and added the singularly Palestinian culture influenced by the crushing Israeli occupation. They sang about women's rights and murdered children, checkpoints and Walls, invasions and curfews, all of it straight out of the updates and press releases I wrote every day about real people trapped, humiliated, killed so regularly it had almost become banal. Tears came to my eyes more than once.

Then they transitioned to music about pride, resistance, art as a way to stand up and express your humanity, and the unbreakable spirit of the Palestinian people who have survived and thrived against all odds. An affirmation of existence, an undeniable message that we cannot and will not be treated this way. We're mothers, we're artists, we're kids—we're human beings. If you don't respect us, you don't respect yourself. You can say we don't exist, but here we are.

The crowd went wild.

MEANWHILE, A FEW miles to the west, a very concrete point of pride was taking shape. Jayyous had been the first village to mount regular protests against the Wall, and several other villages were now taking up the mantle.

Bil'in, a village west of Ramallah, was currently the most active front. Five hundred of Bil'in's olive trees had been uprooted for construction of the Wall, and the Wall's route was set to isolate half the village's land, including twenty thousand olive trees, from its owners. The massive settlement of Modiin Illit was expanding on that land. Since February 2005, the villagers had been organizing protests every Friday after midday prayers and were often joined by international and Israeli activists. It was such an inspiration to see the weaker side take the high road, Gandhi-like, even as outmatched, oppressed, and splintered as they were. It was well past time I saw this phenomenon for myself.

When I got to Bil'in on Friday, August 12, I decided to skip the orientation lecture and walk around town instead. It was beautiful to see Israeli activists walking freely in this traditional Muslim town wearing T-shirts with Hebrew slogans. Shy Palestinian girls ventured a few friendly *Shaloms* in their direction. Several Israelis had taken over a spot in the shade next to the central market, and a Palestinian man was walking up the road toward them. When he heard the group speaking Hebrew in the middle of his town, he lit up in one of the warmest smiles I had ever seen.

"*Salaam alaykum!*" he said with an amazed kind of gratitude.

They answered enthusiastically, "*Wa alaykum al salaam!*"

My heart filled with lightness and rare hope.

At 1:00, right on schedule, about two hundred people marched to the outskirts of town. Several were carrying a huge chicken-wire model of the Wall covered with posters. A scarecrow-like figure was being strangled by it. Every week they created a different artistic manifestation of their situation. The previous week it had been a giant black snake symbolizing the Wall.[13]

A handsome young man named Rani Burnat, who had been shot in the neck by Israeli soldiers and paralyzed during a demonstration in Ramallah in 2000, manned the front lines in his motorized wheelchair. Off to one side, a Palestinian journalist was interviewing an eloquent young Israeli woman from Anarchists Against the Wall. She explained

---

13. When the movie *Avatar* came out in 2009, the people of Bil'in donned blue face and body paint and dressed up like the Na'vi people (http://wp.me/pExvW-7T). You can view my photos from another Bil'in protest in 2009 here: http://wp.me/pExvW-5g.

to them (in English with a heavy Hebrew accent) why she was there in solidarity with the Palestinians and how the Israeli government did not represent her values.

As usual, no mainstream Western or Israeli journalists were present.

The soldiers had put up a razor wire barrier in the middle of the gravel road that led to the site where the Wall was being built. As a punishment for previous protests, they had declared the land between the roadblock and the construction site to be a "closed military zone."

A tall, skinny young man handed me a section of raw onion as we were walking toward the roadblock. I looked at him in confusion. He smiled knowingly. I thought he was making fun of me somehow—the old "hand the foreigner an onion wedge" trick?—so I impaled it on some barbed wire as I passed and forgot about it.

After pausing at the razor wire roadblock, chanting and singing, we split into two cordons. The one I followed swept down a dirt road toward the Wall. When the soldiers tried to stop us, the people in front sat in the dirt road and refused to move. The soldiers began beating and arresting them. I moved toward the less-enthusiastic rear-guard crowd to observe and take notes.

Soon other soldiers began shooting tear gas canisters at the crowd along with the occasional flash-bang grenade (also called concussion grenades or sound bombs), which make a terrifying noise but don't throw deadly shrapnel. Some of the flash-bang grenades started small fires when they exploded in the dry underbrush between olive trees. Young men with *keffiyas* wrapped around their faces were stamping out the flames. A few Palestinians managed to pick up tear gas canisters that were still spewing gas and throw them back at the soldiers, which sent the soldiers scattering. Several protesters were sniffing onion wedges, and I realized with a pang of embarrassment that it must be a way of partially neutralizing the effects of tear gas.

Suddenly, without warning, the soldiers began shooting projectiles toward my group. I turned to run, and as I did, something heavy struck the back of my right calf so hard my leg almost buckled. I felt no pain, only the shocking weight of the impact. I barely kept my footing and managed to keep running.

Time acted strangely in the moment between the impact and the explosion. It had an indefinable, dreamlike quality that seemed to stretch in order to give me time to consider what the next moment might bring. There were three possibilities: (1) Tear gas, in which case the worst that could happen was that I'd pass out and possibly asphyxiate if the cloud was too thick and the wind not strong enough and help didn't come fast enough, or if I had a stronger-than-normal reaction to the gas. (2) Flash-bang grenade, which might set my clothes on fire and cause contusions and burn injuries. A woman trying to get through a checkpoint to Jerusalem had recently had a flash-bang grenade thrown at her face by a soldier, and it caused terrible burns and bruises. Or (3) a live grenade, in which case shrapnel might lodge in my spine or kidneys or tear off my right leg at the knee—the leg I kicked soccer balls with. I had no way of knowing until it exploded and solved the mystery.

I never heard the explosion. I could only infer that it had happened because I was partially deaf for several hours afterward.

After running fifty yards or so, I was able to calm down and take stock. I was still conscious, and the leg was still there. I examined my body, and the only injury I found was a deep, black, baseball-sized bruise on the back of my right calf and a stinging abrasion that made walking painful for days.

I was lucky. It had only been a flash-bang, and it hadn't exploded on impact. But my nerves were shattered and my spirit was crushed. There's nothing like a military-grade projectile hitting your body to remind you that this is not a game. People's rights really are being denied, and this denial is backed up and can only be backed up by overwhelming physical violence against living human bodies.

Soon an excruciating cloud of tear gas enveloped me, and I ran again and kept running until I was back in the village.

None of this fazed the veteran demonstrators. All in all I was told it was more sedate than usual. The next week's demonstration was not even allowed to happen. Israeli soldiers raided the village preemptively with tear gas, sound bombs, and rubber-coated steel bullets. Bil'in had apparently been declared a "no chanting zone."

But the protests went on the week after that, and the week after that. In the years that followed, Bil'in became an international symbol of the Palestinian popular struggle. In 2007, the Israeli High Court would hand Bil'in a rare victory: It ordered the Israeli military to move the route of the Wall and return about half the land isolated by the Wall to the village. It was only a partial victory, but "the villagers danced in the street," said Emily Schaeffer, an Israeli lawyer who worked on the case, in 2009. "Unfortunately, it has been two years since the decision, and the wall has not moved."[14]

In the summer of 2009, Jimmy Carter, Desmond Tutu, Mary Robinson, and other international luminaries visited Bil'in and praised their campaign, holding it up as an example for all. But the people of Bil'in pay a terrible price for their nonviolent resistance: beatings, curfews, closures, and midnight arrest raids that punish the entire community. Some leaders of nonviolent resistance have been jailed for a year or more, and since 2005 at least twenty Palestinians have been killed at protests against the Wall, including eleven children.[15]

DISENGAGEMENT FEVER

For months, Jewish extremists had been clashing with Israeli police and soldiers, blocking intersections, throwing nails onto busy highways, and calling Israeli soldiers and police "Nazis" to their faces—all without a single rubber-coated steel bullet or flash-bang grenade being fired at them. Several thousand West Bank settlers had

---

14. Ethan Bronner, "Bil'in Journal: In Village, Palestinians See Model for their Cause," *The New York Times*, August 27, 2009.

15. More than 1,500 Palestinians and several Israelis and internationals have also been injured, some severely, including an American named Tristan Anderson, who suffered brain damage when he was shot in the forehead by a high-velocity tear gas canister, and a young Jewish artist from New York named Emily Henochowicz who was shot in the face with a tear gas canister and lost her left eye.

infiltrated the Gaza settlements and seemed intent on fighting. One group of teenaged settlers claimed they'd surf out to sea and drown when the soldiers came to throw them out. Some parents pinned orange Stars of David to their children's clothing and took pictures of them walking out of their settlement homes with their hands up, as if the Disengagement were comparable to Jews being seized from their homes during the Holocaust.

Two rogue soldiers were caught planting a fake bomb in the Jerusalem Central Bus Station. Prime Minister Sharon's life was threatened on numerous occasions, and former Prime Minister Yitzhak Rabin's grave was defiled. Some protesters threw eggs and paint and acid at soldiers, tried to stab them, or threatened them with needles they claimed were infected with AIDS. Settlers also terrorized the West Bank worse than usual, knowing the police were too busy with the riots in Israel and the media were too busy with the settlers' impassioned and brightly colored sideshow to pay them any mind.

It all reached a crescendo on August 4 when a nineteen-year-old settler named Eden Natan-Zada boarded a bus in Shfaram, a town in northern Israel, and opened fire. He killed four Palestinian-Israelis (two Christians and two Muslim sisters in their twenties) and wounded twenty more before running out of bullets and being tackled and beaten to death by horrified bus passengers. Israeli police arrested three of the killer's teenaged buddies from his settlement of Tapuach near Nablus. They were charged with membership in an outlawed organization and conspiracy to commit a criminal act. But there were no plans to bull-doze the young man's family home, invade his town and blow down doors in dead-of-night arrest raids, assassinate Jewish extremist lead-ers, or impose a full closure on Israel.

Two weeks later, an Israeli from the Shiloh settlement opened fire on Palestinian workers and killed four men. He said he wasn't sorry and he hoped someone would kill Ariel Sharon as well. Sharon joked that he might have his first meeting with Abbas in Ramallah because he'd need fewer security guards in Ramallah.

Living here was like living in a house of mirrors. If irony could be bottled and sold, the Holy Land would be richer than Saudi Arabia.

WHAT CEASEFIRE?

Days before the Disengagement was set to begin, the Israeli army raided Tulkarem, a city north of Qalqilia, and killed five people. The army claimed the victims were all wanted terrorists involved in a suicide bombing by Islamic Jihad. But an investigation by *Haaretz* and B'Tselem found that three of the dead were seventeen-year-old high school students, one of whom was epileptic, with no record of membership in any terrorist organizations. The adults, aged eighteen and twenty-six, were unarmed low-ranking operatives who could have been arrested instead of shot at close range in a largely enclosed court-yard.[16]

A visibly weary Abbas told an outraged Palestinian public, "At a time when the Palestinian Authority is trying to maintain calm, this murder intentionally seeks to renew the vicious cycle of violence." But he called on Palestinians "not to respond to provocations by Israel so as not to give it a pretext to escalate its aggression."[17]

When Ariel Sharon had first assumed power, he'd suspended talks with Arafat and chosen instead to negotiate with Washington over unilateral Israeli moves. Now that Abbas was in power, it was hoped that Sharon would negotiate with him about the terms of the Disengagement, which would boost Abbas's legitimacy.

But Sharon had already "dismissed Abbas as a 'weak' leader with whom Israel cannot do business," according to Henry Sieg-man, a senior fellow at the Council on Foreign Relations and for-mer head of the American Jewish Congress. Siegman called "the failure of Israel to coordinate its imminent withdrawal from Gaza

---

16. Arnon Regular, "IDF Chief to Probe Tul Karm Raid that Killed Five Palestinians," *Haaretz*, September 7, 2005.
17. Greg Myre, "Abbas Says Raid in West Bank Undermines Peace Efforts," *The New York Times*, August 25, 2005.

with Palestinian leadership" a "crisis . . . With less than four weeks to go, not one of the issues that will determine whether the pullout will be a success or a disaster has been resolved."[18]

These issues included whether air and sea ports could be built in Gaza, who would control the Gaza/Egypt border, and whether Palestinians would be able to travel freely between the Gaza Strip and the West Bank. No one had any idea what would be in store after the Disengagement. A World Bank–funded fantasyland of construction and tourism? Mogadishu-style chaos? Total Israeli lockdown? A massive Israeli air assault? Would Palestinians be allowed to import and export and rebuild their economy? No one knew anything.

Meanwhile the occupation seemed to be running along, nose to the ground, full speed ahead, as if all talk of peace were a passing fancy—a dangerously self-fulfilling prophecy.

DRINKING BY THE SEA IN GAZA

It was difficult for me to imagine life in the Gaza Strip. It seemed less an actual place than a metaphor for human suffering, the modern world's dirty little secret, a forbidden, forgotten, crowded, besieged penal colony that vied handily for Most Miserable Spot on Earth. Over a million people squeezed into a twenty-seven-by-five-mile strip of land choked by settlements, "security zones," sniper towers, and military bases, like a super-concentrated version of the West Bank.

The Gaza Strip is only thirty miles from the West Bank, but their trajectories have diverged steadily since 1948. Gaza has only one city, three towns, a handful of villages, and eight refugee camps. Two-thirds of its residents are refugees, compared to only 6 percent of West Bankers. Gazans depend much more heavily on humanitarian aid and Islamic charities for basic survival. West Bankers have more dealings with Jordan and the west, while Gazans gravitate toward Egypt and its Muslim Brotherhood.

---

18. Henry Siegman, "Israel is Still Blocking the Road to Peace," *International Herald Tribune*, July 25, 2005.

The brutality of the occupation is also much worse in Gaza. An Israeli officer had recently admitted the army's raids into Gaza were characterized by chaos and the indiscriminate use of force. "Gaza was considered a playground for sharpshooters," he explained.[19] Schools and homes, roads and restaurants, fields and beaches—nowhere was safe. The Gazans' framework had become so warped, many of them truly couldn't fathom why Israelis were so scared of Qassam rockets. They could only dream of their only torment being an occasional barrage of unguided missiles with a half-percent kill rate.

I arrived at the Erez crossing, the gateway between Israel and northern Gaza, on Thursday, September 8, not entirely sure whether I hoped I'd be allowed in or turned back. Two guards called to me and asked to see my passport. I gave it to them. They nodded at each other and directed me to a building further on.

Inside the building, a friendly Israeli guard took my passport and luggage. I waited in a small room with other aid workers and journalists, many of whom had probably been forced to misrepresent themselves in order to have any hope of access. I certainly hadn't mentioned anything about my job in my application. We all avoided eye contact, fearful that anything we said might be used against us.

Half an hour later I was called up, given my passport back, and directed to the entrance to the Gaza Strip. I gathered my bags and made my way to the rather intimidating portal, a shabby affair of chipped concrete and metal bars. It led to a passage enclosed by concrete walls, a tunnel-like path that stretched on for nearly a mile. My feeling of fear and desolation intensified the further I walked down that Kafkaesque lane into God knew what.

Presently I came upon a closed metal gate. An unseen Israeli soldier was making blowing noises over a microphone. The blowing noises stopped as I approached. I tried the gate. It was shut tight. I looked around the empty hall.

---

19. Conal Urquhart, "Israeli Soldiers Tell of Indiscriminate Killings by Army and a Culture of Impunity," *The Guardian*, September 6, 2005.

"Hello?" I ventured. Nothing. Feeling silly, I knocked on the gate. Still nothing. "Hello?" I banged on the gate. I knew they could see me. It was unnerving to be trapped, watched, ignored. I felt very much like a gerbil in a cage. Were they waiting for me to do something? Entertain them? Hop on one foot? Say the magic word? I suppressed an almost irresistible urge to intone, "Open Sesame."

Finally I gave up and sat on a concrete block and started playing with my cell phone to pass the time. Twenty minutes later, several Palestinian workers approached from behind me.

"*Salaam alaykum*," I greeted one of them, and he returned the greeting. "I've been waiting here twenty minutes," I complained in Arabic.

He was unimpressed. "Sometimes we wait half an hour, one hour." He shrugged.

Five minutes later the gate creaked open. A soldier barked unintelligible orders over the loudspeaker. I grabbed my bags, and we all made our way through.

At last I neared the end of the tunnel. Two Palestinian women in *hijab* greeted me with shy smiles and warm Arabic pleasantries. As they carefully recorded my passport information in a tattered green volume, my fear began to ease. A familiar feeling of calm and safety settled over me. It was unmistakable: I was back in Palestine.

I caught a cab into Gaza City. It looked similar to Ramallah but more flat and dense, larger and more overwhelming. A banner across a main intersection declared in dark green letters, PALESTINIAN UNITY IS A MUST. It was signed in red, HAMAS.

A friend had recommended I stay at a hotel on the beach, the Grand Palace, one of many swank venues built after Arafat returned in 1994. It was airy and elegant with white arches, spacious verandas, and fantastic sea views. With its air conditioning, satellite TV, hot showers, and soft beds, it was startlingly easy to forget I was in a conflict zone on the verge of historic upheaval. Gaza's economy had been valued at $1 billion before the second Intifada, and the service sector was its largest segment. This hotel was a symbol of what could have been—an entire service industry, an international vacation destination, lost.

I WENT FOR a walk on the beach the next morning and said hello to a family sitting in a circle of lawn chairs enjoying coffee and cakes. They invited me to join them. A plump, friendly woman fished a pan of crumb cake out of her beach bag and insisted I sample it. I happily obliged, and we chatted and laughed for nearly an hour. When I got up to leave, they expressed the usual mock outrage that a guest should think of doing anything other than sitting with them and accepting their hospitality until the end of time. I thanked them over and over, and they made me promise to find them if I ever came back to the beach, or to Gaza, again.

Gaza's seaport came into view next, a small harbor surrounded by a stone breakwater. Ramshackle fishing vessels bobbed on the wavelets—a deceptively idyllic scene. Gaza fishermen are routinely fired on by the Israeli Navy if they venture past the limit of twelve nautical miles imposed in 2002—far less than the twenty-mile limit agreed to under the Oslo Accords.[20] Old photographs show Gaza's fish markets overflowing with red mullet, bream, flounder, tuna, sea bass, sardines, squid, shrimp, and crabs. The market today was a sad, scrawny shadow of those days. Everyone hoped Israel would remove the restrictions, which forced Gaza's fishermen to overfish young populations near shore, and allow the construction of a deep water port to serve larger fishing, cargo, and passenger vessels after the Disengagement.

My primary concern on this aimless day was whether and when the Abu Holi checkpoint would open, the main barrier between the northern and southern Gaza Strip. I'd have to cross it to get to Rafah, Gaza's southernmost city, by most accounts one of the friendliest and most brutalized towns in the Palestinian territories. I had a contact named Nader, a friend of an American Jewish journalist friend, waiting to meet me there.

Rafah had seen the worst of Israel's violence, home demolitions, and restrictions. Even though the city is two miles from the Mediterranean, the settlements' "security concerns" prevented the residents

---

20. As of 2012, the limit is down to three nautical miles.

of Rafah from accessing the beach. When the last soldiers left at the end of the Disengagement, Rafah's residents would no doubt flood the long-forbidden settlements and run to the long-lost sea. If the checkpoint stayed closed, I would miss the extraordinary moment.

Abu Holi had been closed almost continuously for the past several days, open only at midnight on weekdays and all day Fridays. But on this Friday it was shut tight. No reason was given, no timetable made public for when it might open. Everyone was left to hope and wonder. Rumors were flying, and the most widespread and persistent was that it would open at 11:00 PM.

As eleven o'clock approached, I found a service taxi that was heading south. I and a few other hopefuls crowded in and took off.

The landscape around the Abu Holi checkpoint was monitored by a monolithic sniper tower. Acres around it had been bulldozed bereft of homes and trees and fields. The checkpoint was a prime target for suicide bombers, which meant security was on a hair trigger. A bad read of a soldier's hand signal could mean a quick and pointless death. I held my breath as our service taxi inched toward it. To our relief it was open, and we made it through in a little over an hour.

Nader met my taxi in Rafah and introduced himself briefly as we walked toward his house. He was a lanky young man with a crooked nose and a wary, almost manic friendliness.

"We will probably meet some militants before we get to my house," he informed me. "But don't worry, you are with me."

Before I had a chance to respond, we turned a corner and came face-to-face with half a dozen masked gunmen, probably from Hamas. All of us froze like deer in headlights. Nader said something sarcastic in Arabic. The militants looked at each other. If it was possible for a gang of masked men sporting assault rifles to look sheepish, they did. We continued on to his house without another word.

He insisted I have some tea before we turn in, then he offered me a foam mattress on the floor to sleep on. I fell asleep gratefully, exhausted but euphoric. Somehow I had made it to the least accessible of the least accessible places in Palestine in one of its most historic times.

NADER'S MOTHER FIXED us a breakfast of falafel, hummus, yogurt, and fried potatoes, then Nader and I ventured outside, where I got my first heart-stopping glimpse of the destroyed neighborhoods of southern Rafah. The area is famous for the huge number of homes obliterated in the hundred-meter-wide "buffer zone" along the border with Egypt to deter smuggling tunnels. What had once been a neighborhood was now a rocky, uneven field covered in scrub brush.

More than 4,500 Palestinian homes had been demolished in the Gaza Strip since September 2000, most of them in Rafah.[21] Nader's house was in the last row of homes that hadn't yet been totally destroyed, though one of the back walls of his house had been blown out by tank shells. The roof of the house to our left was caved in. A black water tank, salvaged satellite dish, and clotheslines hung with laundry indicated that someone lived there anyway. A house farther to our left leaned at a forty-five-degree angle, and kids were climbing on it like it was a colossal jungle gym. Every exposed wall was riddled with bullet holes. Across the street a man and his two young kids were starting a fire with dry brush, perhaps to make tea or cook. Their house had one wall busted out so that you could see into the bathroom. When I held my camera up to ask if I could take their picture, the father smiled as if he were standing in front of a proud home instead of squatting over a makeshift fire in a dusty street next to wreckage.[22]

Nader said, "Come, I will show you a place they really destroyed."

---

21. Twenty-two thousand more homes were partially destroyed or damaged. See: "Razing Rafah: Mass Home Demolitions in the Gaza Strip," Human Rights Watch, October 17, 2004.

22. In May 2004 the head of Israel's secular-liberal Shinui Party, Tommy Lapid, said to the Israeli cabinet, "The demolition of houses in Rafah must stop. It is not humane, not Jewish, and causes us grave damage in the world . . . At the end of the day, they'll kick us out of the United Nations, try those responsible in the international court in The Hague, and no one will want to speak with us." He said seeing a picture of an elderly woman searching in the debris of her bulldozed home for her medication reminded him of his own grandmother, who had perished in the Holocaust. See: Gideon Alon, "Prominent Israeli Denounces Home Demolitions in Gaza," *Haaretz*, May 24, 2004. His comments were met with outrage by other Israeli politicians, and the demolitions continued.

He directed me to some quarters of Rafah that had been bull-dozed in the course of a recent military incursion. It looked like ground zero of the Apocalypse. A few wire-reinforced concrete support beams stood crookedly, but everything else had been pulverized into thick, grey, ashy dust. My brain clicked off, as if some outer layer of judgment had been blown away in self-defense. All that was left was a childlike observation and acceptance of what I was seeing with no pass through the limbic system to attach emotions to it. I found a child's marble and a small blue bathroom tile half-buried in the dust. I pocketed them as mementos of this scene and the feeling of horrible numbness it evoked.

When we emerged from this netherworld, we walked to the Rachel Corrie Center, which hosted art classes, after-school pro-grams, an Internet café, and summer camps for local youths. The community center was named in honor of a twenty-three-year-old American college student who was crushed to death by an Israeli bulldozer on March 16, 2003, while trying to prevent the demoli-tion of the home of a Palestinian pharmacist in Rafah. The Israeli army claimed there was a smuggling tunnel inside the home. A few months after they crushed Rachel, they destroyed the house. No evi-dence of tunnels was found.

After walking through the center and checking our emails, Nader seemed at a loss for what to do next. "Why don't we check out the zoo?" I suggested. I'd heard there was a zoo in Gaza, but I didn't think I would fully believe it until I saw it for myself.

Nader said apologetically, "We can go, but the old zoo was much nicer."

"Old zoo?"

"Yeah. Before the Israelis bulldozed it."[23]

My mouth fell open. "They bulldozed a *zoo*?"

"Yeah."

"What happened to the animals?"

---

23. Chris McGreal, "The Day the Tanks Arrived at Rafah Zoo," *The Guardian*, May 22, 2004.

"They killed some of them, and others escaped and we had to try to find them. The fountain was destroyed, and the pool, and the games and slides for kids." He shrugged. "We built it again, but it's not as nice."

When we got there, he insisted on paying my three-shekel (seventy-cent) zoo entry fee, and we walked into a courtyard surrounded by cages. A boy about eight years old was riding a Shetland pony trailed by two friends. Among the exhibits was a twelve-foot boa constrictor, dozens of colorful birds, rabbits, puppies, house cats, and a young mountain lion, which the zookeeper proudly said came all the way from America. A monkey lived alone in a cage in the center of the courtyard. He'd taken to an endless routine of jumping up on one wall, jumping back to the ground, spinning around twice, then climbing to the ceiling and screaming. Nader and I watched him in silence. The parallel was almost too obvious, but Nader said it anyway.

"You know, I call the whole Gaza Strip the Gaza Zoo," he said. "We are like this monkey. We can't go left or right, we have nowhere to play. We are trapped here, and the world looks down at us like we are insects."

"At least the monkey doesn't have to worry about invasions or home demolitions," I started to say, but I stopped myself. This monkey may have been here when Israeli bulldozers demolished his previous home. He certainly heard the F16s and Apache helicopters screaming overhead, the gunfire, the explosions, the tanks rumbling by, and the omnipresent unmanned Israeli drones with their psyche-destroying buzz, like mosquitoes the size of elephants. Maybe these terrifying events had driven the monkey mad.

Nader sighed. "OK, what next?"

"I'd love to see the airport."

Gaza's international airport opened with much fanfare in 1998 only to be shut down when the second Intifada started and the Israeli army bombed the control tower and destroyed the runways. Only the passenger terminal was left standing. It was an elegant edifice with modern check-in desks, handsome decorative arches, and marble walls and floors inset with mosaic tile designs. It was the prettiest little airport I had ever seen. Nader and I took pictures of each other as if we were tourists. But we were the only travelers wandering its ghostly interior.

WE AWOKE THE next morning—Sunday, September 11—to an explosion. Nader snapped awake, and we walked blinking into the sunlight. A crowd had gathered a few houses north of us. A white car emerged from the crowd. Three young men were in the back, but I could only see one clearly as the car sped past us. His face and arm were covered with blood.

Nader looked at me and grinned disconcertingly. "The Israelis must have shelled us one last time." I nodded, though the whole scene seemed psychotic, as if bleeding kids were just one of Gaza's quintessential experiences, like how Wisconsin has cheese.

"What is the matter, *ya Bamila*?" he asked.

"I don't know," I said. "It's just . . . they're everywhere, they might—"

"Don't worry," he interrupted with apparently total confidence. "If they try to shoot any one bullet at you, you won't even see what I will do."

I smiled wryly. Was that supposed to be comforting? Oddly enough it was, in a giddy, dangerous way.

In the evening we sat on Nader's roof watching the sun set over what we hoped would be the last day of Israel's occupation of the Gaza Strip. Nader's nephew Mohammad joined us on the roof. He was a handsome boy of about eleven with a haunted innocence in his eyes that seemed disconnected from his calm words and shy smile. I asked him what it was like when Israel invaded. He said, "The house always shakes when the F16s and helicopters bomb the area."

"Does it scare you?"

"Of course. I peed myself five times." He shrugged. "But after a while it's normal. I mean, not normal . . ." He trailed off and looked away, unsure how to put it into words. He was disconcertingly unashamed and unemotional talking about such things.

"You know, you look a little like Ronaldo," I said in Arabic, trying to change the subject.

"Ronaldo?" The way he tasted the word in his mouth, it was clear he had no idea who I was talking about.

"You know, Ronaldo," I said. "The soccer player from Brazil."

"Brazil?" He looked even more confused.

Nader cuffed his neck. "The country, not the camp, you idiot."

I had forgotten there was a refugee camp nearby called Brazil Camp.

"Is it nice?" he asked, referring to the country Brazil. "Better than here?"

"I don't know, I've never been there," I said, feeling depressed. "But I hear it's beautiful." He blinked and nodded, considering this.

After the sun went down, we went back inside for dinner. Just as we were finishing, another deafening explosion rocked the air a few hundred yards away. We all instinctively ducked, but no one was willing to go outside and find out what had blown up this time.

We later found out that it had been the Israelis demolishing one of their own sniper towers. Gaza's neighborhoods had been watched and controlled by these towers for years, plagued by the horror of being surrounded by faceless soldiers who had the power to end your life with no repercussions and little oversight.

Never again, we hoped, after tomorrow.

IT WAS SCORCHING hot the next morning when we stepped outside and looked, hopefully, toward the border with Egypt. The buffer zone between Nader's house and the border had been a closed, forbidden, deadly military zone for as long as anyone could remember. Two Palestinian policemen walked gingerly into it and planted a small Palestinian flag on a mound of earth halfway between the last row of houses and the rusty border wall.

Young boys, heedless of the danger, ran around gathering the millions of spent cartridge shells that blanketed the field to sell for scrap metal. A juice vendor set up shop for the spectacle. I bought an ice cold cup of carob juice, and its refreshing sweetness sang through my body. A few more people began cautiously walking toward the border, gaining momentum as they became more confident no one would shoot them. Soon a steady stream was walking toward the wall, and Nader and I joined the strange pilgrimage. I wore a headscarf to blend in. It was still obvious that I was a foreigner, but no one paid me any mind.

A section of the border wall had been pulled apart, and we walked through it into the No Man's Land between the Palestinian and Egyptian border walls. The space between was as wide as a football field, a featureless stretch of land rutted with tank tracks. Men in black from both Fatah and Hamas scaled the walls to plant their flags. Several vans and pickup trucks rolled by loaded down with masked militants sporting rocket-propelled grenades as a show of power. It was probably also an attempt by Hamas to claim credit for the Disengagement.

We walked down the barren thoroughfare until we saw a section of wall on the Egyptian side that was only five feet high and topped by a chain-link fence. Palestinians and Egyptians who hadn't interacted in years were saying hello and clutching each other's fingers. Many of the kids looked in astonishment at seeing Egyptian people for the first time. Everyone was cheerful and excited. It was a day of rare freedom.

The next day they would tear down this wall and cross at will. Hundreds of stranded students, travelers, and medical patients streamed over the wall to get out or get back home. Egyptian customers made it all the way to Gaza City to shop for apples and blankets while Gazans came back from Egypt with goats and sheep and cigarettes they had bought for a fraction of the usual cost. Shops on both sides sold out of their goods in a matter of hours, indicating how badly both economies were distorted by the hermetic separation enforced by Israel and the widely despised Mubarak regime in Cairo.

We continued walking until our view opened up to a white sand beach and an aquamarine sea fading to deep blue at the horizon. We joined hundreds of Palestinians, children bobbing in the shallows and

young men splashing and laughing in the waves or seining for min-
nows. It was the first time many of them had ever seen the sea, and the
younger ones were especially ecstatic.

After taking in this scene for several happy minutes, we hired a
cab to take us to one of the destroyed settlements. Caravans of trucks
and donkey carts met us on the road carrying anything of even mar-
ginal value that had been left behind in the settlements, including roof
tiles, sections of chain-link fence, pipes, wiring, rebar, doors, insula-
tion, siding, and chains. Israeli garbage was apparently rich pickings.
Some of the children on the donkey carts bore traces of deep poverty—
the kind that stunts growth. They had probably come from the nearby
refugee camps, where raw sewage runs down the middle of alleys and
the brackish drinking water causes major health problems. Or from
Mawasi, a formerly productive strip of land near the beach that for
many years had been locked away behind a ruinous checkpoint and a
string of Israeli settlements.

The settlements had until recently featured horse riding trails,
a tourist hotel, and a golf course. Now they looked like an upscale
version of the pulverized neighborhoods of Rafah. Bushes, trees, and
flower beds surrounded rubble-strewn wastes. A half-destroyed school
still had kids' paintings tacked up on the crumbling walls. Palestinian
policemen in blue camouflage uniforms watched as people had a curious look or hunted for anything of value. There wasn't much they could
do to prevent the looting. Turning arms against their own desperate
people for stripping illegal buildings on their own land would have
been devastating to their fragile popularity.

A feeling of hope and wonder hung in the air along with a faint,
alarming stench of toxic burning. It was hard to believe the occupation
might really be over, that people could roam their Gaza prison without
the terror of Israeli snipers, that they could finally repair their broken
and bullet-scarred houses without fear that the next wave of violence
would destroy everything again.

The next day, astoundingly, Nader and I were able to catch a taxi
directly to Gaza City in broad daylight. The trip took only half an hour.

The Abu Holi checkpoint had ceased to exist—as if that all-powerful obstruction had merely been a bad dream.

I found a gift shop and bought a commemorative mug with a picture of a dove and a Palestinian flag on it. The mug said, CONGRATU-LATIONS FOR THE EVACUATION OF GAZA . . . AND HOPEFULLY FOR THE WEST BANK . . . It was a lukewarm victory cheer, but I supposed Palestinians were used to taking what they could get.

Triumphant Palestinian flags flew everywhere, and Nader and I soaked it all in, a feeling of pressure being released, of hamsters being given a slightly bigger cage with fewer daily cruelties and a hope, however slim, that things would continue to improve.

It's heartbreaking now to remember how we felt standing there, holding our breath and hoping.

CHAPTER 12

The Last Ramadan

When you have had a glimpse of such a disaster as this . . .
the result is not necessarily disillusionment and cynicism.
Curiously enough the whole experience has left me with
not less but more belief in the decency of human beings.

—George Orwell, *Homage to Catalonia*

There was no time for rest or reflection when I returned home from Gaza. After two days of frenzied catch-up work, it was time to renew my fucking visa again.

Following a long weekend of borders and buses and pointless travel in Jordan, I arrived back at the Israeli border too tired to think. When the woman at passport control started questioning me, I mumbled something about an internship in Jerusalem.

"If you're not a tourist," she said, "I can only give you a two-week visa. You'll have to talk to the Ministry of the Interior if you want to stay longer."

I stared at her in dull disbelief. From what I'd heard about the Ministry, they would grill me to within an inch of my life and probably deny my request for a visa extension. If I went to another border instead, those guards would wonder why I had only gotten two weeks at the last border. They might follow suit and give me only two more weeks, or they might deport me altogether.

This one careless mistake might be the end of my life in Palestine.

The next day at work I was so delirious and miserable, I felt almost drunk. The thought of going through that border again in two weeks was more than I could bear. In a haze of desperation, I sprinkled water on my visa paper and tried to scratch off the part where the border guard had crossed out "3 months" and written in "2 weeks." When I was done it no longer clearly said "2 weeks." But it did look completely and deliberately mangled.

Brilliant. I'd gone from having a legitimate but inconvenient two-week visa to having no valid visa at all. My ears burned with the stupidity of what I had done.

As if things couldn't get worse, I looked at a calendar and realized Taybeh's First Annual October Fest was two weekends away. I had been looking forward to it for months. There'd be tours of graceful white churches, ancient hilltop ruins, and the brewery that made the famously unexpected beer. There'd be live music, dancing, and stalls with local arts and crafts, perfect for Christmas presents. Because of one woman's power trip, my fun-filled beer fest weekend would be replaced by another expensive, stressful visa trip and possible deportation.

I started having flu-like symptoms, but I was so far behind in my work I couldn't take any days off. Everything was infused thickly with the dread that these might be my last two sick, miserable weeks in beautiful Palestine. I didn't know whether to tie up all my affairs or not, whether to say tearful good-byes to good friends or not, whether to pack for a weekend or forever. I might be back in three days or I might be barred for the next five years. It was all up to the shrewdness and moods of the Israeli guards.

I kept thinking this kind of thing should be classified as a type of psychological torture.

I KNEW MY chances at the border would increase the less I looked like an activist. So I ironed my nicest clothes, put on makeup, let my hair down, and found a reasonably priced faux Louis Vuitton rolling carry-on bag to replace my beat-up backpack. As for the visa, I decided my best bet was simply telling the border guard I'd lost it.

At the northern crossing near Beit Shean, I clicked smartly across the linoleum to the passport control window in high heels and shiny lip gloss, my entrails sodden with dread.

"*Shalom*," I said brightly as I handed my passport to the neatly dressed and intelligent-looking woman behind the counter. "I'm really sorry, but I lost my—"

"Mmm . . ." She grabbed my passport and turned to her computer.

"Here, I have the Jordanian stamp to prove—"

"*Lo, lo.*"

"But I—"

"Pssh!"

"Can you—"

She waved her hand dismissively, tapped a few taps on her computer, stamped a visa paper, handed it to me, and said with friendly sarcasm, "Don't lose this."

I nodded, speechless. It was the easiest border crossing in my long and colorful history of them. I practically floated across the bridge to Jordan.

But by the time I got back to Ramallah, I felt like something was beginning to break in my psyche. So many thoughts, experiences, and emotions kept building up in my head like static electricity. There was never time to process anything before more piled on. I had no idea how Palestinians dealt with this year after year after year.

Besides, this break from routine had become a kind of routine in itself—constant death, destruction, and deadlock, writing article after article that told the same story over and over, and nobody listened and nothing changed. The only place I had any real leverage, as a U.S. citizen, was also the main power broker in this conflict: Washington, D.C. And I had a tremendous amount to learn about the machinations of power and the culture and motivations of Beltway insiders—a culture at least as inexplicable to me as that of the Middle East had been. I couldn't bear the thought of leaving Palestine. But it was time to shake things up again. It was time to do something even harder than leaving: going home.

I called Nick, who'd been thinking about leaving as well.

"I just got a three-month visa that expires in December," I told him. "Why don't we go to the Sinai then? There's this little backpackers' resort town called Dahab. It's right on the water. I can't really explain it, but I promise you'll love it. Then we can go home. What do you say?"

"Yeah," he said, sounding haggard and worn out. "I think it's about time."

Islamic Jihad vs. Hamas vs. Fatah

A few days later John and I met at Sinatra Café, a little cake shop run by Palestinians who'd lived in San Francisco for several years. The weather was mild and perfect. We chatted and watched the sun set as we shared divine homemade chocolate maple cakes. The hills faded to their sunset rose color, the sweeping views of green trees and white houses faded to dusk, and the sky fanned out in a glorious cloudless sunset rainbow. We drank it all in like sweet wine.

The next day we were hit simultaneously with Ramadan, winter, and daylight savings time—the trifecta of outdoor nightlife death.

Meanwhile, the aftermath of the Disengagement was starting to take shape. Although the settlers had cried and screamed and protested and carried on, in the end they had been evacuated and the sky had not fallen. No soldiers were killed, and only one settler died because she set herself on fire. Soon even Israelis were making fun of the weeping, wailing, posturing settlers. One popular cartoon showed a traffic cop pulling over a speeding Israeli driver. Imitating the settlers (who kept wailing, "How can a Jew kick another Jew out of his home?"), the driver whined, "How can a Jew give another Jew a traffic ticket?"[1]

---

1. Kimberly Dozier, "Real surprise in Gaza yet to come," CBS News, August 26, 2005.

But all Israelis were waiting to see if the Gaza pullout would pay off in terms of bringing them more security. If it didn't, there would be little political will for a similar pullout from the West Bank, unilateral or otherwise.

At the same time, Palestinians were waiting to see if Sharon's plan was indeed a smoke screen for continued settlement expansion in the West Bank, as his advisor Dov Weisglass had said, delaying negotiations indefinitely, and turning Gaza into an open-air prison.

All in all, between the ceasefire at Sharm al Sheikh and the end of 2005, Islamic Jihad was responsible for four suicide bombings and the deaths of 31 Israelis, nearly all civilians. Fatah's Al Aqsa Martyrs Brigades killed 7 civilians and a soldier. Hamas killed one Israeli civilian. And Israeli soldiers killed 130 Palestinians, including 35 children.

The Shin Bet, Israel's internal security and intelligence service, credited the sharp decline in violence in 2005 to the truce and Hamas's desire to enter the political arena. The Shin Bet admitted that the Wall was "no longer mentioned as the major factor in preventing suicide bombings, mainly because the terrorists have found ways to bypass it. The fence does make it harder for them, but the flawed inspection procedures at its checkpoints, the gaps and uncompleted sections enable suicide bombers to enter Israel." The main reason for the drop in attacks was "the fact that Hamas, in general, stopped engaging in terror activities . . . Its focus on the political arena and the preparations for the Palestinian parliamentary elections have limited its active involvement in terror to a large extent."[2]

The army had already admitted to the Israeli High Court that the Wall had been routed based on settlement development plans. Now the internal security service was claiming the Wall was not an effective security measure anyway. It appeared Yusif's words back in

---

2. Amos Harel, "Shin Bet: Palestinian Truce Main Cause for Reduced Terror," *Haaretz*, January 2, 2006. Of the seventy-five Israeli soldiers who died on duty in 2005, thirty-three of them committed suicide. Most of the rest died of traffic accidents and illnesses. See: Gideon Alon, "Fewer Officers to be Armed as Suicide Becomes IDF's Top Killer," *Haaretz*, December 14, 2005.

2003 had been correct: The Wall's purpose was more about annexing land than about security.

Ahmed's Heart

On the first day of the post-Ramadan Eid al Fitr holiday, a twelve-year-old boy named Ahmed Khatib in the Jenin Refugee Camp woke up before his brothers and sisters to help his mother make tea.

"He always tried to help me because he felt sorry for me having to do all the housekeeping and cooking," said his mother, Abla.

Then he dressed up in his new holiday clothes and headed to the mosque.

Three years earlier, Ahmed had witnessed the destruction of the heart of the Jenin Refugee Camp by the Israeli army, which left at least fifty-nine Palestinians dead. Now, on the first day of the holiday, when rambunctious kids were enjoying their break from school, excited about new toys and clothes and special meals and holiday spirit, the Israeli army invaded again. Ahmed was with a group of boys, and one of them handed him a plastic toy gun.

The next thing his parents knew, someone arrived at their door telling them that Ahmed had been shot in the back of the head and the pelvis. When his mother arrived at the hospital, she knew her son wouldn't survive for long.

"His body was full of fragments," she said. "Part of his brain was on his clothes. Did they have to shoot him twice? Couldn't they just have shot him in the leg?"

As their son lay dying in an Israeli hospital in Haifa, Ahmed's parents made an agonizing decision. As heartbroken as they were, they believed some good should come of their tragedy. So they donated the boy's organs for transplant. Within hours Ahmed's heart, kidneys, liver, and lungs were transplanted into six Israelis, five of them children and four of them Jewish.

"To give away his organs was a different kind of resistance," said his mother. "Violence against violence is worthless. Maybe this will reach the ears of the whole world so they can distinguish between just and unjust. Maybe the Israelis will think of us differently. Maybe just one Israeli will decide not to shoot."[3]

Dinner with a Suicide Bomber's Family

A few nights later, as I was walking home from work, I ran into an older gentleman with watery eyes and a big grey moustache named Abu Zaid. I knew him from one of the shops I frequented. He had invited me to harvest olives on his land several times, and I felt bad because I'd never had time. This time my evening happened to be free, and when he invited me to dinner with his family, I happily accepted.

He drove me to his house and introduced me to his charming wife and one of his daughters, Noura. She had a pretty face and a long, sleek ponytail, and she spoke English with an American accent. When I asked about her accent, she said, "I used to work in Florida!"

She talked chirpily for several minutes about how much she'd loved living in Florida and working as a receptionist in a hotel there. When she finally took a breath, I asked, "So why'd you come back?" I expected an answer along the lines of, "Oh, I just realized I loved Palestine more."

Instead she froze. An empty look crept across her face.

"Well . . ." she said slowly. "I came home for a visit one time, and I was watching the news with my family, and we . . ." Her voice faltered. "We saw that my brother Zaid had . . . exploded himself." She looked at me pleadingly, as if hoping I would tell her it was a ridiculous idea, that surely it hadn't really happened. I didn't know what to say. She sighed and looked down. "It changed everything in my family. After this I never wanted to leave home again."

I looked up the bombing later. It had taken place in a settlement and wounded several people but not killed anyone other than Zaid. Hamas claimed responsibility. I'd been calling Noura's father "Abu Zaid" all this time without even wondering who Zaid was. Now I knew.

3. Chris McGreal, "Ahmed's Gift of Life," *The Guardian*, November 11, 2005.

"My brother used to laugh and joke," Noura said wistfully. "He was very outgoing. But as things got worse, he changed. We used to live in a house near a settlement, and sometimes the Israelis would fire on our neighborhood. It was easy to tell the difference between the Palestinian fire—*tck tck tck*—and the Israeli fire—*BOOM BOOM*. One time our friend Abu Ibrahim from Hebron, his house seemed to be the target of intense fire. My brother came back from the mosque, and he looked very strange. He was afraid for Abu Ibrahim. Later we learned that Abu Ibrahim had been killed." Noura shook her head. "My mom used to comfort my brother when these things happened. This time it was my brother who comforted my mom.

"Things were also bad for him during university. He couldn't get past the Surda checkpoint to get to Bir Zeit most of the time. One time at Surda he saw Israeli soldiers push a blind man down in the rain and force him to walk over the mountains above the checkpoint alone. It made my brother cry. He felt so helpless. But the worst thing was . . ." She took a deep breath. "My brother used to paint houses, and he had a boss who was one of the best people he knew. He was always honest and good in his dealings. He never overworked or underpaid his employees. And he had an eight-year-old son who he loved so much."

She sighed sadly. "One time he was painting his son's room, so his son was on his parents' bed playing with toys. A sniper from the Psagot settlement shot him in the head through the window and killed him. When my brother saw on Al Jazeera what had happened, he was crying very loudly. This time mother had to comfort him. After this he didn't seem normal . . ."

Noura looked down. "Sometimes I am OK. But it's different for moms. My mother can never hear my brother's name without crying." Her face hardened. "I hate Hamas. They take pure people willing to sacrifice for a just cause and manipulate them. My brother wasn't thinking straight. He wasn't himself. And they ask him to do something like this . . ."

Suddenly we heard from the kitchen, "*Yalla ya binat, al akel jahez!*"

Noura's face changed, brightened, as if she had put her anger and sadness away for another time. "Oh, the food's ready! Come, you'll see, my mother is an amazing cook . . ."

SETTLER LOGIC

Kyle, an ex-wrestler friend from Stanford with blue eyes and red hair, was passing through Israel on his way home from travels in India in mid-November and asked if he could drop by. I told him I didn't have any vacation days left, but I still had weekends and a few places I wanted to visit before I left Palestine, and he was welcome to come along.

I'd been itching to visit a settlement called Elon Moreh on a hilltop northeast of Nablus, and when he arrived, I suggested we start there. Elon Moreh's "administrative district" is three times larger than its built-up area, and the Area C land around Elon Moreh is many times bigger still. I couldn't help but wonder what the view looked like from up there. Was it possible, from that distance, to blind oneself to the humanity of Palestinians?

Kyle and I made our way to the Jerusalem Central Bus Station and caught a settler bus back up north to Elon Moreh. Our contact was an American settler named David. I had found his number on a settlement website and told him we were Christian Zionists[4] who'd read about Jews being evicted from Gaza and wanted to see what life was like in the settlements that were still standing.

I was surprised how run-down the settlement looked. The lawns were scrubby and unkempt, and the beige plaster on many homes was peeling under red-tiled roofs. The dusty streets were virtually deserted.

---

4. Christian Zionists are mostly American Evangelicals who believe Jews must control the entire Biblical "Land of Israel" so the Messiah can return. They represent a vocal and moneyed political constituency in America with strong ties to Congress and the White House. They oppose any compromise with Palestinians because they believe it might forestall the battle of Armageddon. For more information about Christian Zionists, their ideology, and their influence on American foreign policy, see this astonishing article: Jane Lampman, "Mixing Prophecy and Politics," *The Christian Science Monitor*, July 7, 2004.

David, a man in his sixties with a white beard and *kippah*, met us in the street in front of his house. He greeted us, not with smiles and warm welcomes and invitations to tea and dinner as a Palestinian would, but merely with a wary nod. He didn't seem to know what to do with us, so I suggested we walk to a vista point where we could take in the surrounding countryside. We saw Nablus spread out below us, which he referred to by its Biblical name, Shechem.

Curiosity overcame prudence, and the first question I asked was, "What do you think about the Arabs?" I was careful not to say "Palestinians." Many settlers don't acknowledge their existence as a people, and simply saying *Palestinian* can get you branded as a "leftist."

He shrugged. "The best option is obviously to persuade them to leave peacefully. They have fourteen Arab countries they can live in. Why do they have to live here? But as far as I'm concerned, they're welcome to stay as long as they accept that they're living on Jewish land and stay in their areas and don't cause trouble or demand any privileges."

"Kind of like putting them in Indian reservations?" I suggested.

"Yes," he said without hesitation. "I think America has the right idea."

Kyle and I shot each other a sideways glance.

"So what brought you to Elon Moreh?" Kyle asked.

"I used to live in New York," he said. "But I'd wake up every morning and look in the mirror and feel that I wasn't where I belonged. When I came here . . ." He looked around and pointed at a random stone. "You see that rock? I belong to that rock, and that rock belongs to me. This is my home. This is where I belong."

When it was time to go, he handed us envelopes and told us how we could send a donation if we liked. As we prepared to leave, I realized I hadn't planned an exit strategy. We were going to Nablus next, so it seemed absurd to take a settler bus all the way to Jerusalem and then take Palestinian buses and service taxis all the way back up to Nablus. That would be a trip of a hundred miles and more than four hours to get to a place that was just down the hill from where we were standing. Yet we couldn't simply walk into Nablus. The settlers would want to know why we were passing their security perimeter on foot, and the Palestinians would wonder why we were approaching from a settlement. We'd run a risk of being arrested, kidnapped, or shot.

Then I remembered a traffic circle called the Tapuach Junction where settler roads and Palestinian roads intersected. I asked David what was the best way to get there.

He seemed to have warmed to us a bit by then, and he told us kindly, "My daughter is going to Tel Aviv soon. She can drop you off there."

His daughter was a pretty young woman named Miriam with straight brown hair and an appealing Hebrew accent. She'd obviously been raised there, unlike her father, whose accent was pure Brooklyn. After another round of thanks and farewell, she drove us down the hill and through a Palestinian village.

Kyle said in surprise, "You feel safe driving through the West Bank like this?"

"It's OK," she said. "They don't cause us too many problems anymore."

"But there was violence before, right?" I asked innocently. "Why was that?"

"I don't know!" She seemed genuinely surprised. "When I was a kid, the Arabs would clean our houses and work in our yards and build things for us, and everything was fine. Then they started blowing themselves up in our buses and cafés, you know? They even kill children. It's crazy. I don't understand it."

"So it's not strange driving through the West Bank like this?" Kyle asked again.

"I mean, at first it was weird to see Arabs picking olives and working in the fields and that kind of thing." She shrugged. "But now I am used to it."

Kyle and I glanced at each other again. It was frighteningly easy from the settlers' point of view to see Palestinians merely as dangerous and unwanted elements of the landscape who occasionally caused problems, not as human beings with jokes and dreams and families and pain every bit as real as their own. One of the biggest threats to peace all over the world is how people get so identified with the stories in their heads, they become unwilling or unable to deal with reality as it actually occurs.

Miriam dropped us off at the junction with a kind good-bye. Other than her strange ideology and selective blindness, I liked her. It was sad that we couldn't be honest with her—that if we were, she would probably think we were brainwashed, or worse. I wished there were a way to bridge the divide. It seemed increasingly impossible.

The traffic circle was also a major checkpoint manned by soldiers and Jeeps. Two dozen settlers were waiting for buses and a group of Palestinians were waiting for service taxis within twenty yards of each other. My ears burned as we gingerly passed from the amorphous "Israeli" bus stop area to a group of Palestinians waiting for taxis. No one seemed to notice our deviant behavior.

Once we were safely in Nablus, Kyle said in amazement, "I can't believe how 'normal' everything is! I mean, settlers driving through Palestinian villages, Palestinians standing next to settlers waiting for taxis . . . I thought these people hated each other."

"Well, they don't exactly love each other," I said. "But they've been living side by side for a long time. Before the Intifada, lots of Israelis shopped in Palestinian towns because it was cheaper. You can still see Hebrew signs in some of the villages where Israelis used to shop. Now settlers and Palestinians have learned to ignore each other for the most part and go about their business as if the other didn't exist. Except when they're attacking each other." I sighed. "It's bizarre, I know."

I pointed out a group of black tents on a hilltop northwest of Elon Moreh. "That's a settlement outpost," I said. "It's a type of unauthorized settlement expansion." I told him the Israeli government officially opposes the outposts, but it usually tolerates them and provides security, infrastructure, and ex post facto authorization. On the rare occasions when they do dismantle an outpost, the settlers usually return and build again. About 100 outposts and 130 authorized settlements are scattered throughout the West Bank.

"How do they justify all of this?" asked Kyle.

I told him about the beginnings of the settlement enterprise shortly after the 1967 war when the Israeli government started building settlements along the Jordan Valley and on hilltops they considered militarily strategic. The most heavily populated areas in Israel—the coastal plains to the west and the Galilee to the north—are fairly flat, while the West Bank is hilly. Aside from its rich Biblical history and important water resources, the West Bank is a valuable strategic asset. Even secular Israelis tend to think of the West Bank as historically Jewish land, and they're told the settlements are built on "public land" or land that was purchased legally. Many Israelis today were born or immigrated to the country after 1967 and don't even know where the Green Line is. I told Kyle that my Russian-Israeli friend Dan had showed me the map he bought when he first moved here. It didn't have the Green Line on it. The only indication that Palestinians existed at all was that the 17 percent of the West Bank designated as Area A, which Israelis aren't allowed to visit, was shaded in grey.

"The settlements just look like part of Israel, and no one goes out of their way to set anyone straight," I said. "Israelis tend to think of them as suburbs or bedroom communities, not illegal colonies."

By now the settlers had become a major political force in their own right. According to Jewish journalist Amos Elon, "It is not difficult to imagine what the settlers' lobby means in a country with notoriously narrow parliamentary majorities. Though 70 percent of Israeli voters say in the polls that they support abandoning some of the settlements, 400,000 settlers and their right-wing and Orthodox supporters within Israel proper now control at least half the national vote. They pose a constant threat of civil war if their interests are not fully respected. At their core is a group of fanatical nationalists and religious fundamentalists who believe they know exactly what God and Abraham said to each other in the Bronze Age."[5]

---

5. Amos Elon, "Israelis & Palestinians: What Went Wrong?" *The New York Review of Books*, December 19, 2002.

The office of Prime Minister Ariel Sharon had recently published a report by Talia Sasson on government involvement in the establishment of unauthorized settlement outposts. The Sasson Report revealed corruption and misappropriation at the highest levels. Pro-settler politicians fought to control key ministries such as Construction and Housing, National Infrastructure, and Transportation so they could direct money to settlements.[6] The Housing Ministry had supplied four hundred mobile homes for outposts on private Palestinian land. "As far as law enforcement is concerned," Sasson wrote, "the political echelon sends a message of no enforcement when it comes to the [Palestinian] territories. Felons are not punished. The overall picture draws the conclusion that no one seriously wants to enforce the law."[7]

But one had to wonder: What was the settlers' endgame? Did they think the Palestinians would simply vanish one day or acquiesce to living in ghettos forever?

Israeli justice minister Tommy Lapid told American journalist Jeffrey Goldberg, "They believe there will come a point in the critical clash between us and the Palestinians when it would come time to transfer the Palestinians to Jordan; the second thing they hope for is the great American *aliyah*—a million more Jews coming to Israel. The third, and by far the most stupid, thing is that they believe God will help them."[8]

As much as the settlers live in a fantasy world, their takeover of the Israeli agenda comes at a very real price. It costs billions of dollars to build, maintain, and secure settlements, while serious housing shortages and poverty exist in Israel.[9] No one knows just how

---

6. "No One Knows Full Cost of Israel's Settlement Ambitions," *USA Today*, August 14, 2005.
7. Talia Sasson, "Summary of the Opinion Concerning Unauthorized Outposts," Office of the Israeli Prime Minister, March 10, 2005.
8. Jeffrey Goldberg, "Among the Settlers: Will They Destroy Israel?" *The New Yorker*, May 31, 2004.
9. The poverty rate in Israel is one of the highest in the developed world at roughly 20 percent. The poverty rate of Holocaust survivors is even higher, at approximately 30 percent. See: "NGOs: One out of every Three Holocaust Survivors Lives in Poverty," *Haaretz*, September 11, 2009.

many billions because "much of the building was financed through winks and nods, an opaque state budget and secret military spending that in some cases violated Israel's laws and undercut international peacemaking efforts. Among the methods used . . . were government subsidies, shadowy land deals, loopholes in military spending, and an auditing bait-and-switch in which U.S. aid was used to free up billions of dollars for spending on the settlements formally opposed by the United States."[10]

But perhaps the greatest cost is that it makes peace increasingly impossible. An editorial in *Haaretz* stated:

> The settlements put up in the heart of Samaria [the
> northern West Bank], including Ofra, Elon Moreh and
> Kedumim . . . were scattered throughout the heart of
> the Palestinian area to prevent any political agreement.
> Building a security fence around those settlements . . .
> broadening their jurisdictions without consideration while
> chopping down olive groves and stealing private property
> shows that the need to be generous in withdrawal and
> the future settlement to enable the Palestinians to live
> honorably on their land has not been fully grasped yet on
> Israel's side . . . All the harassment of the Palestinians in
> this interim period, harming their source of livelihood,
> their lands, homes and freedom of movement, will only
> sow more hatred. Ultimately, no separation fence route
> will be able to defend Israel from that hatred.[11]

"So eventually all the Jews will have to be kicked out of the West Bank," Kyle said. "It's either that or there will never be peace?"

I thought for a moment. "No. The problem has never been whether

---

10. "No One Knows Full Cost of Israel's Settlement Ambitions," *USA Today*, August 14, 2005.
11. "The Battle for the 'Fingernails,'" *Haaretz*, April 20, 2005.

or not Jews can live here. I know a Jewish Israeli woman who lives in Ramallah with her Palestinian husband. Another Jewish friend married a Muslim from Jayyous. An Israeli journalist named Amira Hass has lived in Ramallah and Gaza City. If Jews want to come and buy land and live under the same laws as Palestinians, they're as welcome as anyone else. The problem isn't religion. It's the systematic injustice of what's going on."

OUR LAST STOP was Jayyous. We joined Qais and Shadi and their grey-eyed mechanic cousin, Karim, for a *nargila* on the porch as we watched the sun sink into the Mediterranean. I knew it would be the last time I would see them for a long time. My eyes stung whenever I thought about it, so I tried not to think and just enjoyed these last hours.

I asked Qais how his mother was. He said she was better but she still had some paralysis on one side. I asked if I could say hello to her, and Qais led me into the house. She was sitting in the living room watching television. She smiled crookedly when she saw me. Her family had been so kind to me, and I wanted to express how much that had meant to me. I took her hand, and we smiled through tears. She nodded, and I nodded, and all was understood.

I went to Rania's house next to say good-bye. Rania would go on to graduate from college, marry a man from Tulkarem, and have two beautiful children, a boy and a girl. The girl would be born while her husband was serving a one-year sentence in an Israeli jail, though he was guilty of nothing.[12]

LEAVING RAMALLAH
I arrived at my office the next day to the news that Captain R, the Israeli soldier who had killed thirteen-year-old Iman al Hams in October 2004 and then pumped her body full of bullets, had been

---

12. Pamela Olson, "An Arrest on the West Bank," *Mondoweiss*, August 20, 2009.

cleared of all charges. Captain R's defense claimed that "confirming the kill" was standard Israeli military practice.

After the verdict was announced, Iman's father said in disbelief, "This was the cold-blooded murder of a girl. The soldier murdered her once and the court has murdered her again. What is the message? They are telling their soldiers to kill Palestinian children."[13]

It was predictable that an Israeli soldier would not be punished for killing a Palestinian civilian. But this was the most clear-cut case imaginable. And they didn't even bother to slap him with light or symbolic charges. It was a profoundly depressing punctuation mark on my year and a half of reporting from Palestine.

I WORKED LIKE crazy during my last few weeks to find my replacement, get everything ready for her, and tie up all loose ends. Some friends from the PLO Negotiations Affairs Department took me to Sangria's to celebrate my last day of work. The owner joined us. Everyone was talking about the Palestinian Legislative Council elections, which had finally been scheduled for January (with a strong push from the Bush Administration despite Fatah's misgivings). All the parties were scrambling to find their footing with the voters.[14]

The owner said half jokingly, "If Hamas wins, *khalas*, I will have to find another line of work."

We laughed, but in some ways we were genuinely concerned. After Hamas won municipal elections in Qalqilia, they'd done very little except to cancel an international folk festival because it featured mixed men and women dancing. This hurt Qalqilia's economy and alarmed people all over Palestine.

Yet such was the near orgiastic hatred of Fatah—who had done virtually nothing to end corruption and certainly hadn't made any headway toward good-faith negotiations with Israel—that by the last

---

13. Chris McGreal, "Not Guilty. The Israeli Captain who Emptied his Rifle into a Palestinian Schoolgirl," *The Guardian*, November 16, 2005.

14. All except Islamic Jihad, who weren't running because they knew they would lose. They were well aware that only conflict kept them relevant and gave them any power or legitimacy.

vote in December, Hamas surprised even Hamas by winning full or partial control of councils in most major towns and cities, including, most shockingly, Bethlehem.[15]

Hamas was running on a platform of ending corruption and stopping chaos and lawlessness in the territories, as well as the old standbys—health care, education, and infrastructure. Their slogan was "Change and Reform," not "Islamism and Violence." They knew there was little support in Palestine for an Islamic state, and people were desperately weary of violence. Though Hamas's moderate wing was quieter than its more belligerent wing, it was manifestly there. Even Sheikh Yassin, before he was assassinated, had talked favorably of ending violence if Israel withdrew from the West Bank and Gaza and honored a truce for a hundred years. It was a face-saving way to end the conflict without officially surrendering. By the time a hundred years had passed, Hamas likely wouldn't exist anymore.

In an interview with *Haaretz*, Hamas leader Dr. Mahmoud Zahar was asked what he would consider an achievement in the January elections.

"We will be happy with any result," he replied, "but elections without fraud are a good basis for the future. We are prepared to be a strong opposition."[16]

Little did any of us know that Hamas would win 44.5 percent of the popular vote in January—enough to defeat Fatah's 41.5 percent and take over the Palestinian Legislative Council outright. A stunned world, not understanding the evolving dynamics of Palestinian politics, would assume the Palestinians had voted for terrorism and refuse to recognize the new government. This would precipitate a series of numbing disasters, beginning with closures and sanctions aimed at punishing the Palestinian people for their democratic choice, which would decimate the last remnants of Gaza's economy and evolve into a strangulating siege. The siege would tighten after Hamas captured an

---

15. In the second round of local elections in May, Hamas had won handily in Jayyous as well.
16. Arnon Regular, Nir Hasson, and Aluf Benn, "Mohammed Zahar: No Truce Beyond 2005 if PA Reneges on January Elections," *Haaretz*, October 31, 2005.

Israeli soldier named Gilad Shalit in the summer of 2006 to bargain for the release of thousands of Palestinian prisoners.

Then in the summer of 2007, "President Bush, Condoleezza Rice, and Deputy National-Security Adviser Elliott Abrams backed an armed force under Fatah strongman Mohammed Dahlan, touching off a bloody civil war in Gaza and leaving Hamas stronger than ever."[17] Hamas would end up violently taking over the Gaza Strip, which gave Fatah free rein to attack Hamas in the West Bank, leaving the territories estranged and divided.

In the last days of the Bush presidency, Israel would bomb Gaza to pieces in another attempt to stop Qassam rocket fire and try to punish and weaken Hamas. The campaign, dubbed Operation Cast Lead, destroyed thousands of homes, schools, businesses, and mosques and killed 1,400 Gazans, most of them civilians, including 320 children. What it did not do was weaken Hamas or end the Qassam threat.

In all of 2006–2009, 54 Israeli civilians (including 8 children) and 29 Israeli soldiers would be killed. In the same period, nearly 3,000 Palestinians would be killed—more than the population of my hometown of Stigler, Oklahoma—including 632 children. Despite the stunning drop in Israeli casualties (which reached a sharp peak in 2002 and was in the low single digits by 2009), the rate of Palestinian deaths was slightly greater in 2006–2009 than it was during the height of the second Intifada in 2001–2004.[18]

There would be no hope, and nothing new, for many years—not until the culmination of several threads of awareness-building and activism would begin to turn the global Boycott, Divestment, and Sanctions campaign into a force to be reckoned with.[19]

As IF TO mock my decision to leave, the weather turned gorgeous after Ramadan, an Indian summer. Ziryab's fireplace was warmly lit on

---

17. David Rose, "The Gaza Bombshell," *Vanity Fair*, April 2008.
18. Sources: B'Tselem and the Israeli Ministry of Foreign Affairs.
19. See, for example: Naomi Klein, "Enough. It's Time for a Boycott," *The Guardian*, January 10, 2009. See also: www.bdsmovement.net and www.whoprofits.org.

breezy nights, and the beer once again flowed like wine. A new restaurant called Al Makan (The Place) opened in Ramallah. Its white stone terrace enclosed a fountain, tasteful wall displays of stone, wrought iron, pottery and flowers, and two graceful olive trees that just brushed the ceiling. The trees and walls were hung with old-fashioned lamps, the *nargilas* were smooth, and the food was excellent.

I couldn't wait to get home and see friends and family. And I was anxious to find out what new lessons I could learn in the world's most powerful capital. But I was definitely in love with Ramallah. There's nowhere in the world quite like it.

I was in a kind of denial about the fact that I was leaving Palestine. I knew I'd break down if I went around saying good-bye to everyone. I wouldn't even be able to hold it together if I said good-bye to the guy who sold me my cappuccinos every afternoon. So I left quietly one day, taking my memories and lessons with me, packed securely in my heart where no soldier could pull them out and examine them, pass judgment or confiscate them.

SINAI REFLECTIONS

Nick and I made our way to the Sinai in the first week of December. After a late lunch in Dahab we set out on the camel trail to the Bedouin village in the north. I couldn't wait to return to the place where Dan and I had spent such wondrous times two years before, and to show Nick the galaxy over the gulf.

One odd thing about the eastern shore of the Sinai is that you never really see the sun set. The mountains to the west gobble up the sun long before it hits the horizon, and the day fades lazily away without anyone really noticing. The sun was behind the mountains, but not down yet, when the translucent, almost-full moon rose over the dusty rolling Saudi mountains in a hazy pale pink and blue sky.

As the twilight deepened and the moon began to shine more confidently, its reflection on the silky calm gulf waters took my breath away. Gently, brilliantly, the soft white moonlight glittered off the clear aquamarine gulf and shone like a spotlight on one area in the middle, like a stage where spirits dance. The reflection trailed in a shimmering line toward us like a path.

The Sinai is a haunted place, in the best sense of the word. I have no trouble believing someone named Moses once felt a great presence here.

The moon climbed higher as we made our way north until the Bedouin camp came into sight. We approached a group of four men sitting on mats on the beach. They motioned for us to join them and offered us tea. We sat with them and looked toward Dahab. The mountains vanished to a point where the lights of Dahab softly glowed, where the sea, sky, and mountains met. Two years ago I'd been here during the new moon. Now the moon was nearly full. When I closed my eyes and then opened them, my old memory was replaced by the present scene, with a bright moon lighting up the hills and changing all the colors.

We found a hut facing the gulf, and the Bedouin owner prepared a reasonably priced fish and rice dinner for us. As we ate, looking at the dark water and the bright stars by the light of two candles, Nick said reverently, "When you described this place, I assumed it was some kind of tourist trap. But now . . ." He looked around, as helpless as I was to put it into words.

AFTER TWO TIMELESS days, we walked back to Dahab, which came to feel like our own personal tropical island. Behind us was forbidding desert. Ahead of us, though the Saudi shore was only fifteen miles away, it might as well have been another planet. Palm trees, stars, flowers, cushions, a bonfire, red wine, and wild kittens were our nightly companions, with a soundtrack of Bob Marley and Pink Floyd.

One afternoon, sitting under the palm trees of our favorite open-air restaurant looking over the blue water, Nick seemed unusually quiet and pensive. I asked if something was bothering him. He hesitated, then sighed heavily. "I am not a happy camper, Pam."

"Why?"

"Well, I told you I was a Christian. I was. But it's all gone now. I feel like . . . There's no meaning. No morality. We're just lost in a jungle of guns and politicians. I don't want to be selfish or cynical, but the world almost demands it, you know?"

I sighed too. These were questions I'd been wrestling with since I lost my own faith when I was fifteen. My biggest fear had been that I would turn into an amoral monster. To my surprise, life had gone on pretty much as before. I experienced no sudden impulse to become a lying, covetous, idol-worshipping murderer. It took me a while to realize that the Bible was, after all, written by humans. Even if there was no God, something had prompted them to write it, some instinct that billions of people recognized and embraced.[20]

I later read about a study in which Israeli children were told the story of Joshua attacking the town of Jericho. Joshua's army "utterly destroyed all in the city, both men and women, young and old, oxen, sheep, and asses, with the edge of the sword . . . And they burned the city with fire, and all within it; only the silver and gold, and the vessels of bronze and of iron, they put into the treasury of the house of the Lord."

Sixty percent of the children approved of Joshua's actions.

But when a virtually identical story was told to other Israeli children, in which an ancient Chinese general sacked and destroyed cities and murdered their inhabitants because he dreamed a deity told him to, 75 percent of the children disapproved.[21]

It's scary to realize how easily we can be manipulated to justify immoral actions, even by books that claim to be moral guideposts. But the study also points toward hope. It suggests that tribally based immorality isn't innate; it has to be conditioned. And history is full of examples of people who managed to see beyond their conditioning. Even in the most indecent of times, you always have whistleblowers and dissidents and people who choose to behave with decency. No

20. See Marc Hauser's book, *Moral Minds: How Nature Designed Our Universal Sense of Right and Wrong*, to learn about one fascinating theory of a universal "moral grammar" imprinted in us by evolution. For an overview see: Josie Glausiusz, "Discover Interview: Is Morality Innate and Universal?" *Discover Magazine*, May 10, 2007.
21. Paul Vallely, "Faith & Reason: How Joshua Claimed a 20th-Century Victim," *The Independent*, December 13, 1997.

matter how deep my anger or grief, the main thing that kept me from feeling or doing anything too extreme was the shame I would feel when so many Palestinians were maintaining their humanity, their ability to love and not to hate, under such unimaginable circumstances.

I asked Nick what precisely had done him in.

"I'm an idealistic person," he said. "I'm the kind who's willing to put myself on the line for my beliefs. And if I'd been born in Nablus, I definitely would have defended my city. Which means I'd probably be dead by now. If I'd been raised on Messianic Judaism, I might be one of those dudes on the hilltops. I could see myself doing what any of these people are doing if only I believed strongly enough."

He sighed again. "But what's really depressing is that the rest of the people, the ones who try to live with integrity, whose 'beliefs' are all about peace and fairness . . . It seems like they're basically suckers. They're history's losers." He stared into the middle distance, his eyes losing focus as he considered the full implications of what he'd just said.

"That's true up to a point," I said. "But one thing that's different about the modern age is that we no longer have to accept this as inevitable. People are becoming more sophisticated, more aware of what's happening and why. They're starting to realize they have choices other than to suffer in silence. Individual human consciences have more power than they've ever had in the history of humankind. We just need to figure out how to organize and use this power effectively. Once people figure this out, weapons and real estate aren't going to be enough to protect the powerful. We can either take from this a siege mentality that guarantees endless conflict or figure out a new way to relate to the world."

"Don't you think it's a tad racist to expect America or Israel to behave better than anyone else does when they get power?" he asked. "Every empire oversteps and declines. It's the nature of things."

I shook my head. Nick seemed to be wearing his cynicism like a Boy Scouts badge he'd earned by living in Nablus for a year. It's true that your childhood dreams are expected to die at some point. You're supposed to learn to bow to inevitability, however it is defined in your time, or risk being ridiculous. As if "growing up" were a matter of witnessing cruelty and madness and finding ways to rationalize and accept them.

But the Realist worldview—that what *is*, is the best we can do— seems inherently lazy to me. When I look at history, at the Spanish Inquisitions or the slave trade, I admire the people at the time who said, "This is insane and cruel. We can and should do better than this," more than those who said, "This is insane and cruel. And here's why it's the best we can do and it's impossible to do anything better." The first is the voice of an active agent of history. The second is just storytelling, apologizing.

"Just because something's unprecedented doesn't mean it's impossible," I said. "For the first time in history we have international laws on the books as a rampart against barbarity.[22] The idea was unthinkable until very recently."

"International law didn't save the Darfurians," Nick said. "It didn't protect the Rwandans or the Tibetans."

"Or the Palestinians," I pointed out. "At least, not yet. But America is the most powerful country on earth. More than anyone else we have a chance to try to perfect these instruments. By ignoring and violating them, we're fulfilling our own prophecy that no one will take them seriously. Where will that leave us when we're not in a position of dominance anymore? Anyway, look, you don't have any cultural, national, racial, familial, or religious connection to the Palestinians. Yet you care about them. You care if they're treated badly. My parents did, too, once they saw what was going on. This is the most natural instinct in the world. It actually takes a lot of brainwashing and distortions and covering up of basic facts to keep people *from* caring about other people. It's the only way things like this occupation can be allowed."

He looked at the water again. I smiled fondly at his troubled profile. Nick could have gone straight to a law firm and lived in a nice suburb and been fine. But he was choosing a lonely life in a way, experiencing things

---

22. The Preamble to the Universal Declaration of Human Rights, to which Israel is a signatory, reads: "Whereas it is essential, if man is not to be compelled to have recourse, as a last resort, to rebellion against tyranny and oppression, that human rights should be protected by the rule of law."

most of his peers never would. The Holy Land brought out the best and the worst in people. It was inspiring and beautiful and terrifying and horrifying in equal measures. The absurd and the sublime constantly together. Like a giant Rorschach test, it was up to each of us which aspects we saw, which instincts we followed. Just like life, only compressed and made quick and urgent. This, I think, was one of the main reasons why we fell for it so hard. Because it never for a moment permitted us the luxury of forgetting.

In mid-December it was time for Nick and me to part. We caught a bus from Dahab to a town forty miles to the north called Nuweiba. From there he would catch a ferry to Jordan and fly home from Amman. I would continue on to Israel and catch my plane in Tel Aviv.

We were silent as our bus wound its way through the Precambrian Sinai Mountains. As usual in these most intense of times, there was nothing to say.

When we reached Nuweiba, he grabbed his backpack, smiled disconcertingly, and said, "See ya around, Pammy." I smiled, too, my head tilted back, not wanting to spoil the moment with any mawkishness.

And then he was gone.

I had known it would hurt. But I didn't expect it to hurt this much. It wasn't just him I was saying good-bye to. He was my last tie to the life I'd had in Palestine.

A woman a few seats in front of me must have overheard my broken sobbing. She leaned back and asked gently, "Are you OK? Do you need a doctor?"

"No," I hiccupped. "I'm fine, I just . . . said good-bye to someone."

She pursed her lips and nodded, the light of understanding in her eyes. Now she was my ally. If anyone else approached, she would wave them off and explain. I was left comfortably alone with my quiet storm of emotions.

Author's Note: More happened in these two years than could possibly fit in one book. To read the stories that were cut for reasons of length, and to view photographs of some of the people, places, and events portrayed in this book (along with links to all references cited), visit www.pamolson.org and click "Chapter Companions." You'll also find maps and suggestions for further reading and research.

Glossary of Terms

Abu: Arabic for "father." Parents are usually referred to as "Mother of" (Umm) and "Father of" (Abu) their firstborn son.

Abu Ammar: Yasser Arafat's nickname.

Abu Mazen: Mahmoud Abbas's nickname.

Ahlan wa sahlan: "Welcome!"

Al Mubadara: The Palestinian National Initiative, a political party founded in 2002 by Dr. Mustafa Barghouthi, Professor Edward Said, Dr. Haidar Abdel-Shafi, and Ibrahim Dakkak. Its platform is based on fighting corruption, building inclusive democratic governance, strengthening civil society, negotiating peace with Israel based on international law, and engaging in nonviolent resistance if Israel continues to violate international law.

Al Manara: Central traffic circle of Ramallah. The word means "lighthouse."

Al Quds: The Arabic name for Jerusalem. Means "The Holy [City]."

Allah: Arabic for "God" among both Muslims and Christians.

Allahu Akbar: "God is greater."

Al Aqsa Martyrs Brigades: An armed offshoot of Fatah.

B'Tselem: The Israeli Information Center for Human Rights in the Occupied Territories, a well-respected Israeli NGO that works tirelessly to expose human rights violations (www.btselem.org).

BDS: Boycott, Divestment, and Sanctions. On July 9, 2005, Palestinian civil society called on the international community to boycott, divest from, and sanction Israel until it complies with international law.

DCO: District Coordinating Office, the office responsible for coordinating security and humanitarian cooperation between Israelis and Palestinians.

Eid: Muslim holiday or festival.

Erez crossing: The main crossing point between Israel and the Gaza Strip.

Fatah: The dominant Palestinian faction of the PLO; the party of Yasser Arafat and Mahmoud Abbas. Fatah means "opening" or "beginning" but can also mean "victory" or "conquest." It is the backwards acronym for *Haraka al Tahrir al Falastini*, the Palestinian Liberation Movement.

Green Line: The border between the West Bank and Israel.

Habibi (f. habibti): "My beloved" or "darling."

Hajj: Pilgrimage to Mecca. Older people, whether they have made the pilgrimage or not, are often referred to as "Hajj" (f. Hajja) as an honorific.

Hamas: "Hamas" is the Arabic acronym for *Haraka al Muqawama al Islamiya*, or "Islamic Resistance Movement." It was founded in 1987 at the beginning of the first Intifada. Hamas means "zeal" in Arabic.

Hamdulillah: "Thanks to God."

Haraam: "Forbidden" in a religious sense, or generally something that seems wrong.

Haram al Sharif: "The Noble Sanctuary," a thirty-five-acre plaza that takes up one-sixth of the Old City of Jerusalem and is home to the Dome of the Rock, the most iconic structure in Jerusalem, and the Al Aqsa Mosque.

Hijab: Female head covering.

IDF: Israeli Defense Forces, which is what Israel calls its military.

Iftar: The sunset meal that breaks the day's fast during Ramadan.

Insha'Allah: "God willing."

Intifada: A word for "uprising" that literally means "shaking off." The first Intifada was a popular and largely nonviolent uprising by Palestinians against Israeli occupation that took place between 1987 and 1993. The second Intifada was much more militarized and took place between 2000 and 2005.

Islamic Jihad: A smaller, less powerful, and more militant faction than either Hamas or Fatah.

Kadima: An Israeli political party that split from Likud in order to proceed with the Gaza Disengagement. Likud was vehemently opposed to it.

Keffiya: Traditional Palestinian black-and-white checkered headscarf commonly worn by farmers and made famous by Yasser Arafat.

Khalas: "Enough," "Stop," or "That's it."

Kippah: A small round skullcap worn by religious Jews (plural: kippot). Also known as a yarmulke.

Knesset: Israeli parliament.

Kunafa: A warm, cheesy dessert covered in spiced shredded wheat, smothered in vanilla-citrus syrup, and topped with crushed pistachios.

Labor: Israel's principle left-of-center political party.

Likud: Israel's principle right-wing political party.

Mabrook: "Congratulations!"

Maqlouba: A casserole of baked chicken, fried cauliflower, and eggplant embedded in a mound of rice plumped with broth and cinnamon and spices. The word means "upside down," so named because of the way it's served.

Nakba: "Catastrophe," the Palestinian term for the war and ethnic cleansing of 1948 that led to Israel's creation.

Nargila: Palestinian word for "hookah."

Oud: "Lute," a twangy stringed instrument that can convey a vast range of mysterious emotions.

PA: Palestinian Authority.

Palestinian Legislative Council: Palestinian parliament.

PLO: Palestine Liberation Organization, founded in 1964 and widely recognized as the sole legitimate representative of the Palestinian people. It has enjoyed observer status at the United Nations since 1974 and is made up of several Palestinian political factions such as Fatah, the PFLP, and the DFLP.

Quran: Muslim holy book, also spelled "Koran."

Seder: The meals and rituals during the Jewish holiday of Passover (Pesach).

Settlement: An Israeli colony built on Palestinian lands occupied by Israel since 1967. Such colonies are illegal under international law, and this illegality has been affirmed by United Nations resolutions.

Shebab: "Youth" or "young men."

Sheikh: "Elder." Refers to someone wise and respected and/or a scholar of Islam.

Shukran: "Thank you."

Souq: "Market."

Temple Mount: The Jewish name for the Haram al Sharif, believed to be the former site of the First and Second Jewish Temples.

Umm: "Mother of."

UNRWA: United Nations Relief and Works Agency for Palestine Refugees in the Near East, charged with assisting, protecting, and advocating for Palestinian refugees in Jordan, Lebanon, Syria, and the Palestinian territories.

W'Allah: "By God," usually used to mean "Really," "Definitely," or "Seriously?"

Wadi Nar: "Valley of Fire," a remote road in a dry canyon used as a route to bypass Jerusalem since green-plated Palestinian cars aren't allowed to drive on Jerusalem roads.

Ya: A word that means you are speaking to the person addressed. Somewhat redundant but really nice and kind of poetic once you get used to it.

Yalla: "Let's go."

Maps

ISRAEL/PALESTINE REGION

TURKEY

NICOSIA

CYPRUS

SYRIA

Mediterranean Sea

BEIRUT

DAMASCUS

IRAQ

ISRAEL

JERUSALEM

AMMAN

CAIRO

JORDAN

SINAI

SAUDI ARABIA

EGYPT

Red Sea

N

0   100 mi

0   100 km

Israel and Occupied Territories

[RIGHT] The "Israel-expanded East Jerusalem boundary" is the area Israel illegally annexed in 1980. This annexation is not recognized as legitimate by the international community.

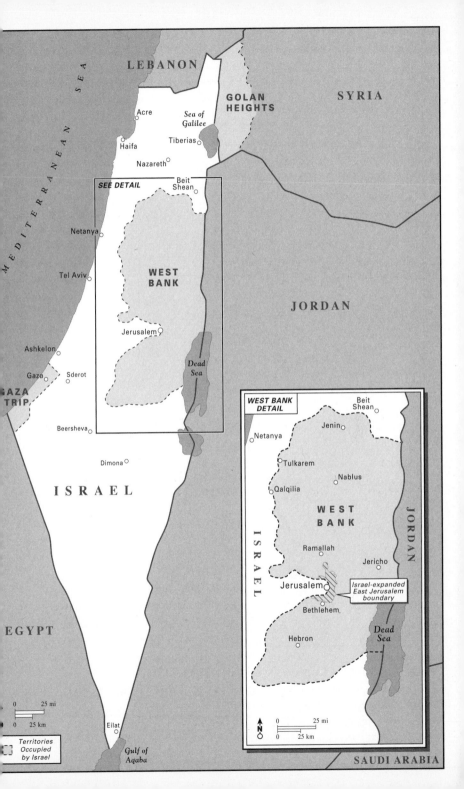

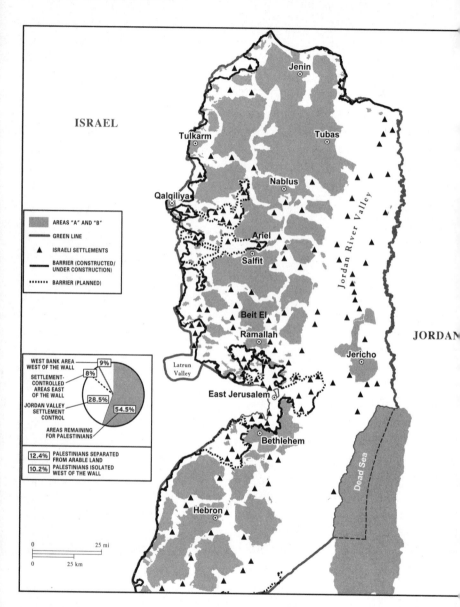

[ABOVE] For a detailed view of the cities, villages, and settlements in the West Bank and Areas A, B, and C, see B'Tselem's indispensable map [PDF] at bit.ly/g1b1af

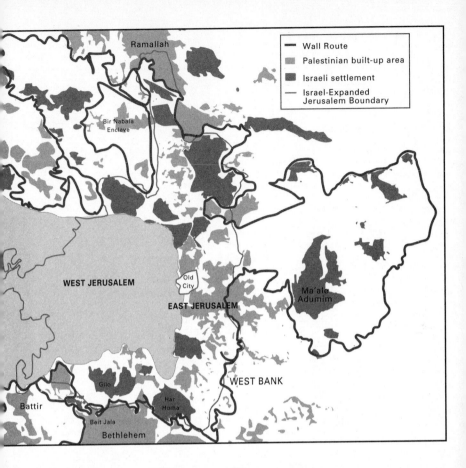

East Jerusalem Wall and Settlements

[ABOVE] The Wall weaves around to sever many Palestinian areas from East Jerusalem while seizing several settlements and large tracts of West Bank land. It also surround Bethlehem, isolates much of its land from its owners, and severs the ancient link between Bethlehem and its sister holy city Jerusalem.

The Ma'ale Adumim settlement (and the Wall around it) threatens to isolate East Jerusalem from the rest of the West Bank and to make travel between the northern and southern West Bank difficult. The Wall also separates several adjacent Palestinian neighborhoods from each other.

You can find a color version of this map here: fasttimesinpalestine.files.wordpress.com/2009/10/map9.png

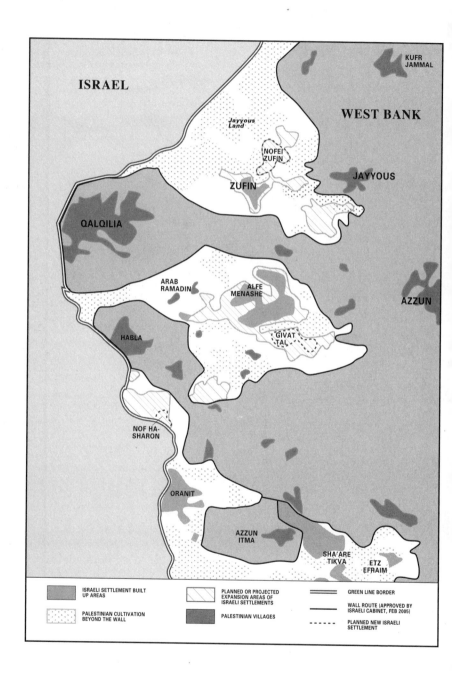

ISRAEL

WEST BANK

KUFR JAMMAL

Jayyous Land

NOFEI ZUFIN

ZUFIN

JAYYOUS

QALQILIA

ARAB RAMADIN

ALFE MENASHE

AZZUN

HABLA

GIVAT TAL

NOF HA-SHARON

ORANIT

AZZUN ITMA

SHA'ARE TIKVA

ETZ EFRAIM

	ISRAELI SETTLEMENT BUILT UP AREAS		PLANNED OR PROJECTED EXPANSION AREAS OF ISRAELI SETTLEMENTS	GREEN LINE BORDER
	PALESTINIAN CULTIVATION BEYOND THE WALL		PALESTINIAN VILLAGES	WALL ROUTE (APPROVED BY ISRAELI CABINET, FEB 2005)
				PLANNED NEW ISRAELI SETTLEMENT

WALL IN THE QALQILIA AND JAYYOUS AREA

[LEFT] A close-up of the Wall in the Qalqilia and Jayyous area. The Wall isolates most of Jayyous's land from its owners. A settlement called Zufin has already been built on that land, and another settlement called Nofei Zufin is planned. The Wall surrounding Qalqilia is a 25-foot-tall concrete structure punctuated by sniper towers.

According to the UN Relief and Works Agency, "Jayyous and neighbouring Falamyeh were well known for their intensively-irrigated agriculture which produced vegetables and citrus fruit, together with figs, apricots, loquats, mangoes and almonds. There are also thousands of olive trees... Four thousand trees were uprooted for the Barrier and 125 acres of land leveled. The Barrier isolates some 9,000 dunums, representing between 75 to 90 percent of its fertile land. Also isolated are 120 greenhouses belonging to Jayyous and Falamyeh and six water wells. Jayyous now shares water with Azzun from a well located between the two villages, which covers less than 50 percent of its needs, with water rationed to two hours per day in summer."

Source: "Profile of Jayyous—The West Bank Barrier," United Nations Relief and Works Agency for Palestine Refugees in the Near East (UNRWA), February 28, 2006.

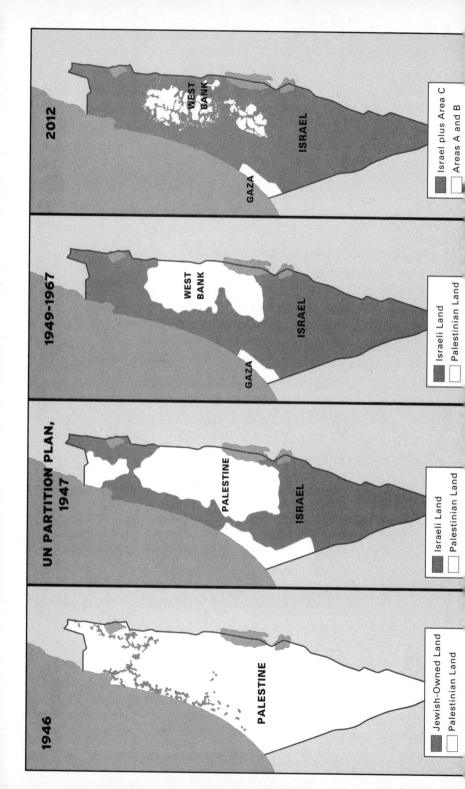

PALESTINIAN LOSS OF LAND, 1946–PRESENT

[LEFT] In 1946, Jewish residents of Palestine owned approximately 7% of the land and made up about one-third of the population (most of them fairly recent immigrants). In 1947, the UN proposed a partition plan in which 55% of the land would be given to Jewish sovereignty. The Palestinians and surrounding states refused, but they were no match for the well-armed and -organized Zionist forces. After a war in which 750,000 Palestinians fled or were expelled from their homes, the state of Israel was declared on the dark area in the third panel.

In 1967, Israel occupied the West Bank and Gaza. The white "islands" in the fourth panel show Areas A and B as delineated under the Oslo Accords of the 1990s. These areas represent the less than half of the West Bank that falls under even limited Palestinian control. Israel claims much of Area C (the remaining 60% of the West Bank) as Israeli territory, in contravention of international law, and continues to fill it with illegal settlements.

For larger, full-color versions of these maps and more, visit the maps page on my blog: wp.me/pExvW-2k

Acknowledgments

They say it takes a village to raise a child. The same is true, it turns out, for writing a book.

Thanks to Dan in Israel for his outstanding hospitality and exceptionally open mind, and to Fayez in Jordan for his humor and patience with a blank slate like me. Thanks to Yusif and Sebastian for letting me tag along and to the people of Jayyous—the mayor Abu Nael and his family, Amjad and Amir, Rania and her family, Qais and his family, and countless others—for taking me in. Thanks to Muzna, Dr. Barghouthi, and Yasmine in Ramallah for helping me find my footing in the big city and to John for the chats over cheesecake while watching the sunset at Pronto.

Many thanks to my lovely agent Helen Zimmermann for finding this book a perfect home, to Brooke Warner at Seal Press for believing in my book, and to Laura Mazer for midwifing it through to publication. Thanks also to my fabulous copyeditor, Kirsten Janene-Nelson, and my publicist, Natalie Nicolson. It's amazing to have such an all-star team behind this book!

But the book never would have made it this far without the people who were kind enough to make discerning comments about early drafts, including Amy, Emily, Holly, Nora, Anne, Pat, Ra'anan,

Ahmed, Leen, Tanya, Steve, Mali, Dan, Jeff, Drago, David, Dr. Dell, Miko, Patricia, Rush, Nafis, Kyle, Mom, Val, Rich, Ian, and Susan and Katie. And thanks for the warm welcome in New York from Nafis, Peter, Nora, Noor, Fadi, Phil, and Max.

I owe a special debt of gratitude to my parents, who were brave and open enough to visit me in the West Bank and supportive of this book from the very beginning. Thanks for all the books and for not letting me watch television until 7:00 PM when I was a kid.

I have to thank Mrs. McAdoo for forcing me to write in a journal every day in ninth grade. I haven't stopped since. And Patricia Ryan Madson of Stanford University, who taught Improvisation for Theater as a practicum in Taoism and changed my life profoundly. Thanks to Columbae, the Stanford Jujitsu Club, Michel, Magic, and Tony.

Thanks to Carl Sagan, Henry David Thoreau, Lao-tzu, and Keith Johnstone for helping me find my way back to the world and to myself and making me want to be a writer, if only to pay it forward just a little. Thanks for helping me find the will to follow my own path and the common sense not to be satisfied with unsatisfying explanations.

Thanks to Ahmed (again), Kevin, Tarin, Skye, JB, Dr. Woodson, Ali, Tony J, Caroline, Liz, Charlie, Tino, Maeve, Jon, Ben, Gudge, Nader, Hisham, Majed, FZ, Andy, Olivier, and Ronan.

I couldn't have done any of this without the humor, generosity, and grace showered upon me by the Palestinian people. From Gaza to Bethlehem, from Nablus to the Hebron, from Jayyous to Ramallah, you taught this self-centered, frightened, ignorant American so much about what it means to be a good person and find a pocket of peace in this mixed-up world. I don't have the vocabulary to describe what it means to me. I hope this book at least begins to explain.

For more people than I can name, more thanks than I can ever give.

About the Author

Pamela Olson grew up in small town Oklahoma and studied physics and political science at Stanford University. She lived in Ramallah, Palestine, for two years, during which she served as head writer and editor for the *Palestine Monitor* and as foreign press coordinator for Dr. Mustafa Barghouthi's 2005 presidential campaign.

In January of 2006, she moved to Washington, D.C., and worked at a Defense Department think tank to try to bring what she had learned to the halls of power—an educational but disillusioning experience. She is currently working on a sequel to *Fast Times in Palestine* called *Palestine, D.C.*

You can reach Pamela via her website, www.pamolson.org.